PROPOSING PROSPERITY?

PROPOSING PROSPERITY?

Marriage Education Policy and Inequality in America

Jennifer M. Randles

Columbia University Press ⟡ New York

Columbia University Press
Publishers Since 1893
New York   Chichester, West Sussex
cup.columbia.edu

Library of Congress Cataloging-in-Publication Data
Names: Randles, Jennifer M., author.
Title: Proposing prosperity? : marriage education
    policy and inequality in America / Jennifer M.
    Randles.
Description: New York : Columbia University
    Press, [2017] | Includes bibliographical
    references and index.
Identifiers: LCCN 2016014662 |
    ISBN 9780231170307 (cloth : alk. paper)
Subjects: LCSH: Family life education—United
    States. | Marriage—United States. | Family
    policy—United States. | Poor families—Services
    for—United States. | Equality—United States.
Classification: LCC HQ10.5.U6 R36 2016 |
    DDC 372.37/40973—dc23
LC record available at https://lccn.loc.gov
    /2016014662

Columbia University Press books are printed on
permanent and durable acid-free paper.
Printed in the United States of America
COVER DESIGN: REBECCA LOWN

To Craig,

from whom I have learned the most about love.

Contents

Acknowledgments   ix

1. Introduction: Learning and Legislating Love   1

2. Rationalizing Romance: Reconciling the Modern
   Marriage Dilemma through Skilled Love   25

3. Teaching Upward Mobility: Skilled Love and the
   Marriage Gap   51

4. Intimate Inequalities and Curtailed Commitments:
   The Marriage Gap in a Middle-Class Marriage
   Culture   81

5. The Missing "M Word": Promoting Committed
   Co-Parenting   106

6. Men, Money, and Marriageability: Promoting Responsible
   Fatherhood through Marital Masculinity   136

7. "It's Not Just Us": Relationship Skills and Poverty's
   Perpetual Problems   169

8. Conclusion: Family Inequality and the Limits
   of Skills   202

   Notes   *217*
   References   *233*
   Index   *253*

Acknowledgments

Just as it takes a village to raise a child, it takes a special kind of village—mentors, colleagues, editors, friends, and family—to write a book. As one member of that village, my dear mentor Arlie Russell Hochschild, once wisely advised me: Create a cocoon of people who will support you and the research you want to do, and don't worry about the rest. Alas, I often did worry about the rest. When I did, those I name in the paragraphs that follow were there to support me unconditionally. They are my village, one for which I am deeply grateful.

First, I would like to thank the marriage educators who allowed me to study the classes that are the empirical focus of this book. Your work and commitment have made a significant difference for many couples and families. I, for one, am a better partner and parent for having taken relationship skills classes. Though my analysis in what follows is often critical of these classes, please know that I strove to provide a balanced perspective of what the programs have to offer and how they might better support those who partner and parent under much less privileged circumstances than my own. Special appreciation goes to the woman I call "Cynthia" for her willingness to let a graduate student critically investigate a program that was her professional and personal calling and for her constant openness to ideas for making the program more useful for low-income parents.

Next, I would like to acknowledge the significant financial and institutional support I received throughout the duration of this project. This research was generously funded by the National Science Foundation (grant no. 0903069) and the following programs of the University of California–Berkeley: the Institute for the Study of Societal Issues; the Center for Child and Youth Policy; the Department of Sociology; the Graduate Division; and the Institute for Governmental Studies. A publication grant from the American Association of University Women and scholarly activities grants from the College of Social Sciences at California State University–Fresno were vital for carving out the writing time I needed to finish and edit the manuscript.

This book benefited early on from the guidance of mentors who taught me how to think with a sociological imagination and how the personal and political intersect in the most intimate aspects of lived experience. I am especially grateful to Barrie Thorne for agreeing to advise this project even before she knew me. She cared about my personal well-being as much as she cared about the progress of my dissertation, recognizing that the two are intricately connected. Barrie's encouragement to focus on the "juice" of the project renewed and enlivened my commitment to this research when I needed it most. Sandra Smith and Cybelle Fox always encouraged me to find the larger sociological hook in the empirical story. Their attention to my professional development is inspiring, and I strive to model it now for my own students. Carolyn Pape Cowan and Phil Cowan's decades of research on couples groups and vast knowledge of relationship strengthening programs have been an invaluable source of guidance. They, in particular, encouraged me to be balanced in my analysis. I am confident that publicly funded relationship programs will increasingly meet the needs of disadvantaged families because Phil and Carolyn are steadfastly committed to that goal. To Deborah Freedman Lustig, David Minkus, and Christine Trost of the UC–Berkeley Institute for the Study of Societal Issues, thank you for the always constructive feedback and for supporting research focused on equality and social change.

Many colleagues read chapter drafts and provided insight that allowed me to better say what I really wanted to in this book. To Jennifer Jones and Leslie Wang, I cannot imagine a better writing group for the formative stages of this project. For reading chapter drafts as the book was taking shape, I am grateful to Orit Avishai, Lynne Gerber, Daisy Rooks, Jennifer Sherman, Jennifer Utrata, Leslie Wang, and Kerry Woodward. To my coauthors of manuscripts related to this project— Orit Avishai, Lynne Gerber, Melanie Heath, and Kerry Woodward— thank you for showing me the value of true collaboration. A special note of appreciation goes to Orit Avishai, my marriage education sounding board and the person with whom I wish I could write everything. Thank you all for being supportive colleagues and collaborators, ones I am privileged to also call friends.

To the amazing editorial team at Columbia University Press, thank you for improving the manuscript in numerous ways. To Jennifer Perillo, you saw the value in this project from the very beginning and advocated for it to the very end. Thank you for working so diligently to maintain my vision of the project. Your support has been invaluable. To Stephen Wesley, thank you for overseeing countless tasks related to the book throughout the production process. To the anonymous reviewers, I am grateful for the careful attention to the manuscript and the truly constructive feedback and insightful critiques. Addressing them, I hope, allowed for a more balanced treatment of the book's subject matter.

To Bennie and Bridget Randles, your love and support have sustained me in so many ways throughout the long duration of this project. You taught me what cannot be learned from books—how to be compassionate, inquisitive, and concerned for the well-being of others. To my grandparents, James and Patsy Clement, thank you for the inspiring example of your almost seventy-year partnership and for agreeing to be interviewed for chapter 4. I cherish daily memories of the late Buddy and Dorothy Randles. To Christine Bailey and Bill Becker, you are more than in-laws; you have become my second set of parents and the family that allows me to feel as though I am never far from home.

To Craig Bailey, everything I learned from this project about what sustains a strong relationship points to you. An expert active listener and ever empathic, you are my model of being relationally skilled. Most importantly, you epitomize equality in every word and action. I cannot fully articulate how much your love and support have meant, so I'll just say that Craig is, indeed, awesome, and that I'll always be grateful for serendipity. To Bridget Christine Randles Bailey, finishing this book coincided with the first year of your life, and the timing could not have been better. May you grow to have a sociological imagination and never forget the privileges you have, just as I promise to never lose sight of the privilege it is to be your mother.

Finally, thank you to the parents who graciously gave me their valuable time and energy to participate in this research. Most of them invited me into their homes. All of them invited me into their personal lives by describing their experiences with love and money, topics neither commonly nor easily discussed with a stranger. Thank you for trusting me to represent your experiences accurately and meaningfully on the page. I hope that I have done justice to them.

1   Introduction

Learning and Legislating Love

I met Gwen and Isaiah at their apartment on Valentine's Day, the holiday for celebrating love and romance.[1] Both twenty-four and African American, they had been together on and off for five years and had just welcomed a son named Joshua a month earlier. No red roses adorned their kitchen table. There were no dinner reservations scheduled for later that night. Flowers, a nice meal out, and a babysitter would have cost a week's worth of their income.

While many other American couples went out for romantic dinners to celebrate their commitments, Gwen and Isaiah spent their Valentine's evening talking separately with me about money and marriage. Even before Joshua came along as an unplanned addition to their family, they had talked a lot about getting married. But since then, Isaiah had been laid off from his factory job and had to quit college because he could no longer afford the tuition and fees. Gwen's hours working as an aid for autistic children were cut back. The strain of living in a constant state of emotional and financial limbo led to more arguments.

After Gwen developed gestational diabetes midway through her pregnancy, her obstetric nurse told her about Thriving Families, a program for low-income, unmarried expectant parents. The nurse told Gwen it was a relationship skills class focused on communication, managing money, and adjusting to having a new baby. Excited that she and Isaiah could "work on their relationship" before Joshua arrived, Gwen eagerly enrolled. Isaiah reluctantly agreed, hoping this would give them an opportunity to address the anger and trust issues that made him hesitant about marrying her.

Several months after they finished the seven weekly Thriving Families classes, I interviewed them about what they learned and if it had helped their relationship. Both enjoyed the classes, especially the opportunity to talk with other couples experiencing the same problems. They both "had emotional walls up," Gwen told me, and the classes encouraged them to communicate about things they had never talked about before, including Isaiah's desire to be a good father because he never really knew his own dad. Yet, by the time I spoke with them that evening, Thriving Families had faded into their memory as a hopeful, yet mostly futile, effort to improve their relationship. The communication and budgeting tips they learned were no match for the stresses they faced: little money, a new baby to support, dwindling optimism that Isaiah would soon find a steady job, and constant uncertainty about the future of their relationship.

Couples like Gwen and Isaiah—not married but living together with children while struggling emotionally and financially—have become one of the primary targets of U.S. policy focused on encouraging marriage by teaching relationship skills. Often referred to as "fragile families," as with Gwen and Isaiah, four in five unmarried couples are still dating when their children are born, and almost half are living together at the time.[2] However, more than three in five of these couples are no longer together when their children celebrate their fifth birthdays, and not many of those who do stay together marry.[3] Teaching low-income, unmarried parents relationship skills is based on the logic that if struggling couples who have children together could strengthen their relationships before likely breakups, more would stay together, eventually marry, and have a better chance of creating an emotionally and financially stable home for their children. Thriving Families, the relationship skills program Gwen and Isaiah participated in before Joshua was born, was funded by the Healthy Marriage Initiative,[4] a federal policy created in 2002 that funded marriage and relationship education programs focused on positive communication, empathy, and constructive conflict resolution.[5] Combined federal and state funding for healthy marriage programs, which have been implemented in almost every U.S. state, have totaled almost $1 billion as of 2014.[6]

Taking an ethnographic on-the-ground approach, this book shows how healthy marriage policy has been translated into concrete practices and messages about family structure and economic success and how the two are interconnected. I observed and participated in hundreds of hours of healthy marriage classes and interviewed low-income couples who took them in order to answer the primary sociological question that drives the empirical and theoretical goals of this book: What does healthy marriage policy reveal about American political understandings of how romantic experiences, relationship behaviors, and marital choices are primary mechanisms of family inequality?

The answer I provide takes the reader inside the healthy marriage classroom to reveal how micro-level practices of state-funded relationship skills programs are reflections of broader macro-level issues of culture, gender, governance, and social inequality. Social policies and programs significantly shape our ideas of what it means to be a good spouse and parent. They also create a structure of opportunities and constraints for putting those ideas into practice. At the intersection of the two, they institutionalize moral prescriptions for how we should act as family members and political ideologies about the root causes of inequality. I found that healthy marriage policy reflects and reinforces the idea that individual choices and behaviors in romantic relationships determine adults' and children's social and economic opportunities. Central to this assumption is that upward economic mobility is teachable and that romantic competence—knowing how to love skillfully and make well-informed intimate choices—allows families to overcome financial constraints.

The classes I studied did not teach couples that marriage will automatically pull them out of poverty, as many detractors of the policy feared. Rather, they taught a more nuanced, though equally dubious, message that disparate family and economic outcomes can be explained in terms of individual capabilities or "skills" for communicating, parenting, and managing money. Marriage was cast as a way to reduce poverty—not just because it allows spouses to pool resources or to benefit from policies that advantage married families, but because it is a normative framework for shaping responsible romantic and financial choices, proper parenting practices, and a middle-class worldview. Beyond communication and budgeting strategies, the classes emphasized particular ways of thinking about how to fall and stay in love, whom to fall in love with, and how parents should invest in their romantic relationships as a socioeconomic good for the benefit of their children. On the surface, these messages seemed like well-intended efforts to help families stay together, stay happy, and create loving, stable environments for children. But a critical analysis reveals how these lessons individualized family inequalities by failing to acknowledge how social and economic circumstances shape relationship choices and experiences. Sociologists have long described how inequalities pervade the most intimate aspects of individuals' lives. The unique contribution of this book is to show how romantic love and interpersonal commitment have recently become direct objects of policy efforts to address these inequalities.

Welfare Reform and Marriage Education

Thriving Families taught Gwen and Isaiah about S.M.A.R.T. goals—which stands for specific, measurable, attainable, realistic, and timely—as a way to create a sense of purpose, happiness, and self-confidence. Once during a typical class focusing on this lesson, Susan, a white instructor in her forties, began the discussion by saying, "We're going to talk about how to achieve your goals. Is anyone really satisfied with where they're at?" Most of the parents in the room vigorously shook their heads no. Susan continued:

> Me either. We should never be satisfied with where we're at. We should always strive for more. If our children see us striving for things and trying to move forward, they learn that habit. . . . If your goal is to see your child go to college, start talking to them about that constantly, so they have that in their mind. I want you to take a few minutes to write down your goals.

One of the fathers volunteered to share what he had written: "Short term, mine is to find a job. Right now, my mom is helping us out a lot, and the government, so I want to find a way to be financially independent from both. In five years, marriage, definitely." His girlfriend groaned and said that she wanted marriage to be a shorter-term, six-month goal. Other parents shared that they wanted to go to college, get a good job, be financially stable, own a house, have more children, and ultimately get married.

In response, Susan asked: "What skills and knowledge will help you get there?" One of the fathers responded that he did not need more skills and knowledge; what he really needed was to finish school and get a job. Susan's husband and co-instructor, José, Latino and in his fifties, interjected: "Though the job situation is really bad right now and school can be expensive, the market always goes up and down, and you should just hold on to your dreams and keep working hard no matter what." Susan added, "If you just keep knocking, eventually a door will open. To move up in life, it takes a lot of determination, sweat, and tears. Consider what's keeping you from accomplishing your goals, and don't let anything stop you."

This goal-setting lesson was one of many I encountered in healthy marriage classes focused on teaching couples behavioral strategies for overcoming economic challenges. The classes taught that goal-setting is a cognitive capacity necessary to achieve major middle-class markers— higher education, stable and well-paid jobs, marriage, home ownership. This ignored how Thriving Families participants' economic circumstances as undereducated and unemployed or low-paid individuals constrained their abilities to realize these goals. Alas, instructors told parents that smart goal-setting was particularly important for exercising "individual responsibility," a political theme that played a major role in the welfare reform legislation that led to healthy marriage policy.

In 1996, Congress passed the Personal Responsibility and Work Opportunity Reconciliation Act (PRWORA). The PRWORA ended a sixty-year history of welfare as an entitlement program. Faced with five-year lifetime limits and work requirements, welfare recipients, mostly single mothers and their children living in long-term poverty, were no longer guaranteed welfare benefits. Claiming that "Marriage is the foundation of a healthy society" and "essential for family and child well-being," the new law encouraged work and marriage to shrink welfare rolls. The PRWORA listed the following four statutory goals for the new cash assistance program it created, Temporary Assistance for Needy Families (TANF):

1. Provide assistance to needy families so that children may be cared for in their own homes or in the homes of relatives.
2. End the dependence of needy parents on government benefits by promoting job preparation, work, and marriage.

3. Prevent and reduce the incidence of out-of-wedlock pregnancies and establish annual numerical goals for preventing and reducing the incidence of these pregnancies.

4. Encourage the formation and maintenance of two-parent families.[7]

To accomplish these goals, the PRWORA earmarked $150 million for healthy marriage and responsible fatherhood grants.

Claiming that marriage produces numerous benefits for adults and children—including less poverty, less crime, greater physical and mental health, and higher academic achievement—the Healthy Marriage Initiative (HMI) was created in 2002 as part of the Administration for Children and Families (ACF) to distribute healthy marriage grants. The HMI's official mission was: "To help couples who choose marriage for themselves to develop the skills and knowledge necessary to form and sustain healthy marriages"[8] in order to "increase the percentage of children who are raised by two parents in a healthy marriage" and "the percentage of married couples who are in healthy marriages."[9] As of 2016, the ACF has continued to fund healthy marriage programs through the "Healthy Marriage, Relationship Education, and Economic Mobility" grants.[10] These grants were intended to support "healthy marriage promotion activities," including "programs that provide healthy marriage and relationship skills designed to change behaviors of individuals and move families toward economic self-sufficiency."[11] Healthy marriage policy therefore assumes that marriage directly creates social and economic benefits for families.

Though the PRWORA and the HMI were the first U.S. policies to explicitly promote marriage, they continue a long American tradition of using marriage to publicly institutionalize private support for families. According to historian Nancy Cott, beginning with colonial poor laws, the U.S. social safety net has included economic incentives for getting and staying married and has penalized those who were not.[12] Welfare policy has historically framed family poverty as the result of a missing male breadwinner and need-based assistance programs as the government stepping in to take his place.[13] As divorced and never-married mothers, especially stigmatized women of color, began to comprise a greater share of welfare rolls in the 1960s, some welfare reform advocates became increasingly concerned that family structure was driving rising poverty rates and that poor women avoided marriage so they would not risk losing government benefits.[14] As sociologist Sharon Hays has illustrated, this concern led to the work and marriage promotion provisions of welfare reform in the 1990s.[15]

Since 1996, the ACF has granted most healthy marriage funding to programs that, like Thriving Families, provide marriage education.[16] As described by the ACF:

> Marriage education, a relatively new approach to preventing marital distress and breakdown, is based on the premise that couples can *learn how* to build and maintain successful, stable marriages. . . . The marriage education approach is based on years of research into the characteristics that distinguish marriages that succeed from those that fail. The difference between couples that survive and thrive in marriage and those that do not lies primarily in how couples understand and accept the fact that at times they will disagree and how they handle their inevitable differences. . . . Marriage education highlights the benefits of strong and healthy marriages for both adults and children. These include being better providers; living longer; earning and saving more money; and being less reliant on government services, such as welfare, health care, and mental health care [emphasis in original].[17]

This description of marriage education points to three primary inter-related assumptions of healthy marriage policy. First, having a good marriage is a knowledge-based proposition; with the right training, couples can learn to modify their behavior in ways that lead to better relationships and more stable families. Second, learning to manage conflict more effectively is the major difference between marriages that last and those that do not. Third, in modifying their behavior to be better partners and spouses, couples act in ways that create other social and economic benefits—they work harder, they save more money, and they become more responsible goal-setters and decision-makers—which reduces poverty and the need for welfare.

First popularized in the United States in the 1970s, marriage educa-tion is premised on the belief that individuals can cultivate attitudes and abilities that sustain happy, long-term marriages.[18] Most programs are short-term, typically lasting from several days to several months, and are either free or low-cost, usually less than $25 per couple.[19] Training requirements vary widely, with some curricula requiring no training, while others require several days of instruction facilitated by the developers of the curricula. Most marriage educators are marriage and family counselors, religious leaders, teachers, or social service providers. The most common class venues are community centers, religious organizations, schools, and social service agencies.[20]

Though many marriage education curricula are intended for all couples, some target specific relationship stages (dating, engagement, remarriage), family types (stepfamilies), or subpopulations (African Americans). The earliest programs served mostly white, middle-class couples who were already married or engaged. Because of government funding made available through the HMI, many recently developed curricula have tailored their messages for specific groups, such as youth, low-income couples, and unmarried parents.[21]

Relationship science, an interdisciplinary field of study devoted to identifying and understanding interpersonal relationship dynamics, serves as the empirical basis of marriage education programs that translate relationship research into teachable skills.[22] Predictors of marital stability have been a primary concern of relationship scientists who study individual and relational factors, including personality traits and attraction, as well as environmental factors such as social norms, laws, and partners' employment opportunities.[23] However, marriage education almost exclusively focuses on interpersonal communication and learning how to develop behaviors that relationship science has revealed as typical of happily married couples, such as empathy and active listening.

The Marriage Gap and Curtailed Commitments

When targeting low-income, unmarried parents like Gwen and Isaiah, healthy marriage programs specifically encourage couples to consider how marriage will benefit their children and their finances. But Gwen and Isaiah had already thought carefully and talked incessantly about getting married before taking their first Thriving Families class. According to Gwen, Isaiah was eager to get married when he was employed. Everything changed after he lost his job:

> When we talk about marriage he asks, "Why would you want to marry me in this situation?" As a man he really wants to provide for his family more. He doesn't see in himself what I see. . . . I don't doubt that he loves me and I love him, it's just money. It's the

reason for him not making the commitment to get married and for us not having a future together.

Isaiah similarly explained why, after dating and living together for almost five years and now sharing a son, he was not ready to marry Gwen:

> The money thing is the issue. I told her when I get work I'll be providing a lot more, and she wants to know when. . . . She'll question my commitment and my love for her, but I'm here every single day. I love her, but I need time. We both need to change. For one, her credit isn't that great, and when they check for a mortgage, they'll check both our credit. I want to have a house. I don't want to have an apartment with kids. I want to have a yard, a playground. It's going to be harder now.

Most of all, both Gwen and Isaiah were anxious about how they could trust one another and give Joshua the life they felt he deserved, including that house with a backyard playground and married parents. Ultimately, neither needed a class to encourage them to think about whether getting married was what they wanted for Joshua's future. They both wanted to get married, but they did not feel that they were financially or emotionally ready to make that commitment.

We cannot understand the full political and social implications of healthy marriage policy without understanding Gwen and Isaiah's dilemma, one that has become common among low-income, unmarried parents. In analyzing the implementation of relationship skills programs as part of welfare policy, I develop broader insight into how the emotional and financial challenges of economically struggling families are linked to changes in the meanings and experiences of love, marriage, and growing social inequality in the United States.

In the mid-twentieth century, Americans were equally likely to marry regardless of class. Now, those living below the poverty line are significantly less likely to marry.[24] Scholars refer to this trend as the *marriage gap*. Americans still almost universally aspire to marriage, but their expectations of whether they will ever be ready for it vary depending on their economic circumstances. Marriage has become ideologically associated with middle-class advantages, namely, finishing college, being securely employed, making decent wages, and owning a home.[25] As sociologist Kathryn Edin and colleagues have argued, because of the growing cultural norm that marriage is what people do once they become financially secure, those living in poverty are especially likely to view marriage as an achievement, a luxury to which they aspire but will likely never achieve.[26]

As marriage became culturally associated with middle-class markers, those advantages became further out of reach for poor and low-income Americans. These changes explain not only why Americans, on average, marry at older ages than those of previous generations, but also why many low-income parents like Gwen and Isaiah delay marriage or avoid it altogether. Previous research on low-income parents has consistently found that if they cannot live up to middle-class ideals of family life, couples do not feel equipped for marriage.[27] I call this phenomenon *curtailed commitment*.

Almost all of the prior research on healthy marriage policy has consisted of program or curricular evaluations, studies that determine if healthy marriage spending is correlated with higher marriage or lower divorce rates, and policy briefs that argue for or against using marriage-focused policies to address poverty. Taking a decidedly different methodological and theoretical approach, this book fills an important gap in our knowledge about healthy marriage policy. It uniquely combines a broad analysis of the dominant messages in a wide variety of government-approved healthy marriage curricula and an in-depth, multiyear ethnographic study of one exemplary healthy marriage program for low-income families. This approach allowed me to understand if the legislative intent of healthy marriage policy reflected the socioeconomic realities of curtailed commitment that shape the relationship choices of couples like Gwen and Isaiah. I discovered an important contradiction. Parents who took healthy marriage classes believed that marriage should come after achieving a greater degree of financial security. Yet, the legislative logic of the policy as reflected in healthy marriage curricula is that marriage itself will help couples achieve this security. This tension is at the heart of major controversies over healthy marriage policy.

Statistics and Moral Politics: Debates Over Healthy Marriage Policy

One major disagreement over healthy marriage policy is an issue of causality. There is a strong correlation between marriage and socioeconomic status: Overall, married people are more educated, make more money, and accumulate more wealth.[28] Advocates of healthy marriage policy have pointed to this evidence to make a case that marriage reduces poverty and that teaching couples the skills associated with happier relationships can improve poor families' lives and prevent social problems associated with poverty.[29] From this perspective, marriage generates more income because it signifies unrivaled commitment to the financial and emotional well-being of an entire family unit, not just one's self, especially among men who tend to work harder and make more money as husbands.[30] Children like Joshua would benefit from marriage, advocates have claimed, because an official, long-term commitment would encourage Gwen and Isaiah to work harder, make mutually beneficial economic decisions, and pool their parental resources to create a more stable household. Critics of healthy marriage policy have expressed concern that marriage classes erroneously teach couples that marriage can solve their economic problems.[31] Just because married people make more money, they have argued, does not mean that marriage causes them to earn more. They pointed to selection effects: People with more education, higher incomes, and more wealth are more likely to marry in the first place. The crux of this debate is whether there is something intrinsic and unique to marriage that has direct economic benefits.

The answer is complicated because the causal arrow points in both directions, and marriage and economic well-being tend to reinforce each other over time. Being college educated and financially secure makes it more likely that a couple will get married and stay happily married.[32] Couples who get and stay married are more likely to experience greater economic well-being as a result of marriage,[33] and this enhances their ability to provide more economic and parental resources to their children.[34] For men, getting married is associated with more paid work and higher wages over time, which in turn is associated with a greater likelihood of getting and staying married.[35] Adults and children struggle less, both financially and emotionally, when they or their parents avoid frequent relationship transitions, which tend to happen less among married families.[36] This is true for both heterosexual and same-sex parents, whose children tend to fare equally well, though the latter have only very recently been allowed to legally marry in all fifty states. As with the children of heterosexual couples, differences in socioeconomic circumstances and family stability account for much of the variation in levels of child well-being among those raised by same-sex couples.[37] Ultimately, family structure and parents' relationship quality significantly shape children's social experiences and life chances because both parents are more likely to stay involved in their children's lives by contributing both care and money if they stay together on good terms.[38]

We should not, however, extrapolate this evidence to conclude that marriage prevents poverty. Several statistical analyses have directly addressed this issue. Adam Thomas and Isabel Sawhill's marriage simulation found that a majority of mothers and children in poverty could rise above the poverty line if the mothers married.[39] Yet, rising above the official poverty threshold—a government measure that estimates the income necessary to meet a family's minimal subsistence needs—does not necessarily entail a meaningful increase in a family's quality of life or socioeconomic opportunities. Wendy Sigle-Rushton and Sara McLanahan found that marriage alone would not lift most welfare recipients out of poverty,[40] while Daniel Lichter and colleagues found that marriage could prevent poverty only if poor women would get married, stay married, and married well, meaning if they were able to marry financially well-off men, which is unlikely.[41]

When low-income, single mothers do marry, they are more likely to marry similarly disadvantaged men with little education, low earnings, and a criminal record;[42] if they divorce, they tend to be economically worse off than before they married.[43] For those who stay together, marriage between two people in poverty who make similarly low (or no) wages is unlikely to improve their financial situation; the fact that almost four million married families lived in poverty in 2014 indicates that marriage does not necessarily prevent poverty.[44] Moreover, not all children living with two married parents benefit equally. Those living with step-siblings do not tend to experience the same level of social and economic benefits,[45] while high-conflict and abusive marriages are often detrimental to both adults and children.[46] Marriage can be beneficial when people get along, have ample resources to pool, and stay together, but inequalities prevent all marriages from being equally beneficial.[47] Consequently, it is important to understand what healthy marriage programs teach about why married families generally experience more social and economic benefits and under what conditions these benefits emerge.

To legitimately claim that they are "evidence-based," marriage education programs should acknowledge that marriage's benefits derive largely from our society's tendency to structure social and economic rewards around the married family ideal. Marriage is a dominant social institution that confers social legitimacy on sexual and romantic relationships and provides norms of socially acceptable behavior, including resource hoarding by married couples.[48] Married couples also receive various benefits from employers, the government, and extended family simply because of their marital status. Thus, many of the advantages associated with marriage cannot be explained by its intrinsic value but rather because we live in a society that stigmatizes and disadvantages those who are not married.[49] As nonmarital cohabitation becomes more socially acceptable, couples who live together tend to enjoy the same psychological and social benefits of marriage,[50] and there are fewer benefits to marriage in countries where cohabitation is more common and less stigmatized.[51] A truly comprehensive marriage education program would also need to address how behaviors and circumstances that predict marriage tend to be those enabled by social and economic privilege, including high educational attainment, mental and physical health, stable employment, high earnings, parental engagement, and equitable romantic and co-parenting relationships.

The healthy marriage programs I studied did not admit this complexity. Instead, they simplistically taught that marriage is socially and economically beneficial without acknowledging the unresolved selection effect issues (and heteronormative biases) of the marital research on which healthy marriage education is based. They also neglected to address in any meaningful way the numerous other social trends— poverty, racism, inequitable access to education, the growing low-wage sector of the labor market—that have a significantly greater impact on children's and parents' life chances than marital status. Throughout I explain why this approach does a disservice to the low-income families targeted by healthy marriage policy and the implications of this strategy for understanding marriage-focused policy efforts to address poverty and family inequality.

Do Healthy Marriage Programs Work?

Another key debate is: Do relationship skills programs actually work to accomplish the goals of welfare reform and healthy marriage policy? It depends on what one means by *work*. Gwen and Isaiah told me that they learned how to communicate better in Thriving Families, but the classes did not change their mind about marriage or help them financially. Similarly, evaluations of healthy marriage programs have found that relationship education classes for low-income couples work to improve communication, relationship satisfaction, and support, but they do not affect marriage or poverty rates. Neither has research investigating population-level impacts of healthy marriage programs found consistent associations between government funding for relationship education and marriage or divorce rates.[52] Both program-level and population-level studies suggest that healthy marriage policy is based on unsupported inferences that because relationship skills education improves relationship experiences, it directly affects family-formation and economic trends.

Much of the evaluation research on relationship skills programs has found that classes improve couples' relationship satisfaction and communication,[53] but most studies have focused on privileged couples—predominantly white, middle class, and college educated—who were already married or engaged.[54] Thus, much of the evidence used to make a case for government support of marriage education programs has been based on the experiences of economically and socially advantaged couples who had already decided to marry. Nevertheless, research focused on low-income couples has found that relationship education programs improve important family outcomes, including communication and relationship quality;[55] co-parenting dynamics;[56] and relationship satisfaction, dedication, and confidence.[57]

Two major government-sponsored evaluations of healthy marriage programs have also revealed some positive results. The evaluation of the Supporting Healthy Marriage program—which targeted low-income, married couples—found that couples who took classes were happier with their marriages, experienced more warmth and support and fewer negative emotions and interactions, and communicated better a year after beginning the program. However, the classes had no effect on whether couples were more likely to stay together.[58] Another HMI-funded, multisite evaluation study—the Building Strong Families project for low-income, unmarried parents—found significant positive impacts on relationship quality and stability at the fifteen-month follow-up and positive impacts on relationship stability after thirty-six months in one program based in Oklahoma City. However, averaged across the eight sites, there were no lasting overall positive effects on relationship satisfaction, co-parenting, or how involved fathers were, even among the couples who attended classes regularly.[59] Couples who took the classes were even slightly less likely to be together after three years, and the classes had no impact on whether they married. Neither evaluation found that program participation helped improve families' financial situation.

Qualitative research on healthy marriage programs for welfare recipients has also revealed mixed findings. Anne Sparks and Melanie Heath separately studied relationship education programs for TANF clients sponsored by the Oklahoma Marriage Initiative. Participants told both researchers in interviews that they thought the information about relationships and communication was useful. Yet, while Sparks found that the classes effectively addressed participants' relationship concerns and challenges,[60] Heath found that single-mother welfare recipients were largely unreceptive to class messages because of the program's focus on marriage and the instructors' middle-class perspective.[61]

As with Gwen and Isaiah, the collective evidence suggests that relationship skills classes do often work to improve couple communication and the emotional experiences of family relationships. This is a worthy policy goal. But this is not the primary justification for devoting public resources to healthy marriage programming. Funding is based on the speculation that teachable relationship behaviors will allow couples to experience greater relationship stability and upward economic mobility because marriage, rather than preexisting socioeconomic advantages, aids "economic self-sufficiency" among those in poverty. To date, there is no evidence that marriage education works to increase marriage and reduce poverty rates. The healthy marriage programs I studied taught that family and financial success are the dual consequences of hard work and making skilled romantic choices. In doing so, they individualize social problems such as poverty by ignoring the social and economic problems that undermine lower-income couples' abilities to realize their family-formation goals, including, in many cases, their desires to marry. Though not an efficacy study per se, this book sheds light on the primary reasons healthy marriage programs have, as of yet, failed to accomplish the goals of welfare reform. It analyzes the logics and methods of government-funded healthy marriage programs in relation to evidence about economic and social inequalities that shape divergent experiences of intimate life, something that evaluation and population-level studies have not addressed.

Marriage and Morality

Sociologist Andrew Cherlin argued that the real controversy over healthy marriage policy is not actually about data or statistics, but morality.[62] By officially endorsing the two-parent married family over all other types, the government sanctioned a particular moralistic view of family life. Yet previous research has revealed little about how that sense of morality takes shape on the ground and what government marriage education programs teach about how family life should be lived. Sociologist Melanie Heath's ethnographic study of the first state-wide marriage initiative in Oklahoma is the exception.[63] Drawing from a variety of perspectives—including state leaders of the initiative and instructors and participants in marriage workshops and classes— Heath argued that marriage education does not just teach communication strategies. She found that, by promoting an ideology that takes for granted the middle-class, white, heterosexually married family as a normative model of social stability and well-being, government marriage classes teach a hidden curriculum that reinforces social boundaries around gender hierarchy, heterosexuality, citizenship, and religiosity.[64]

I found that healthy marriage programs teach people they should marry, not for moral or religious reasons, but because marriage directly creates economic and social benefits. Beyond officially endorsing married families, healthy marriage policy promotes a political ideology that family well-being depends on individuals learning to love in a responsible and rational way that minimizes the economically costly and socially destabilizing consequences of irresponsible, uninformed romantic choices. By participating in marriage education myself, I discovered how the moral politics of family, love, and inequality coincide in the healthy marriage classroom.

Becoming a Healthy Marriage Educator

As a sociologist and ethnographer committed to observing the social phenomena I seek to understand, I decided that the best way to identify the core messages of healthy marriage programs was to participate in trainings and classes for government-approved marriage education curricula. Recognizing that one curriculum would not likely be representative of the many used by healthy marriage grantees, I attended classes that used a purposively chosen sample of government-approved relationship skills education curricula.

When I started this research in January 2008, there were a total of 238 state and community-based Healthy Marriage Initiative grantees receiving federal funding. Using the grant abstracts for these 238 programs published by the ACF, I compiled a list of all the relationship skills curricula the ACF approved for use in healthy marriage programs.[65] Using this list, I created a sample of twenty curricula based on three selection criteria. First, I selected the ten most commonly used curricula nationwide, which included all curricula cited five or more times by HMI grantees. Of these ten curricula, four were general relationship skills curricula (*Active Relationships, PAIRS, PREP,* and *Relationship Enhancement*); two were for youth ages twelve to eighteen (*Connections* and *Love U2*); two were used in conjunction with premarital inventories (*FOCCUS* and *PREPARE/ENRICH*); one was a relationship skills curriculum for unmarried, low-income parents (*Love's Cradle*); and one was a relationship skills and partner selection program for low-income individuals (*PREP Within My Reach*).

Second, because my research was based in California, I included five HMI-approved curricula sponsored by the then-named California Healthy Marriages Coalition, the recipient of the largest HMI grant as of 2008, as well as the largest state-based healthy marriage initiative. These included a partner selection program (*PICK a Partner/How to Avoid Marrying a Jerk*); a marriage enrichment program (*10 Great Dates*); a parenting and relationship skills program for married expectant parents (*Bringing Baby Home*); a program for low-income, unmarried parents (*Caring for My Family: Together We Can*); and a program for low-income couples (*Mastering the Mysteries of Love*).

Third, to account for HMI-approved programs that targeted specific populations and relationship stages, I rounded out the sample with a program for African American couples (*African American Relationships, Marriages, and Families*);[66] a nondenominational curriculum for use in religious organizations (*Marriage Savers*); two divorce prevention curricula (*Divorce Busting* and *The Third Option*); and a program for step-families (*Smart Steps*). This sample included curricula that targeted all relationship stages, including partner selection/dating, premarital preparation, marriage enrichment, parenting, divorce prevention, and re-marriage/stepfamilies. It also included four programs that targeted low-income participants of various relationship statuses: one for low-income individuals, one for low-income couples, and one each for unmarried and married low-income parents.

I attended an instructor training, workshop, or class for eighteen of these same twenty curricula and took copious fieldnotes during the combined 135 hours I spent in them. I participated in instructor trainings for seven, attended workshops at a national marriage education conference open to the public for nine, and attended classes as a participant for two. The remaining two programs were "Teach-Out-of-the-Box" curricula; in lieu of trainings, educators were expected to follow explicit written instructions when teaching. In many cases, the leaders of the classes I attended developed the curricula. I also acquired either leader's manuals or participant workbooks for all but one (*Relationship Enhancement*) of the curricula and analyzed the more than 3,000 combined pages of textual materials for the twenty programs.[67]

Participating in trainings and classes was a unique window into how the curricula were intended to be used by educators in real classroom settings. The trainings lasted one to three days and included detailed instructions for teaching each lesson. Most also required teaching demonstrations and mock class exercises, all of which I completed with a teaching partner or in a group. The workshops lasted about ninety minutes, included a more cursory overview of core lessons, and focused on communication exercises, which I also completed with a mock spouse. During each training, workshop, and class, I was overt about my role as a researcher to anyone with whom I interacted, including instructors and fellow participants. When analyzing my fieldnotes and the texts, I focused on identifying how the curricula defined healthy relationships/ marriages, which behaviors they advocated for developing healthy relationships, and messages about the benefits of marriage.

Scope of the Analysis

There are hundreds of relationship, marriage, parenting, and family life education curricula with widely varying content that have been used and evaluated in the United States and worldwide. Though the twenty curricula I studied are a fraction of this larger universe, they reflect the dominant messages of U.S. healthy marriage policy. I sampled only curricula that were approved for use in government-funded relationship skills programs and included all six major content areas required by the Administration for Children and Families: (1) commitment to healthy marriage, (2) communication, (3) conflict resolution, (4) beliefs about marriage or family, (5) benefits of marriage (for adults, children, community, and society), and (6) qualities of healthy relationships and healthy marriages.[68]

There is a large and growing literature on the wide variety of relationship and marriage education programs, community sites, and evaluation efforts.[69] It addresses how program content varies, how curricula target different populations, and what program characteristics tend to induce specific behavioral and relational changes. These are all important issues outside the scope of this analysis. Findings from evaluation research have often been presented as decontextualized statistics and outcomes rather than in relation to people's lived experiences, feelings, and choices shaped by inequality. The unique contribution of this book is an analysis of the dominant messages of healthy marriage policy and how low-income, unmarried parents understood and made use of them in the context of these experiences.

Thriving Families: Relationship Skills Training for Low-Income Parents

In the service of this goal, I studied in-depth the Thriving Families program attended by Gwen and Isaiah. Because I wanted to understand the program from multiple perspectives, I conducted 150 hours of participant observation in Thriving Families classes and recruitment sessions; three focus groups with fourteen total Thriving Families couples; in-depth interviews with forty-five parents who graduated from the program; and in-depth interviews with nine instructors and six staff, including the program's founder and executive director, the director of educational services, the program coordinator, and three recruiters. As part of the curricular analysis described above, I also attended a ninety-minute workshop for the curriculum used by Thriving Families.

Thriving Families was coordinated by a community-based healthy marriage organization that sponsored various marriage education classes for individuals and couples. The organization, which I refer to hereafter as Healthy Marriages, received a five-year $2.5 million federal HMI grant for 2006–2011 to create Thriving Families for low-income, unmarried couples who were expecting a baby or had a child younger than three months old. In 2009, the ACF designated Thriving Families as an exemplary healthy marriage program and as one of only three programs nationwide qualified to provide technical assistance to other programs within the same grant area. During my research, the federal Office of Family Assistance also selected the program as one of the top twenty-five best practices healthy marriage programs in the country.

Thriving Families was based in a midsize city of approximately 500,000 residents. Like Gwen, most participants were referred to the program by health care or social service providers, including those working with the Women, Infants, and Children nutrition program, pregnancy and new mother support groups, and Child Protective Services. The program compensated participants $10 per couple, per class for transportation costs, served a full catered meal during each class, and gave couples a $100 "graduation stipend" if each partner attended fourteen hours of class time. To qualify for these incentives, couples had to meet a low-income requirement and could not be legally married at the beginning of the first class. Couples qualified as long as one parent was pregnant or had custody of a child younger than three months old; the other parent was not required to have a biological or legal connection to the child, only to be currently involved in an ongoing relationship with the child's other parent. Couples could choose to attend seven weekly two-hour classes on weeknights or two seven-hour classes on consecutive Saturdays.

Eighty-four percent of those who enrolled in the program were on some form of public assistance, including food stamps or TANF. More than half, 53 percent, reported household incomes of less than $1,000 per month, while only 13 percent had household incomes of at least $2,000. Fewer than 3 percent of participants lived in households that collectively brought in $3,000 per month or more. Most of the parents had more than one child, and many lived with their own parents and partners. Because a three-person household that made $17,600 or less in 2008 was considered poor, most Thriving Families participants lived well below the poverty line.[70] One-third of participants had not graduated from high school, and half had only a high school diploma or GED. Fewer than 20 percent had some college education. Most Thriving Families participants were parents of color: 40 percent identified as Latino/a; 24 percent as African American; 22 percent as white; 3 percent as Asian/Pacific Islander; 2 percent as Native American; and 9 percent as multiracial or "other."

Thriving Families classes typically took place in family resource centers located in the city's low-income neighborhoods. Once the program started offering cash incentives for participation, class sizes grew significantly from one to four couples to as large as ten to fifteen. Classrooms contained dry-erase boards, long folding tables and chairs, and wall posters with pictures of families and captions such as "No one told you being a parent was going to be this hard." On the first day of a new class series, instructors passed out "memory books"—participant notebooks containing lesson outlines and worksheets—along with markers, magazines, scissors, and glue that parents used to decorate and personalize their book covers. Instructors took a Polaroid picture of each couple on the first day of class to place on the cover, and many parents attached sonogram pictures. About half of the women in the classes were visibly pregnant, many only a few weeks away from their due dates. Baby carriers and diaper bags often sat atop the tables. Older children went to the "play care" room during classes to watch movies, play with toys, or color and draw. Though child care providers were also available to take care of babies during class, many parents preferred to keep their infants with them. Parents, mothers especially, often multitasked by listening to the instructors while rocking fussy babies, filling out worksheets while watching over naptime, and participating in group discussions while breastfeeding.

Each class had two instructors—in most cases, a married couple like Susan and José, and always one man and one woman. There was also a staff person present during each class to take attendance, call absent couples, arrange and clean up after meals, and distribute incentives. Healthy Marriages recruited instructors through Craigslist, a popular online classified ad website, and trained them during a two-day workshop that included an overview of the curriculum and a teaching demonstration. As indicated in the job ad, the two-day training and a personal "commitment to healthy marriage" were the only requirements. Instructors earned $25 per hour to teach the classes.

Because the curriculum was designed to be twenty-four 60-minute lessons, and Thriving Families class series were only fourteen hours long, instructors selectively used lessons from their leader's manuals. They tended to focus on five lessons: goal-setting, managing money, the importance of fathers, communication skills, and the benefits of a healthy marriage. Instructors stood or sat at the front of the classroom and used a teaching style that aimed to elicit discussion from parents.

Though they sometimes read from their manuals and jotted down key points on the board to introduce a new topic, instructors focused more on role-playing exercises, group and couple activities, and sharing personal anecdotes. This semi-structured approach allowed a lot of time for parents to share about their relationship experiences as well.

At the beginning of each class I observed, instructors introduced me as a researcher. Except in the few instances when instructors asked me to pair off with one of the parents whose partner was unavailable, I did not participate in couples' exercises. I did, however, have my own participant workbook and filled out the same worksheets instructors asked participants to complete, which allowed me to discreetly take extensive fieldnotes during lessons and break-out exercises. Though I was overt about my role as a researcher, parents and instructors easily and completely incorporated me into the classes, and I participated in group discussions and exercises when life experiences allowed. I participated, for example, in discussions about what we learned from our parents about trusting people in romantic relationships. I sat with couples during class and, while on break, ate meals with them, held babies, played with older children, and chatted with instructors and recruiters. This gave me opportunities to observe participants, instructors, and staff during classes, as well as interact with them more informally.

Because I also wanted to understand how parents reflected on their experiences in the classes, I interviewed a subset of Thriving Families graduates who had completed a full fourteen-hour class series six to eight weeks after they graduated. Those I observed in classes overlapped to some degree with my interview sample. As the program offered several class series simultaneously, I had observed fourteen of the forty-five parents in classes prior to the interviews. The forty-five parents I interviewed ranged in age from seventeen to fifty-seven, and most were in their twenties or thirties. Twenty-three were women and twenty-two were men, which included both members of twenty-one couples. Nineteen of the interviewees (42 percent) identified as African American, eight as Latino/a (18 percent), seventeen as white (38 percent), and one (2 percent) as Asian American.[71] At the time of the interviews, forty of the parents were still romantically involved with the partners with whom they had taken the classes, half (nineteen) had children from previous relationships, and thirteen (eight of the women and five of the men) were employed. All but four of the interviews took place in parents' homes or cars.

Outline of the Book: Going Inside the Healthy Marriage Classroom

The following chapters take the reader inside the marriage education classrooms I studied to reveal the dominant messages and strategies of healthy marriage policy. Chapters 2 and 3 draw on my participant observation research in trainings and workshops and the textual analysis of the twenty government-approved relationship skills curricula. Chapter 2 analyzes how the classes and curricula emphasized what I call *skilled love*, a type of romantic love that is logical, competent, and controlled. Educators taught that individuals can learn to love in line with long-term marital commitment by developing rational romantic values, emotional competencies, and interpersonal habits. Chapter 3 shows how classes promoted skilled love as a strategy for preventing risky and financially costly relationships choices and, consequently, as the essential link among marriage, financial stability, and upward mobility.

Chapters 4 through 7 focus on my research in the Thriving Families program to show how the logic of healthy marriage policy and low-income parents' understanding of marriage conflicted. The policy assumed that learning and using relationship skills leads to better marriages, which in turn modify individuals' behavior in ways that lead to greater financial prosperity. Yet, for parents, marriage represented the culmination of prosperity, not a means to attain it. In chapter 4, I describe how cultural and economic changes in marriage throughout the twentieth century have created what I call a *middle-class marriage culture* in which low-income couples are less likely to marry for both ideological and financial reasons. I introduce several emblematic Thriving Families couples who told me they could not afford or prioritize marriage until they were no longer economically struggling. Their relationship stories illustrate how financial challenges lead to curtailed commitment, especially when marriage between two economically unstable partners seems like a bad financial risk.

How then did the Thriving Families program reconcile the tension between parents' views of marriage and the policy's goal of promoting marriage as a route to greater economic and family stability? Chapter 5 shows how instructors deliberately avoided talk of marriage and instead emphasized committed co-parenting as the primary resource parents have to support their children's life chances. In doing so, staff and instructors emphasized the value of something parents presumably had within their control—the quality of their relationships and parenting—over the jobs and money they did not. In chapter 6, I analyze how the Thriving Families classes also encouraged marriage by promoting what I call *marital masculinity*. This is the idea that, for men, marriage often comes before rather than after financial success and best encourages low-income fathers to become manly, successful providers by inspiring them to work harder and earn more money.

Chapter 7 offers a unique perspective on the healthy marriage policy efficacy debate about whether relationship skills program work. Although Thriving Families classes did not change couples' views of marriage or help their finances, parents did overwhelmingly find the classes useful. While couples' economic challenges made it hard to practice the skills, they experienced the classes as a rare opportunity to communicate free of the material constraints that shaped their daily lives and romantic relationships. Hearing other low-income couples talk about their challenges with love and money also normalized parents' intimate struggles and allowed them to better understand how relationship conflict and unfulfilled hopes for marriage are shaped by conditions of poverty.

I conclude in chapter 8 by describing the benefits and limitations of relationship skills policies for low-income families. Publicly sponsored relationship education could be a valuable social service in a highly unequal society where stable, happy marriages are increasingly becoming a privilege of the most advantaged couples. The classes I studied focused on teaching low-income couples to emulate the relationship experiences and behaviors more typical of middle-class couples. This strategy simplifies and vilifies the relationship choices that couples like Gwen and Isaiah make, while ignoring how social inequality and economic constraints shape those choices. Low-income parents' experiences with healthy marriage classes suggest that relationship policies would be more useful if they focused more on how economic stressors take an emotional toll on romantic relationships and less on promoting the dubious message that marriage directly benefits poor families. In highlighting their perspectives, this book makes a case for relationship policy and programs that reflect how intimate inequalities lead to curtailed commitments.

2 Rationalizing Romance

Reconciling the Modern Marriage Dilemma
through Skilled Love

I met Dorothy on day one of my first marriage educator training. Along with six married couples, we spent two weekends in an expansive suburban church becoming certified to teach a new relationship skills program promisingly titled *Mastering the Mysteries of Love.* As the only other person enrolled in the training not there with a partner, Dorothy, a kind and soft-spoken white woman in her early seventies, was my mock spouse for the partner exercises. She had been happily married for five decades and was planning to teach the program as part of her church's marriage ministry. Relaying a quote she first heard in a sermon when she was a newlywed, she told me she wanted to become a marriage educator because she believed that "Marriage sustains love as much as love sustains marriage."

I learned by observing more than 300 hours of marriage education over the following three years that Dorothy's motivation hinted at a central logic of healthy marriage policy. In a love-based marriage culture such as that of the United States, romantic love or its absence justifies getting married, getting divorced, or never marrying at all. Because romantic love can undermine family stability and social order, the policy presumed, it is in the government's interest to generate and channel a type of love that best supports long-term marital commitment. In this chapter, I explain how relationship skills education was a political strategy focused on teaching couples the values and behaviors associated with this type of love—what I call *skilled love*—which is presumably more durable and less subversive to social order because it is logical, competent, and controlled.

Our *Mastering the Mysteries of Love* instructor, Cathy, a spirited white woman in her fifties who led a government-supported healthy marriage organization, began the training by emphasizing the value of marriage for children, adults, and communities: "According to social science, children who grow up in two-parent married families are significantly less likely to be poor, commit crime, make bad grades, and become unmarried parents themselves." She quickly shifted to describing why marriage allows couples to experience the highest form of romantic love and how relationship skills training can help couples stay in love for a lifetime: "Marriage means having a witness to your daily life, someone who knows your deepest sorrows and joys, someone you can learn to love more deeply with each passing day despite the inevitable challenges you'll face." She then asked for two volunteers for the first exercise.

One of the married couples, Christine and Bill, eagerly offered to participate. Cathy asked them to stand with their backs to one another at the front of the room. Christine faced the north wall away from the group, while Bill faced south looking at us. Cathy asked Christine to describe what she saw. Christine described the whiteboard, the clock above it, and several inspirational posters hanging on the wall. When Cathy asked Bill to do the same, he described smiling people, chairs, tables, and a window that looked out onto a sunlit view of the church playground. "Are there any smiling people in your view?" Cathy asked Christine. "No," Christine replied, "only a whiteboard." Turning to Bill, Cathy inquired, "Is your wife crazy or wrong because she doesn't see the chairs, the tables, and the window that you just described?" Bill tentatively shook his head no. "Christine, turn around and look over your partner's shoulder. Now, what do you see?" "I see the smiling people. I see the chairs and tables. I see the sunny window. I see what Bill saw," Christine said.

"Exactly!" Cathy exclaimed. "Does it ever seem that your partner lives in an entirely different world? Do you ever wish that your partner would look at the world from your perspective? Do you wish you could feel that passionate, exciting love you felt when you first met? This program will teach you the skills to do that." This, Cathy enthusiastically described, is the heart of marriage education. By learning to see the world from our partner's viewpoint, we can experience true empathy and face the world together. Once we learn to truly express ourselves and listen to and validate our partner's perspective, she explained, we can experience real romantic love, the kind that grows rather than fades over time. Consequently, Cathy concluded, our relationships will become more secure as we learn to love better and longer.

Through instructional lectures, videos, and many teaching demonstrations and communication exercises with Dorothy over those two weekends, I began to learn what marriage educators meant by *relationship skills*. The foundational premise of the marriage education curricula I studied is that most relationship problems could be significantly improved if couples would learn to communicate and resolve conflict in a skilled way. Though the skills presented in each curriculum differed somewhat, all the programs generally entailed learning how to follow a series of conversational steps intended to allow couples to experience more empathy, manage conflict and negative emotions, and get at the deeper emotional roots of words and actions.

I talked about many relationship issues with Dorothy, most hypothetical, some painfully real. The most challenging was the topic of our final exam, for which we had to pretend that we were a long-married couple struggling with one partner's (played by me) addiction to online pornography. We both tried to channel the actual emotions that a couple would likely have in this situation and used our newly learned skills to discuss it. First, we used our "showing understanding skill" by alternately listening to one another with compassion. Next, we practiced our "expression skill" by naming our thoughts, feelings, and concerns about the problem. Finally, as the partner who was doing the hurtful behavior, I employed my "self-change skill" by creating a plan for how I would stop watching pornography and be more attentive to Dorothy. I promised to honestly communicate with her about my desires, to try to empathize with her emotional experience of feeling rejected and belittled, and to seek professional help for my addiction if necessary. The conversation was both challenging and comforting. Though it was awkward, Dorothy and I connected deeply and talked constructively about a devastating and common marital problem. Consequently, I started to understand how the communication techniques taught in relationship skills classes could help generate greater intimacy, trust, and warmth among couples. But I also ultimately questioned how effective these strategies would be when discussing something real—especially issues as painful as addiction, infidelity, and lack of trust—with an actual spouse in whom I was emotionally, socially, and economically invested.

The *Mastering the Mysteries of Love* training introduced me to a core assumption of healthy marriage education: Through instruction and practice, couples can cultivate the knowledge and emotional capacities necessary to maintain love throughout a lifetime of marriage, especially when conflicts and challenges arise. To use Dorothy's words, I learned that healthy marriage programs focused on teaching that marriage can sustain romantic love when couples learn how to control and channel it. This orientation to intimate relationships reflects an understanding of romantic love that has emerged in tandem with larger changes in the social meanings and practices of marriage.

Romantic Love and the Modern Marriage Dilemma

That romantic love and relationship skills have become central to public policy focused on stabilizing families and preventing social problems reflects how marriage has dual, often contradictory, demands. It is at once both a personal relationship and a social institution. As historian Stephanie Coontz has shown, most of marriage's history is not a story about romantic love, free choice, or personal fulfillment, but one of obligation to family and survival through economic, political, and religious ties.[1] Many of the social and economic reasons that used to compel people to marry and avoid divorce have been eclipsed by the desire to stay married only as long as marriage is emotionally and intimately fulfilling for two individuals.

This shift has been a double-edged sword. It is unlikely that many would welcome a return to the older social foundations of marriage, which included a starkly gendered division of labor, parentally arranged marriages, prohibitively restrictive divorce laws, and draconian customs that ostracized the never-married and divorced. However, as Coontz described, these changes have stripped the institution of traditional bases of social support and prescriptive rules for individual behavior without establishing new ones in their absence.[2] This leaves a void that marriage educators seek to fill.

Healthy marriage policy tacitly acknowledges that emotional satisfaction is a precarious foundation for a social institution. The policy's focus on relationship skills training reflects that a fundamental tension between individual freedom and commitment now shapes contemporary experiences of matrimony. Historian Rebecca Davis called this tension the *modern marriage dilemma*.[3] It pits marriage's personal role as a primary site of emotional and sexual expression against its communal role as an anchor of economic interdependence, co-parenting relationships, and sexual legitimacy. Contemporary marriage is thus characterized by a paradox: It is now more satisfying but less stable.[4] Without social pressures holding couples together, there are more inducements to leave and fewer reasons to stay when marriage ceases to be emotionally gratifying. This shift signals what sociologist Andrew Cherlin termed the *deinstitutionalization of marriage*, which is now increasingly individualistic and fraught with a dizzying array of options about whom to marry, when to marry or divorce, and how to be married.[5]

Resulting from a proliferation of marital choices, this dilemma creates a profound sense of emotional ambivalence about marriage. Sociologist Robert Bellah and colleagues described how the tension between individual freedom and social obligation leaves "Americans . . . torn between love as an expression of spontaneous inner freedom . . . and . . . love as a firmly planted, permanent commitment, embodying obligations that transcend the immediate feelings or wishes of the partners in a love relationship."[6] As marriage continues to structure much of family life in the United States, couples—and policymakers—seek strategies to navigate this high-stakes tension rooted in simultaneous desires for both personal satisfaction and social stability.

These changes in marriage demand a much greater personal obligation of emotional effort and investment in intimate relationships.[7] As social rules, roles, and rituals exert weaker influence on marriage and as sentiment forms the basis of commitment, every family decision must be discussed, deliberated, and negotiated.[8] It is not surprising, then, that a policy focused on strengthening intimate relationships would target emotional experiences of marriage and interpersonal communicative habits. Whereas social stability used to be anchored in family members sharing labor, it now depends on couples sharing emotions.[9] Marriage education's emphasis on empathy, affective awareness, and interpersonal negotiation reflects the growing perception that emotional effort, cooperation, and compromise are necessary if marriages are to survive. As sociologist Karla Hackstaff argued, in a divorce culture where marriage is viewed as optional and contingent on emotional happiness, many couples adopt a marital work ethic—the belief that marriage requires ongoing reflection and relational work—to cope with the uncertainty and fragility of marriage.[10] Analyzing the rise of couples counseling in the United States, historian Kristin Celello similarly illustrated how the belief that marriage requires therapeutic work to survive and thrive has become a key part of the American collective consciousness.[11] Healthy marriage policy reflects and reinforces this ideology that marital work is necessary to sustain a gratifying marriage.

It also points to how, as sociologist Arlie Russell Hochschild theorized, subjective emotional experiences within marriage are subject to norms of emotion management and feeling rules shaped by cultural, economic, and political forces.[12] Cultural values, economic circumstances, and social policies influence how couples feel and share the emotions that support the do-it-yourself relationships of modern marriage. Though affectively experienced as haphazard and deeply personal, romantic love as a legitimate basis of marriage is the result of patterned and widely accepted social customs—what scholars call romantic beliefs.[13] Romantic love is often thought to exist only as a private feeling, one that mysteriously emerges as a result of inexplicable and natural emotions unconnected to larger social forces.[14] Yet, it is deeply implicated in social norms and practices shaped by laws, such as healthy marriage policy, that institutionalize romantic beliefs emphasizing personal happiness, interpersonal compatibility, and communication skills as requisites of a successful marriage.

By promoting skilled love, healthy marriage policy sought to intervene in marital relationships at the nexus of two dominant emotional paradigms that characterize Americans' matrimonial experiences. According to sociologist Ann Swidler, *mythic love* casts intimacy with that one special person as all-encompassing, everlasting, and able to overcome any obstacle. It coexists with the more mundane concept of *prosaic-real love* that couples draw on to work through the everyday challenges and foibles of ongoing relationships, such as deciding who will take out the trash.[15] This less idealistic view of love necessitates willingness to compromise and change over the course of a marriage as two people continuously recommit to working through intimate challenges. The American culture of love that combines these two emotional paradigms flourishes, Swidler argued, because it helps people manage the emotional tension at the heart of the modern marriage dilemma: the simultaneous desire for both passion and permanence. It also supports American couples' commitment to marital work and developing the romantic beliefs and emotional capacities—or *skills* in healthy marriage policy parlance—now deemed necessary to sustain and manage ongoing relationships in a social context where institutional pressures no longer hold marriages together.

The perspective exercise with Christine and Bill during our *Mastering the Mysteries of Love* training exemplified how healthy marriage education focused on teaching couples how to reconcile these mythic and mundane experiences of marital intimacy. The purpose of skilled love is to allow spouses to continuously adapt to one another and create a dynamic stability based on neither social pressure nor economic interdependence, but rather on empathic intimacy generated through structured communication and conflict resolution. By focusing on relationship skills, healthy marriage policy institutionalized a rational paradigm of romantic love that combines commitment to both individual satisfaction and social stability. This paradigm, skilled love, promises to resolve the tension at the heart of the modern marriage dilemma and thereby support long-term, happy marriages.

Rationalizing Romance to Promote Marriage

By studying twenty government-approved marriage education curricula, I learned that U.S. healthy marriage policy did not just focus on promoting marriage and teaching people how to be better communicators. It also encouraged participants to develop relationship beliefs and tools that would presumably allow them to transform individual desires for emotional satisfaction and personal happiness into instruments of marital permanence. In short, it focused on teaching couples how to love in line with long-term marital commitment.

Sociologist Elizabeth van Acker found that marriage education policies in Australia adopted a highly rational view of marriage, one that ignored the importance of romance in couples' marital experiences.[16] Couples believe that their relationships are held together by romantic bonds comprised of ineffable and intuitive emotions that operate outside the realm of rational discourse—while governments, she argued, seek to regulate and control marital interactions by teaching pragmatic skills that have little to do with romantic feelings. Van Acker concluded that romance should thus be a central part of public marriage education programs. I similarly found that U.S government–supported healthy marriage education was an attempt to intervene in intimate relationships using pragmatic and systematic communication strategies. Yet, rather than ignoring or dismissing romance, government-supported marriage education in the United States co-opted couples' expectations of romantic love as central to modern marriage and taught them to apply rational techniques of emotional management to their romantic experiences. That is, rather than discounting romance, the classes I studied rationalized it by promoting skilled love as a cultural script for pro-marriage relationship beliefs and practices.

The emergence of relationship skills education as a political strategy to encourage happier and longer marriages reflects the growing cultural emphasis on romantic love as a basis of marriage combined with the rising influence of social scientific experts on family life. Ironically, as sociologist Eva Illouz argued, now that marriage is no longer organized based on the values of planning, calculation, and reason, but rather emotional satisfaction and love, it has become an object of rationality and scientific scrutiny.[17]

Starting in the early twentieth century with the development of domestic science and home economics, social scientists, especially psychologists, became the recognized experts on marriage and parenting.[18] Concerned that something as fleeting as romantic love had become the basis of marriage, sociologist Ernest Groves advocated for marriage education as part of standard educational curricula for all youth as early as the 1920s.[19] Many answered his call. From the 1930s through the 1960s, most American colleges and universities had some form of marriage education in their academic curricula. Proponents of marriage education—mostly social scientists, like Groves, who specialized in marriage and family—argued that lay forms of marital knowledge, such as elders and religious institutions, were no longer adequate to provide youth with the "functional" and practical information necessary to create and sustain modern healthy marriages.[20] Healthy marriage policy continued this American tradition of educational and therapeutic initiatives that seek to improve relationships by teaching couples to apply social scientific findings to their intimate lives. Relationship science, the empirical basis of marriage education, identifies patterns in the behaviors of happily married couples. Relationship skills education translates these findings into systematic rules of interpersonal interaction that promise to help couples temper or intensify romantic feelings to sustain satisfying marital commitment.

This is a case of what sociologist Max Weber described as the rationalizing tendencies of modern social life. Weber theorized that rationality is the process whereby scientific knowledge organizes belief and emotion and abstract rules shape behavior. Intellectualization, consciously naming and reflexively reasoning about our social experiences, is central to rationalization. Science, Weber argued, is ill-equipped to show us how to live or what to value; rationality can inform the means, but not justify the ends, to which our conduct is directed.[21] Healthy marriage education ultimately tried to do both by teaching couples how to rationalize and intellectualize relational experiences to strengthen marriage and pro-marriage ideology. The rationalizing tendencies of marriage education are focused on teaching people how to generate feelings of romantic love, channel them toward the appropriate people, and restrain them when they might lead to socially or economically destabilizing choices, such as divorce. The problem with rationality, Weber concluded, is that it undermines emotional intensity through disenchantment, the tendency for scientific explanations to cognitively and emotionally distance us from our lived experiences. When we begin to view something like romantic love as governed by psychological and social laws, we no longer view it as a transcendent experience shaped by grand, mysterious forces. Yet, as Illouz argued, rationalization need not be understood as a cultural logic opposed to emotion.[22] Though rational thought and emotion are often portrayed as mutually exclusive experiences, rationality often works in conjunction with and through emotion. As the case of healthy marriage education illustrates, rationality has shaped the cultural scripts through which emotions are felt, understood, and used to motivate behavior. Healthy marriage policy and its implementation through relationship skills education signifies how romantic love as a culturally acceptable basis of marriage has been rationalized as an emotion that can and must be skillfully managed.

As reflected in healthy marriage curricula, this rationalization of romance involves several core tenets. First, scientific relationship experts use medical metaphors to categorize relationships as either "healthy" or "unhealthy," implying that some relationship behaviors are normal, while others are pathological. Presented under the guise of scientific authority and neutrality, moral statements about good versus bad relationship choices and values become seemingly objective accounts of what people should do in relationships as a matter of what is "healthy" and scientifically justified, rather than what is normative. Second, it is assumed that the romantic bonds uniting couples can be studied and evaluated using impartial scientific criteria and that people can learn to use these criteria to develop relational knowledge about themselves and their mates. Finally, therapeutic techniques—in this case, relationship skills training—translate these criteria into teachable knowledge and skills that promise to help individuals develop "healthy" relationship behaviors. By learning to identify, interpret, and manage emotions, individuals become objects of self-reflexive inquiry that monitor their relational behaviors in line with the "healthy" relationship norms that privilege marriage both as the ideal family form and the socially acceptable context for romance. The end result is skilled love, a rational cultural script of romantic love that endeavors to equip people with the emotional capacities and cognitive tendencies presumed to be necessary for long-term, love-based marital commitment.

Learning to Love Skillfully

Alison Krauss's song, "Baby, Now that I've Found You," was piping through the overhead sound system when I walked into the large hotel conference room for my first day of PREP (Prevention and Relationship Enhancement Program) training. The room was bustling with over 150 people—social workers, teachers, welfare caseworkers, religious leaders—who had traveled to the conference from around the country and various parts of the globe to become certified to teach the program. Given that PREP focused on mutual commitment, it was ironic that the song was about the heartache of unrequited love. Yet, two lines of Krauss's tune poignantly captured what I would learn about that day. She sang, "Baby, baby, when first we met/I knew in this heart of mine." The song's reference to knowing something in one's heart foreshadowed the dominant message of this class and the many others I studied: A healthy marriage is largely a matter of developing the understanding and skills—what many educators referred to as *heart knowledge*—necessary for well-informed relationship choices and behaviors.

Not surprisingly given the goal of the program to strengthen inter-personal relationships, the audience for the training was not optimistic about the current state of marriage and family in America. When the workshop leader asked us all to draw a picture illustrating modern family relationships, I drew two nondescript stick figures playing in a tree-lined park with two similarly nondescript smaller figures repre-senting their children. In my picture, the family was together—committed, if not married, as I did not think to specify in the image—and most importantly, they were happy. My family was normative in the sense that it consisted of two adults and two kids, but the figures were neither gendered nor racialized. (I still have the picture among my fieldnotes. The adults are green, and the kids are blue.)

However, my fellow trainees had a much more calamitous view of contemporary family life. Many drew pictures of couples in the middle of heated arguments. One drew a picture of two spouses traveling on different roads headed in opposite directions, while another drew two balls sitting together and then bouncing apart. The woman who sat di-rectly to my right sketched the most dismal image I saw. It depicted a couple stumbling around in darkness in a shaky house that was falling apart and crumbling to the ground. Commenting on the woman's drawing, one of the workshop leaders noted that becoming certified for *PREP* would help us teach couples to "turn on the lights" in their rela-tionships by learning how to be skilled communicators and better partners.

I learned a lot in the three days that followed, including how to use the *PREP* speaker–listener technique, the value of using time-outs during arguments to better resolve conflict, and the importance of emotional and physical safety in relationships. Though they targeted different aspects of dyadic interaction, all the *PREP* lessons taught that loving well is a learned skill. Likewise, all twenty healthy marriage edu-cation curricula I studied taught that romantic love is something that can and must be continuously recreated through acquiring knowledge, developing healthy relationship behaviors, and devoting significant time and effort to practicing relationship skills with a willing partner. They stressed that "real" love—the kind necessary for a lifelong, happy marriage—is the deliberate result of a conscious cognitive process rather than an ephemeral emotional state. I show throughout the re-mainder of this chapter how the marriage education curricula I studied rationalized romance by teaching that a healthy marriage is one in which spouses have the ability to generate and maintain skilled love that is logical, competent, and controlled.

The Logic of Skilled Love

Speaking to a packed room of workshop attendees interested in teaching his partner selection program, *How to Avoid Falling in Love with a Jerk*, counselor John Van Epp proclaimed that he had an effective way to teach the "logic of love."[23] Called the Relationship Attachment Model, or RAM, Van Epp described it as an "empirically derived model of intimacy" that teaches people about the five fundamental dynamics of attachment: knowledge, trust, reliance, commitment, and sexual involvement. Love becomes blind and irrational, he explained, when the five dynamics get out of sync. Using RAM as a "template for healthy relationships," the program promised that one could learn "to balance the logic of the head with the passion of the heart." The fundamental premise of RAM, the "safe-zone rule," is that the five relationship dynamics have a specific order and logic: Sexual involvement with someone should never come before or outpace the degree to which you know, trust, rely on, and are committed to that person. As he noted in his book outlining RAM, "When the safe-zone rule is followed, then your relationship grows in healthy and stable ways and the potential for making a lasting marital choice is maximized."[24] The take-home message was clear: People who allow lust to overtake logic in relationships risk getting too attached to the wrong person and falling in love with and marrying a jerk. This is why, Van Epp noted, "Research has found premarital sex to be associated with higher divorce rates and infidelity rates in people's future marriages."[25]

Van Epp's message to our audience reflected one of the core principles of relationship science that serves as the empirical basis of marriage education: Healthy relationships have an objective logic, structure, and sequence. Healthy marriage classes vow to teach couples these universal principles of successful interpersonal interaction as part of a scientifically based core of relational knowledge. As the *Third Option* divorce prevention curriculum leader's manual similarly explained:

Just as the physical universe is governed by the laws of physics: gravity, momentum, centrifugal force, etc., so the world of relationships is governed by the "laws" or principles of relationships. . . . Even if we do not know the skills for good relationships, and hence do not practice them, we are affected by them nevertheless. If we do not practice good relationships skills, we will have problems in our marriages.[26]

This implies that universal relationship laws, such as the five fundamental dynamics of relationship attachment described by Van Epp, operate beyond the context of individual relationships. The curricula and instructors I studied claimed that because of this, relationship scientists can identify, measure, and study the effects of these laws. Most importantly for the purposes of educational relationship interventions, marriage educators claim they can translate these universal laws into teachable relationship skills that everyone can use to improve their odds of creating and maintaining a healthy marriage. As described by the *PREP Within My Reach* curriculum for low-income individuals:

We know more than ever before about how people move in and out of relationships, and those patterns affect their prospects for lasting love and stability. The very best news is that a lot of the research in the field can be directly translated into skills and insights that people can learn and use to make their lives better. There's no magic answer when it comes to love, but everyone can become wiser and more skilled in relationships and marriage.[27]

As evidence of these universal laws and skills, all the curricula I studied included references to numerous research studies that had identified or tested how particular relationship qualities—such as empathy, active listening, and humor during conflict—tend to influence dyadic interaction similarly across couples. The other type of research most frequently cited in the curricula was program evaluations, often conducted by the authors themselves, which generally found that couples who had participated in the programs reported better communication and greater marital satisfaction after taking classes using the curricula. This is what curricular developers meant when they made claims about their programs being "evidence-based." Trainers repeatedly emphasized these findings in the workshops. They frequently noted how research had confirmed that relationship skills training lays the foundation for a happy and prosperous marriage by teaching people how to prevent passion, infatuation, and other impulsive emotions from disengaging the intellect when making relationship choices. In other words, to paraphrase Van Epp, relationship skills keep people from letting their libidos and hearts override the better judgment of their heads.

Many of the curricula specifically distinguished between real love, a rational and deliberate foundation of relationship commitment, and infatuation, an inferior and chemically driven form of attraction and affection. The *Love U2* curriculum for youth described infatuation as an emotional experience distinct from the real love that supports healthy relationships and smart, successful life choices:

> When you come into contact with a person who highly attracts you, your brain becomes saturated with amphetamine-like neurotransmitters that trigger incredible side effects. . . . You are in a drugged state. . . . Remember those "love chemicals" might keep you from seeing some problem behaviors. Where do you think the phrase "love is blind" comes from? But, there is nothing fake about infatuation. It is what gets love going, but it is not love initially. It can be the first step of love, but it is not love itself.[28]

Several curricula even included lessons on brain anatomy and neurochemistry, warning of the dangers of letting the biochemical and physical experiences of infatuation overcome rational thinking. Understanding the neurobiological aspects of passionate attraction is important, many trainers and curricula claimed, because couples who mistake infatuation for love risk making costly life decisions when they become emotionally and physically intimate before commitment. The *Mastering the Mysteries of Love* trainer explained that infidelity and divorce are often the result of people seeking new partners to maintain the "love high," a cocktail of hormones associated with the early stages of a relationship. The *PAIRS (Practical Application of Intimate Relationship Skills)* curriculum described how emotional experience and rational thought happen in different parts of the brain, the neocortex and limbic system, respectively; this is why emotions often cause us to make irrational relationship choices. Lori Gordon, the program's author, explained: "The part of the brain that causes us the most havoc in relationships is the part that deals with emotions . . . because they have their own logic, quite distinct from the logic our intellect uses to puzzle our way through day-to-day life."[29]

Healthy marriage classes thus urged participants to conceptualize infatuation and companionate or "real" love as distinct emotional experiences that activate different physiological and cognitive processes. Instructors taught that infatuation develops swiftly, ends shortly thereafter, and causes intense preoccupation with and idealized views of the beloved. Grounded in interdependence and commitment, companionate love is less haphazard, more resilient, and most conducive to long-term marriages. The skilled love advocated by healthy marriage educators was characterized as a better-informed type of companionate love that incorporates the elation and passion of infatuation. Its primary benefit is that it presumably allows couples to deliberately and rationally balance the excitement of first falling in love with the durability of long-lasting commitment.

To do so, curricula claimed, individuals must learn to recognize the warning signs of infatuation and the benefits of a real love that relies on knowledge, reason, and logic. As the *Active Relationships* curriculum emphasized, relationship skills training involves teaching participants to understand the difference between an "angry-reactive brain" that makes bad relationship decisions and a "calm thinking brain" that knows how to use time-outs and speaker–listener techniques to strengthen commitment.[30] According to the classes, healthy relational behavior is *learned* behavior grounded in rational skills people need to override their emotional tendencies to become obsessed with new love interests, get sexually intimate before commitment, and speak harshly during the heat of an argument.

Trainers emphasized that this skill set was even more important now during an era of marriage based on sentiment and individual satisfaction. Many claimed that by compensating for waning institutional constraints that once systematically controlled love impulses, a rational approach to romance and marriage based on relational knowledge can help manage the modern marriage dilemma. Parents and other authority figures used to arrange marriages on behalf of youth, and couples often stayed married because of social norms, family obligation, and religious beliefs. Now individuals are left to their own devices to choose a partner and sustain a lifelong marriage. Many of the trainers lauded the greater degree of personal choice in contemporary romantic relationships and the end of an era when arranged marriages were based on a rational logic of social similarity and economic interdependence without regard for emotional compatibility. But they also warned of the greater tendency for couples to break up when interpersonal conflicts arise. For example, the *PREP* curriculum noted that:

> People can put more emphasis on their personal choices in the role of building and keeping a great marriage. For some, it can make leaving abusive relationships easier. That's surely a good thing. On the negative side, with fewer economic, legal, and moral barriers to divorce, more people choose this option—even when faced with difficulties that many couples could overcome with the right kind of effort. That doesn't mean a couple just survives their problems, but rather that they are learning how to thrive in the relationship.[31]

To promote greater individual satisfaction and family stability simultaneously, many curricula advocated embedding the rational logic of arranged marriages into the interpersonal dynamics of communication and commitment. Van Epp articulated this most explicitly:

> Arranged marriages were designed to maximize a rational approach to marriage: bringing together a couple who were similar in cultural, religious, and ethnic backgrounds; compatible in social status and family values; and beneficial for not just the two who were marrying but also the extended families involved. This historical approach to the choice of a partner was not really about love, romance, attraction, or intimacy. It was a practical arrangement that was directed by a rational plan. You could sum it up in just one word: *think*. Not until the last few centuries were planned marriages replaced by marriages where individuals chose partners based on romantic attraction and feelings of love.[32]

The goal of relationship skills education generally—and tools such as Van Epp's Relationship Attachment Model specifically—is to provide a rational, systematic understanding of love and intimacy based on the "universal laws" of relationships. In an era of deinstitutionalization, modern couples bear a tremendous responsibility as family guidance and social constraints have given way to autonomous choice and interpersonal negotiation in marriage. From this perspective, now that the options for meeting people are endless and the potential dating pool exceedingly and confusingly diverse, emotional and sexual attraction can pose a threat to social stability when ill-informed infatuation compels people to marry or have children too soon or with the wrong partners. A foundational premise of healthy marriage education is that learning to love skillfully, which entails deliberately and logically evaluating personal feelings and interpersonal compatibility, allows individuals to prioritize autonomy and emotional satisfaction while forming stable marriages. To do so, the healthy marriage classes I studied tried to teach individuals that they must develop specific relational competencies based on the findings of relationship research, namely, the abilities to regulate their emotions and control their intimate behaviors.

The Competencies of Skilled Love

The *Wait Training: It's All About M.E. (Marriage Education)* curriculum for youth included several lessons on how to bond effectively to ensure a lifelong, happy marriage. The research cited by the curriculum indicated that bonding was more difficult when someone has had multiple premarital sexual partners. The instructor's manual included detailed instructions for how to illustrate this important finding to middle- and high-school students using the tape exercise. An instructor asks a male volunteer to come to the front of the classroom and says: "Pretend that he's going to have sex for the first time in front of us."[33] The volunteer rolls up his shirt sleeve and wraps a piece of tape representing his girlfriend around his arm. The instructor asks: "Class, is it possible for this guy to marry this girl some day? Yes, it's possible, but is it probable? No. So that means that at some point you're going to have to break up with her." Next, the instructor tells the volunteer to pull the tape off his arm. "Oooh, class, look at the tape now. What do you see? Our volunteer has left his hair, skin, cologne—even his DNA is on the tape! Yikes. Looks like she's going to need therapy!" The instructor repeats the exercise with two more male volunteers using the same piece of tape and explains to the class:

Ok, class, what is happening to the bonding power of this tape? That's right, it's losing its power to bond. You need to know that when you have sex before marriage you are lessening your power to bond to your future mate. You are losing your sexual cement. I am not telling you if you have already started having sex you have lost your ability to bond. I'm also not trying to make you feel guilty. You did what you knew and now you know better. And when you know better, you do better.[34]

The message is that if young people develop the behaviors research has revealed to be associated with healthy relationships—in this case, sexual abstinence prior to marriage—relational competence can serve as the foundation of a satisfying, long-lasting marriage.

The key link between relational knowledge and marital stability presented here is the ability to regulate emotions that motivate behavior. Trainers used various synonyms to refer to this kind of relational competence: *emotional intelligence, emotional literacy, heart knowledge,* and *relationships smarts.* Popularized by Daniel Goleman's 1995 best seller, *Emotional Intelligence: Why It Can Matter More than IQ,* emotional intelligence refers to the ability to recognize, evaluate, and regulate emotional experiences.[35] According to the *PAIRS* curriculum, someone who is emotionally intelligent:

> identifies and expresses . . . emotions and can listen empathically to them . . . listens without interjecting self-concerns, creates and maintains emotional safety for others, uses anger constructively, and experiences and expresses emotions of a type and at an intensity that appropriately fits and that sustains action in accord with one's purpose, intention, and circumstances.[36]

Other curricula described emotional competence in similar terms, as an ability to constructively express one's self and empathically relate to others by recognizing and regulating emotions in line with relationship goals.

Instructors and curricula noted that relational competence is essential for generating and sustaining the kind of rational, skilled love necessary for a stable marriage. "Learning to love in long term relationships requires great skills, effort, security, discipline, good will and trust. These skills do not come naturally," the *Active Relationships* curriculum explained.[37] It also described how people can learn to remain in love without the initial chemical high, and even experience deeper, more satisfying love, if they develop empathic understanding through relational competence: "Because so many believe the chemistry is love, they do not wait for the real love that comes with knowledge."[38] Healthy marriage classes promised that love grounded in knowledge and skills allows couples to love one another through the ordinariness of daily married life in a way that is as exciting as when they first fell in love. As the *Mastering the Mysteries of Love* manual described:

> Your love often gets lost because you live your lives at the Events level. "Honey, did you take out the trash yet?" "Who's going to pick up the kids from soccer practice this afternoon?" . . . But think back to when you first started to know each other. Did you talk about taking out the garbage? . . . Did you nonchalantly turn toward the stairs and say "See ya?" Probably not—or you wouldn't be here together today. You probably talked about your thoughts, feelings, concerns, and desires. "What did you think of the plot of that movie?" "How do you feel about me?" . . . "What are your dreams and hopes made of?" THOSE are the questions, the mysteries, your love is founded on. . . . The goal of this program is to enable you to feel that love now.[39]

Teaching skilled love as a strategy to promote marriage assumes that individuals can learn to temper romantic and sexual impulses when certain marital values demand it, as with infatuation that might lead to sex outside marriage. It also presumes that couples can learn to intensify these same feelings when they wane and threaten to undermine marriage, as with couples who might divorce because their relationships have become too focused on the mundanities of marital life. By cooling down feelings deemed too hot or heating up ones deemed too cool, skilled love was cast as a technique to keep emotions just right within the socially acceptable parameters of marital commitment.

Because many of the people who attended the trainings were planning to teach healthy marriage classes in government-funded programs, instructors and curricula were supposed to omit any religious content. For the most part, they did. However, even messages about religion were framed in terms of knowing the importance of shared moral and spiritual, if not religious, belief systems for maintaining romance. The *Ten Great Dates* revised chapter on "develop[ing] spiritual intimacy" for use in government-funded classes explained:

When we talk about spirituality, we are referring to your core beliefs and how they affect who you are and what you do. . . . Numerous studies suggest that having a spiritual dimension in your life
has a favorable impact on marriage. For instance, couples who
frequently pray together are twice as likely as those who pray less
often to describe their marriages as being highly romantic. Also
those who are religious are less likely to divorce, have higher levels of satisfaction, and higher levels of commitment. Having a
shared belief system will bind you together in the midst of dealing with problems and day-in and day-out living and loving.[40]

As with *Ten Great Dates*, when trainers and curricula discussed religion and marriage, it was not to preach about marriage as a religious
sacrament, but rather to teach couples that shared religious belief will
strengthen their romantic bonds. The ability to jointly engage in religious
practices, such as prayer and attending worship services together, was
presented as another ability associated with skilled love and knowing
how to keep the romance alive.

Instructors and curricula also described how learning about partners' communication, conflict, and love styles was another essential
competency of loving skillfully. The *Ten Great Dates* program encouraged participants to identify which type of communicators they and
their spouses were by metaphorically associating communication and
conflict-resolution styles with animals, such as "otters," who tend to be
outgoing and egocentric, or "beavers," who are more analytical and
temperamental.[41] The goal of this and similar exercises was to help
couples identify emotive differences so that they could learn to empathize with and embrace those differences. Similarly, John Gottman's
Bringing Baby Home curriculum for expectant and new parents included lessons about the importance of developing partners' "love
maps," which involve "taking the time and energy to . . . [learn] each
other's history, concerns, preferences, daily activities, life dreams, likes
and dislikes."[42]

Several programs taught that becoming relationally competent involves learning to assess relationship quality by tracking and counting
relationship quantities. The *Bringing Baby Home* trainer stressed the
importance of "ritualized connection" and encouraged participants to
build the "magic five hours" into their weekly schedule: ten minutes a
day for partings; twenty minutes daily for reunions and stress-reducing

conversations; five minutes a day for admiration and appreciation; five daily minutes for affection; and a weekly two-hour date to update love maps and engage in problem solving. *Bringing Baby Home* also encouraged couples to think of their relationships as having "emotional bank accounts" into which they make deposits when they do or say positive things. Extending the accounting metaphor, the trainer urged that couples should build up their balance so that they can maintain an account in good standing when negative comments, selfish behavior, or fighting causes them to make emotional withdrawals. Citing the research of John Gottman, co-author of *Bringing Baby Home*, the *Caring for My Family: Together We Can* curriculum for low-income, unmarried parents similarly taught couples that the most successful and happiest relationships are those that have five times as many "positive strokes" as "negative strokes" during conflict and as many as twenty to one in non-conflict situations.

Many lessons from different curricula encouraged participants to develop their relational competence and become relationship problem-solving "experts" by applying their emerging skills to case studies of hypothetical couples with common interpersonal challenges. As the authors of the *Caring for My Family: Together We Can* program described during a workshop: "Couples look at these case studies and analyze them and give them advice. They become the experts and begin to rely back on their own knowledge and really come into the advocacy role for one another as they project out towards helping others, and then they turn back to themselves." Michelle Weiner-Davis, author of the *Divorce Busting* divorce prevention program, similarly noted in a workshop that, "When things are going wrong, people can't just talk about their feelings, they have to learn to negotiate the feelings they have. . . . Rather than teaching highly specific solutions, [*Divorce Busting*] teaches people how to become marriage problem-solving experts on their own."

Ultimately, as illustrated by the tape exercise from *Wait Training: It's All About M.E.*, being a relationship expert did not just mean having the abilities to identify emotions, be an empathic communicator, and negotiate common couple challenges. It also meant having pro-marriage values about intimate relationships and making "smart" relationship choices based on these values. Several of the trainers and curricula even noted that making good decisions about sex, childbearing, and marriage was not a matter of morality, religion, or ideology, but of being knowledgeable about the universal dynamics that govern all healthy relationships. That is, loving skillfully entails valuing marriage because research reveals that married couples have more satisfying relationships and better lives. Accordingly, being relationally competent in this context meant behaving in ways that reflect normative pro-marriage family values—namely, sexual abstinence before marriage, monogamy, and avoiding divorce and having children outside marriage. As the trainer for the *Love U2* youth curriculum noted about the program's insistence on premarital abstinence:

> Obviously the lesson just makes a lot of sense, it's smart. It's not moralistic, it's not prudish, it's just smart. . . . This all just takes understanding and building a more realistic concept of love. . . . It's really giving some guides and frameworks for making decisions, setting boundaries . . . and developing a plan for love and life.

The *Love U2* leader's manual reiterated that the program is "unapologetically pro-abstinence for teens, but not for reasons that have to do with religion, ideology or politics."[43] As similarly described by the *Wait Training: It's All About M.E.* curriculum, learning to love in skillful and competent ways—or "knowing better"—will allow youth to "do better," in this case, abstain from sex until marriage. What connects knowing better and doing better is emotional control.

Loving Skillfully through Emotional Control

"Now we're going to teach you how to empty your emotional jug, which is a metaphor for the emotions that rise up inside of us in our daily living," David, the co-facilitator for the *PAIRS* workshop announced. We should tell our partners what is bothering us, he continued, in a way that "doesn't explode, implode, erode, or corrode, but instead builds a relationship and creates closeness." The purpose of the emotional jug exercise is to let go of "all the things that are held down because they seem inappropriate—anger, rage, fear, sadness. If we have rules that say don't feel sad, don't feel weak, don't feel frightened, don't feel angry because these are bad things, we go around neutral like automatons, and we build up this great big wall," David explained. Lori, the author of *PAIRS* and David's teaching partner, elaborated on how emotional walls can drive a wedge between two people who seek greater intimacy. David and Lori then modeled the emotional jug exercise by talking about David's imagined irritation over politics, his boss, and his grandson. He communicated what made him angry, scared, and sad—the "big three of negative feelings"—which allowed him to "move on to the gladness that will pour out because we've cleared the clouds from the sun and now the sun can shine." In describing how to do the exercise correctly, David emphasized:

> When our partner is emoting, we put ourselves on the back burner and keep a container for that, just like we do when a child is emoting. We don't have to give a response because holding that space and just wanting to know and listening is enough . . . . It isn't about giving any responses and answering it. It isn't about explaining it, justifying it, or telling you not to feel that way. None of those things, just listening and asking for more.

Like other communication techniques taught by the healthy marriage programs I studied, the emotional jug exercise offered couples a systematic framework for controlling the negative emotions that lead to conflict, resentment, and relationship dissolution.

Trainers taught that couples' abilities to control their emotional responses, especially when stressed or fighting, is a defining characteristic of a good marriage. As a promotional brochure for the *Wait Training: It's All About M.E.* curriculum described: "In today's chaotic world of instant gratification and floundering commitment . . . healthy relationships are becoming extremely difficult to develop and maintain. Our culture is losing its belief in the institution of marriage and its values of self-control, integrity, and commitment."[44] The *Third Option* leader's manual likewise explained that the kind of love that supports healthy marriage—"mature love"—necessitates the "self-discipline and self-control [that] are the hallmarks of a mature adult and the raw material from which healthy marriages are built."[45] Those who are prone to relational violence, several curricula noted, lack this important ability to regulate their emotions. The eponymous jerk in John Van Epp's relationship skills program is someone who cannot emotionally regulate, a person who has a "habit of breaking boundaries . . . the utter inability to ever see anything from anyone else's perspective . . . and a dangerous lack of emotional controls and balance."[46] This capacity to control one's emotions is, according to the classes, a key component of emotional intelligence that allows people to love skillfully. As noted in the *Bringing Baby Home* training manual:

> Being emotionally intelligent is more than being able to show your emotions. It is the ability to work with your emotions, or to regulate them. This includes being able to focus your attention towards specific goals even in a stressful situation; being able to stay calm and not show your emotions when appropriate . . . ; and being able to label your emotions and problem solve around them.[47]

The *Active Relationships* curriculum advocated the P.O.W.E.R. technique for emotional regulation: "P = Pause to identify the deepest, most emotional pain; O = Observe the meaning of the obsolete message you are telling yourself; W = Work to wire a new meaning of your value; E = Explain events using compassion for yourself and for others; R = Regulate your reaction to make your long-term goals succeed."[48] Warning that people often try to control external circumstances when focusing on internal ones would be more productive and satisfying, the curriculum emphasized that "each person's ability to manage his own thinking, and therefore his own emotions, will generate relationship success or destruction."[49] To help couples regulate what *Active Relationships* called their "internal emotional climate," many of the curricula offered instruction in stress-reduction techniques, including breathing exercises and massage, that participants could use to develop the emotional control necessary for creating and sustaining skilled love.

Skilled Love and the Modern Marriage Dilemma

By rationalizing romance, the healthy marriage classes and curricula I studied tried to reconcile the modern marriage dilemma by promoting a type of love believed to simultaneously support individual satisfaction, marital longevity, and social stability. More personal freedom in marriage has come at the cost of less marital permanence. Fewer prescriptive social rules now govern marital behavior in a cultural context where divorce rates are high and romantic love holds marriages together. This creates a paradoxical emotional culture that, as described by sociologist Arlie Russell Hochschild, invites us to experience "a richly communicative, intimate, playful, sexually fulfilling love," as part of a "social context [that] warns against trusting such a love too much."[50]

Healthy marriage policy reflects that modern couples must negotiate their own relational rules and make greater emotional investments as they engage in the marital work viewed as necessary to keep a marriage exciting and strong. No longer just a contractual agreement that structures resource sharing, labor, and family roles, marriage is now largely understood to be an organic entity that emerges out of the expressive union of two individuals; it is something that can healthily thrive, merely survive, or die if couples cannot or will not make these investments. Rather than evoking themes of personal sacrifice, social obligation, and familial responsibility, healthy marriage classes and curricula taught about marital commitment in terms of rational personal choice, individual fulfillment, and empathic interpersonal understanding.

Relationship skills as a political strategy for strengthening the institution of marriage is a targeted response to the growing concern that Americans now live in a post-marriage culture where people view marriage as just an emotionally inflected individual preference rather than a socially sanctified relational status.[51] Healthy marriage education responds to the romantic impulses of modern marriage by encouraging couples to uncover and more fully experience their deepest emotions— albeit in logical, competent, and controlled ways—as a conduit of marital satisfaction and social stability. Skilled love, which entails both suppressing and intensifying emotions when marriage requires it, is an emotional paradigm that promises to help couples manage their emotions and relational behavior as they manage the modern marriage dilemma.

As implemented via relationship skills training, the primary objective of healthy marriage policy was not just to promote marriage, but rather to shape individuals' emotional experiences and capabilities in line with long-term marital commitment in a social context where external constraints no longer necessarily hold marriages together. Rather than focusing on teaching couples how marriage will benefit them or society, healthy marriage classes emphasized rituals for reflexive self-assessment and emotional control that translated into prescriptions for intimate and marital behavior. Backed by supposedly objective social science, these rules defined real romantic love—skilled love—as only that which precedes, supports, and sustains marriage. Consequently, healthy marriage classes often disparaged relationships, sexual experiences, and even feelings that do not serve this end. Implicit in the promotion of skilled love as a political strategy for promoting marriage is the directive that lesser forms of attraction and affection must be controlled and subordinated to smarter, more rational ways of loving that lead to and strengthen marriage. As illustrated by sociologists Stephanie Cootnz and Judith Stacey, traditional family values advocates often try to elide ideology by relying on social scientific evidence to convince the public of the economic and social value of two-parent, married families.[52] In a unique iteration of this strategy, healthy marriage education referenced social scientific studies on how happily married couples communicate and interact to teach that loving well leads to marriages that last. Thus, most of the "marriage promotion" that happened in healthy marriage classrooms was not about the social and economic benefits of marriage, but rather the psychological and relational benefits of skilled love as a framework for managing the often conflicted emotional experiences of dating, intimacy, and marriage. Ultimately, by bringing love to the fore in an exceedingly value-laden discourse of healthy marriage that emphasized how to love smarter, better, and longer, healthy marriage education ideologically reinforced the superiority of the married family. It did so, not by teaching that marriage is the best family form, but by teaching that love generated and channeled for marriage's sake is the best way to love.

3 Teaching Upward Mobility

Skilled Love and the Marriage Gap

"Every relationship has problems, and most of them are perpetual, irresolvable problems—in-laws, exes, kids, and especially money," said Cathy, the trainer for the *Mastering the Mysteries of Love* program. Noting a core premise of marriage education, Cathy explained that "Couples' biggest challenge is not that they fight or what they fight about, it's that so many don't know how to fight well." If couples could learn to communicate more skillfully about their relationship problems, she concluded, they would be more likely to get married, stay happily married, and be more productive workers and savers.

As part of our training, we watched a video from *Love's Cradle*, a relationship skills curriculum for low-income, unmarried couples with children that was developed by Mary Ortwein and Bernard Guerney, authors of *Mastering the Mysteries of Love*. One part focused on Dan and Gail, an unmarried African American couple with an infant daughter, who were struggling with "Baby Mama Drama," the title of their video segment. Gail is upset because Dan's ex-girlfriends frequently call their house in the middle of the night. Hoping to eventually get married, Gail and Dan use the skills taught by the program to talk through various challenges they are experiencing. These include not having enough money, job problems, Gail's postpartum disinterest in sex, and, most troubling, Dan's struggle to be involved with his children from previous relationships and the mothers' meddling in his relationship with Gail. We also watched Jason and Nicole, a white couple with a new baby who are also struggling with money problems, co-parenting Jason's two sons from a previous relationship, and Nicole's concerns about Jason's overly critical mother.

My fellow marriage educators-in-training and I watched their "unskilled" conversations as the couples communicated in a hostile and dismissive manner without using the skills, followed by "skilled" discussions as they calmly and rationally talked through the same problems using what they learned in a relationship skills class. One of Jason and Nicole's frequent fights about finances started when, according to Jason, Nicole spent too much money to buy candles, pillows, and other decorative items for their apartment. This unskilled conversation quickly devolves into Jason yelling at Nicole for being wasteful and inconsiderate with the little money they do have. Through their *Love's Cradle* class, they learn to be better active listeners and to see the situation from their partner's perspective. Using her new skills, Nicole is able to calmly communicate to Jason that she spent the money to make their apartment feel like a home. Jason skillfully and lovingly conveys to Nicole that he got so angry because he was really worried about not having enough money for essentials like rent and food. Both now know how to articulate the feelings behind the behaviors that upset their partner.

Ultimately, Jason and Nicole come to understand that their fight was less about having too little money and more about her desire to create a nice home for him and his anxiety about adequately providing for her and his children. A relationship skills class is particularly helpful for couples like Dan and Gail and Jason and Nicole, Cathy explained, because they learn to communicate with each about their perpetual issues in an empathic way that gets at their underlying emotional concerns. From Cathy's perspective, Nicole and Jason's biggest challenge was not their money problems. It was that their money problems took a negative emotional toll on their relationship—and likely their children—because they were not communicating about these problems in a skilled, positive way. Doing so would help them manage those problems as a committed, loving team, Cathy concluded.

The contrast between the "unskilled" and "skilled" vignettes illustrates how healthy marriage education defined a good relationship as one that requires effective communication and a sense of solidarity that can weather family stresses and economic strain. As I described in chapter 2, healthy marriage classes emphasized skilled love—a form of love that is logical, competent, and controlled—to create and sustain a satisfying, stable marriage. In this chapter, I continue to draw from my experience in the healthy marriage classes and my analysis of the curricula to show how healthy marriage programs taught that skilled love can prevent risky and financially costly relationship choices. By imparting that loving skillfully is the link between relational and financial success, healthy marriage classes advocated that disparate understandings and practices of love lead to divergent economic destinies. They described romantic choices as financial choices and urged participants to develop the emotional and cognitive capacities associated with skilled love to achieve upward mobility and financial success. Being unskilled in matters of love and money, instructors and curricula claimed, is often the precursor to bad life decisions—namely, unmarried parenthood and financial mismanagement—that threaten both family stability and economic well-being. Paradoxically, though they linked financial and relational success, the classes and curricula ignored how economic inequalities constrain relationship opportunities and choices.

Marriage, Money, and Skills

As discussed in chapter 2, cultural understandings of marriage have changed from a focus on instrumental goals—pooling resources, increasing extended family networks, and having children—to expressive ones, including romantic love, self-actualization, and companionship. Though couples now view romantic love as the primary basis of marriage, resources significantly influence how couples experience and sustain that love. Economic hardship takes an emotional toll on romantic and family relationships. How happy people are with their relationships—what scholars call relationship satisfaction—affects relationship stability, whether couples remain committed to one another and stay together.[1] Economic circumstances affect both relationship satisfaction and stability, which has important implications for relationship policies and programs that seek to help families and address intimate inequalities.

More economically advantaged couples tend to be happier in their romantic relationships and are less likely to break up, separate, and divorce.[2] Couples who struggle with financial insecurity and those who have less education and fewer economic assets tend to have less satisfying and stable romantic relationships.[3] Stress is one major reason. Economic problems, especially living in poverty, often lead to the deterioration of romantic relationships because financial stress affects how couples interact with one another.[4] In particular, hardship tends to generate interpersonal conflict.[5] As couples face economic pressures—low incomes, high debts, unstable employment, low-status jobs, unmet needs, and few opportunities for upward mobility—they are more likely to experience negative emotions, such as anger, anxiety, and despair.[6] Economic insecurity is especially conducive to fighting, despondency, and emotional alienation and less to warmth, support, and romance.

Sociologist Gay Kitson's study on why couples divorce revealed that economically advantaged couples were more likely to attribute their divorce to lack of communication, incompatibility, partners' selfishness, and changing values; lower-income couples were more likely to cite physical abuse, neglecting household duties, cheating, gambling, criminal activities, and financial and employment problems.[7] This and similar studies have suggested that as couples ascend the class ladder, they are more likely to divorce or not marry for expressive rather than instrumental reasons.[8] Yet, subsequent studies of conflict and break-ups among low-income couples have found that partners rarely cite financial issues as their main problem.[9]

The desire for greater emotional intimacy, especially among women who want more affection and attention from their partners, is a source of relationship strife across the class spectrum.[10] But it is more often motivated by financial constraint among low-income couples. Not only does economic hardship make it difficult to buy the things that couples use to practice romance, such as gifts and date nights out, it can make feeling sustained romantic attraction, affection, and connection more difficult as couples contend with the constant strain of doing without and anxiety over how to make ends meet. This can be a vicious cycle. Breaking up, separation, and divorce often have devastating emotional, physical, and economic consequences, especially for women and children.[11] A supportive partner can be an emotional buffer between a loved one and stressful life events.[12] Yet, faced with managing the persistent stressors of poverty and other social disadvantages such as racial discrimination, low-income couples have fewer coping resources left to negotiate interpersonal conflict in romantic relationships.[13] This suggests that low-income couples like Dan and Gail and Jason and Nicole tend to fight more and marry less and are less likely to stay together, not because they are unskilled communicators, but because constant financial strain depletes the positive emotions that support relationship satisfaction and stability.

Money problems are certainly not the only relationship challenge for disadvantaged couples. Low-income couples disproportionately struggle with mistrust, infidelity, intimate violence, drug and alcohol abuse, crime and incarceration, and ongoing conflict with previous partners with whom they share children.[14] Ethnographic studies of low-income parents have revealed that behaviors deemed irresponsible and destructive to relationship commitment usually play an even greater role than finances in couples' decisions about whether to stay together or marry. This research finds that, when low-income couples do fight about money, it is not typically about their economic challenges, per se, but about one partner's perception that another has behaved irresponsibly in the face of these challenges. In their study of poor unmarried mothers, sociologists Kathryn Edin and Maria Kefalas found that conflicts over money rarely happened because men could not find a job or earn enough. Rather, women believed that men were unreliable providers who were unwilling to keep a job, share income with their family, or spend their money responsibly on necessary family expenses.[15] Though chronic financial problems contribute to relationship tension, Edin and Kefalas illustrated, mothers were more likely to blame fathers' drug and alcohol abuse, criminal behavior, repeated infidelity, and intimate violence as the major reasons they neither trusted men nor followed through on their plans to marry them. Similarly, in her study of rural families living in poverty, sociologist Jennifer Sherman discovered that women had left ex-husbands or boyfriends because of drug use and physical abuse but were willing to stay with men who were unemployed or made little money as long as someone could provide income for the family.[16] Sociologist Judith Levine's study of low-income mothers also found that mistrust surrounding sexual fidelity and sharing financial resources, two primary signs of relationship commitment, was especially destructive in low-income couples' relationships.[17] This line of research suggests that money is a primary topic of disagreement among disadvantaged couples, not just because financial stress creates conditions ripe for interpersonal conflict, but also because of what pooling and sharing money represents: selflessness, responsibility, and dedication to family. The symbolic meaning of money also plays a central role in why low-income fathers mistrust women, as studies have revealed that disadvantaged men often believe women want them only for the money they can provide.[18]

Given that low-income couples themselves cite bad behavior as a primary cause of their relationship instability, it makes sense that healthy marriage classes would emphasize making better relationship choices. But behaviors do not happen in a social vacuum where everyone has equal opportunity to make the same choices and faces the same consequences for behaving badly. What healthy marriage classes tended to ignore is that relationship conflict has both behavioral and structural bases. Poverty and unemployment are strong predictors of criminal activity.[19] Selling drugs, for example, can offer greater access to money and status than low-wage, legal employment. Low-income men's weak labor market position makes it more likely that they will become part of the drug trade.[20] Low-income men of color especially are directly targeted by the criminal justice system and face more arrests and convictions and longer sentencing for criminal behavior.[21] This makes it more likely that they will get caught in a cycle of incarceration that decreases their economic opportunities and their marital prospects. Financial strain, especially frequent unemployment, also increases the chances that men will be perpetrators of intimate violence.[22]

Economic advantages protect more educated, higher-income couples from the negative consequences of romantic choices and behaviors. For example, if someone earns more, they have more to spend as they personally wish *and* contribute to family income. In the *Love's Cradle* video, Jason and Nicole might still have fought over Jason's perception that Nicole spent money irresponsibly if they were not poor and struggling to pay for food and housing. But Nicole's expenditure on candles and pillows would not have had the same financial consequences—and, therefore, likely would not have instigated the same fight (or any fight at all)—if their financial circumstances had more easily afforded food, rent, *and* decorative items for the apartment.

One major problem with the healthy marriage classes I studied is how they framed the connection between strong relationships and social class. Without meaningfully acknowledging the role economic deprivation and stress play in romantic relationships, they explained the marriage gap—the tendency for poor couples to marry less and break up more—as a result of lower-income couples being less knowledgeable about marriage and less equipped to make good romantic choices. The assumption that low-income families struggle both relationally and economically because they in particular lack the skills and knowledge to create healthy families is a neoliberal iteration of the culture of poverty thesis. Neoliberalism is a political philosophy that prioritizes personal responsibility, limited government, and managing social problems such as poverty by teaching individuals how to self-regulate in line with larger political aims. As a policy paradigm, neoliberalism characterizes individuals as rational, self-governing entities who create their own economic well-being and happiness by making prudent personal choices.[23] First named by anthropologist Oscar Lewis in 1966, the *culture of poverty* refers to the idea that people who live in poverty have a unique set of values, attitudes, and abilities.[24] According to this theory, growing up amid poverty and its attendant material hardships—no or low wages, few educational and employment opportunities, and a greater likelihood of being raised by unmarried parents—produces adaptive, yet deviant cultural values that normalize nonmainstream behaviors such as crime, welfare dependence, and single parenthood. As these practices become more common in pockets of concentrated poverty, poor children learn to adopt deviant values presumed to be associated with deprivation, such as apathy and promiscuity, while they neglect to learn skills ostensibly associated with being middle class, such as delaying gratification and working hard. Once created in the context of material hardship, these delinquent values and deficient abilities become the driving forces behind poor behavioral choices and the intergenerational transmission of poverty from parents to children. Central to this neoliberal understanding of poverty is the belief that those in poverty are lacking more than money and middle-class values; it assumes that they are inherently deficient in the skills, knowledge, and competencies associated with being financially stable.

This culture of poverty logic has infused much of the academic and policy discourse on American families and inequality claiming that there are two distinct classes of Americans—one poor, the other prosperous—separated by divergent marital values, behaviors, and abilities. Political scientist James Q. Wilson argued that the more prosperous group consists of two-parent, married families who give their children access to superior education, abundant future job opportunities, and self-advancement. In the other group, single mothers raise children outside marriage, while gang violence, drug abuse, sexual promiscuity, poverty, and uncommitted fathers undermine children's potential.[25] The underlying causes of poverty, Wilson reasoned, are a distorted sense of social morality, one that fails to attach stigma and shame to "out-of-wedlock" childbearing, and the distinct habits and abilities related to family formation this distortion creates.

This understanding of poverty has significantly influenced welfare and family policies in the United States, especially healthy marriage policy. For many Americans, welfare evokes images of promiscuous single mothers, often women of color, who purposely have children outside marriage and deliberately avoid work.[26] This idea originated in the 1950s as never-married mothers, including more African American women, became a larger share of welfare recipients. The belief that low-income Americans' delinquent marital values and deficient relationship abilities are a driving force of poverty became even more popular in the 1980s with the publication of several influential books by conservative policy reformers, namely, Charles Murray's *Losing Ground*[27] and Lawrence Mead's *Beyond Entitlement*.[28] The thinly veiled racialized images of single motherhood portrayed in these writings suggested that the poverty of unmarried mothers and their children was rooted in women's immoral sexual practices and bad relationship choices, especially their deliberate decisions not to marry their children's fathers. This led to policy proposals in the late 1980s that faulted government aid for increasing poverty by creating dependence, specifically by enabling poor, single mothers to raise children without men.[29] These proposals culminated in the passage of the Personal Responsibility Act in 1996 that first earmarked public funding for healthy marriage programs, which reflected neoliberal assumptions that becoming skilled in matters of love and money would help reduce poverty and welfare dependence.

For the most part, the classes and curricula I studied did not assume that individuals and couples living in poverty have nonmainstream values. Many instructors explicitly noted that those living below and above the poverty line share similarly strong commitments to education, work, and marriage. They did, however, teach that responsible behaviors and choices can improve couples' financial challenges and that what couples need is the requisite knowledge and self-control to prioritize marriage and ascend the class ladder. By characterizing couples' primary relationship challenges as communicative and expressive ones, this strategy obscured how relationship behaviors and romantic choices cannot be separated from their social context. Given the unique chal-lenges low-income couples face, teaching skilled love as a route to upward mobility does little to help couples address the mistrust and conflict exacerbated by conditions of economic deprivation and lim-ited opportunity. Though couples' interpersonal conflicts may not be explicitly about these conditions, they are intimately affected by them nonetheless. In addition to communication skills, teaching about this phenomenon—the emotional toll that inequality and disadvantage take on intimacy and romance—would be useful for low-income couples who, much like American public policies and cultural stereotypes of the poor, characterize irresponsible personal behavior as the biggest threat to relationship well-being. Instead, the classes emphasized that people are more likely to be successful in both love and money if they can skillfully pursue family and financial goals.

"Your Love Life Is Not Neutral": Relationship Choices as Financial Choices

Speaking to a packed room of workshop attendees, Marline Pearson, co-author of the *Within My Reach* curriculum for low-income individuals, explained: "Your love life is not neutral. . . . There's noth-ing like a messed-up love life to mess up every other part of your life." By this, Pearson meant that making the right choices about love and marriage is crucial for both romantic and economic success. If people only knew how the "success sequence" worked, she reasoned, they could make deliberate and skilled choices that would keep them out of poverty:

> There are three powerful things you can do to get off the poverty track. Finish high school, bottom line. Be married before having a baby, and make sure you wait until you're over twenty to do those things. Do those three things, mothers, and only 7 percent of those children live in poverty, versus 64 percent of children whose mothers don't do those three things.

The inability to follow the success sequence did not, Pearson clarified, reflect bad family values. Rather, it was a result of inadequate relational knowledge, which lower-income individuals are less likely to have:

If you look at the unwed childbearing statistics, you'll see that that lack of understanding of the sequence and why marriage matters is really acute among those with the least education and the least economic resources. They're the ones who have the most to lose by not having a good solid partnership together first. . . . Even though marriage may be a goal, the behaviors young people engage in tend to take them away from those goals, and they don't understand that.

Pearson further explained that one's love life is not neutral because romantic misunderstandings and missteps can take people off the life course dictated by the script that naturally sequences one's love and work life for being middle class. When people do not have a good sense of this life script that links education, work, and family in an ordered and deliberate framework for major life goals, they lack a mental schema that orients them toward smart, intentional, and rational life choices. People who do not know about the script "drift and stumble . . . and they don't put time into figuring out how to have a good relationship," Pearson concluded.

Scott Stanley, co-author of the *Within My Reach* curriculum, spoke next during the workshop and noted that many of the problems in family life today are because people rarely make deliberate, thoughtful relationship decisions: "They slide rather than decide." He added that they do not consider the ramifications of their romantic decisions on their educational opportunities, jobs, economic futures, and especially their kids. Stanley told our audience:

Young, single mothers just don't think about how the relationship issues and decisions affect their children. We're sliding through transitions that have life-altering consequences. . . . The chemical stuff of love is so powerful people are not seeing clearly for a long time. . . . Then you end up with tons of kids where there's not a mutually committed set of parents. . . . You can always dump the jerk, a loser, a poor match, but if you make a baby with a poor match or a loser, guess who can't dump the person? The child can't dump the parent. Or the child may never even see the parent.

Echoing Pearson, Stanley explained that people so often get into relationships they regret because they lack a script for how to get to know a romantic interest as a potential spouse, lover, and co-parent. Making smart, potentially life-altering decisions about sex, living together, and having a child requires informed, skilled choice: "If somebody is really being wise, they get information about the person, about safety, about values, about the future. They make a deliberate decision." In other words, they *decide* to make a commitment, they do not just *slide* into a relationally ambiguous situation that risks their economic future.

The success sequence, a poverty-reduction strategy conceptualized by psychologist Ron Haskins and economist Isabel Sawhill, featured prominently in the *PREP, Within My Reach, Love U2,* and *Connections* curricula.[30] Though not explicitly in terms of the sequence, the other curricula similarly emphasized the importance of making good relationship and financial choices to avoid poverty. As taught in healthy marriage classes, the message of lessons on the success sequence was that being relationally unskilled disrupts life chances by causing individuals to make bad romantic and sexual choices, namely, having babies before finishing school, holding down a full-time job, and marrying. The logic of the success sequence is, in part, correct. Children benefit when their parents have stable relationships. Moreover, when parents have high-school diplomas and can maintain full-time work, it does keep many, though not all, of their families above the poverty line. But the sequence frames poverty solely as a result of when parents choose to have their children and with whom, without accounting for the significant role of educational and occupational opportunities in determining who can fulfill the sequence.

Lessons on how to make good relationship choices reflected this important omission. Describing his experience teaching the *PREP* curriculum as part of a welfare program, Stanley recounted a class where he asked a group of TANF recipients, " 'How many of you would be in a completely different place in your life right now if you had done something differently in an important relationship in your past?' Every hand shot up. We didn't have to tell the stories of bad relationships. They'd lived the stories." Stanley described to the audience one of the hypothetical couple scenarios he used to teach about what the curriculum called "high-cost slides":

He asked to move in when he got evicted. They had been dating about a month at that point. She thought it would take some of the stress and burden off her to have someone else there. He would help pay the bills and the living expenses. "Life might be easier," she was thinking when he moved in. But there are high-cost consequences: After three months he lost his job. He had an argument with his boss, cussed him out, and got fired. Now he only makes a halfhearted attempt to look for work. He sleeps until noon and often goes out late at night. Meanwhile, she's working hard, taking a class, and scrounging to make ends meet. It feels to her that she has another child.

Participants were supposed to identify when in this scenario the woman started to slide rather than decide—that is, when she started making costly life choices by cohabiting with a man she barely knew. This example portrayed the man as a deadbeat and freeloader and his unemployment as the result of unprofessional behavior (cussing out his boss) and laziness (lack of initiative to look for another job). The research on low-income couples reveals that women especially attribute relationship problems to men's irresponsible economic behavior like that in the scenario. However, as was typical in the classes, what Stanley did not address was why this hypothetical woman felt compelled to ask the man to live with her in the first place: the stress and burden of paying for an apartment on her own. Stanley also ignored how reasons outside the man's immediate control—lack of education, a prior criminal record, a bad labor market—likely would have shaped his behavior if the scenario had been real. It is easy to frame good romantic choices merely as matters of relationship acumen and personal responsibility when they are decontextualized from the social and economic forces that shape actual couples' lives.

The goal of this and similar lessons was to convince participants that relationship decisions have great power to shape socioeconomic opportunities. Susan Blumberg, the final presenter for the *Within My Reach* workshop, explained to our audience that this message was particularly important when teaching relationship skills to lower-income individuals. Pointing to two containers of colored marbles—one full of mostly green, the other mostly red—she told us that the red marbles represented bad things in life, while the green represented the good:

Everybody has been given a life that's a mixture. Nobody gets to choose what they've been handed in life. So what can I do? I can go get more green. I can take out some red. I've changed my odds, but do I have a guarantee that I'm still going to pull out a green? No. We'll learn in these classes that there is no guarantee that things are going to turn out the way you would like, but we do have some control over what happens to us in our lives because we can change the odds. We can pull out reds, and we can add greens. We also teach people that I am not the only one who adds reds and greens to my bowl. Who else?

One of the audience members answered "family." "Yes," Blumberg exclaimed, "who else?" "Romantic partners and friends," offered another. Blumberg responded, "Absolutely. What if I am hanging out with a bunch of people who are continually dumping reds into my bowl? We're giving folks some skills and confidence to break connections with people who are dumping red into their lives."

Stanley then interjected to explain how it was even more important for disadvantaged individuals to be mindful of the consequences of hasty and uninformed relationship choices because those handed a life full of mostly red marbles do not have much of a safety net to fall back on when something bad happens. Pointing to the container of mostly red marbles, Stanley explained:

> If you live in a very chaotic world with lots of economic disadvantage, lots of breakdowns of structure, you have more of this. If you have someone with a red bowl and someone with a green bowl, which person better be paying a whole lot more attention to what they reach in and pull out? . . . If you have a lot of wealth, you at least have a much greater ability to recover in terms of assets and money. If you are already right on the edge, and this is what life dealt you, it's that much more crucial to learn how to make better choices because you have no margin.

Blumberg ended the workshop by noting that *Within My Reach* was designed for people whom life has handed a jar full of red marbles: It teaches them to express and manage their emotions appropriately, to recognize unsafe relationship situations, to take time-outs, and to resist the urge to externalize anger and stress. She concluded, "Angry brains are not smart brains," and you need a smart, controlled brain to make wise romantic choices.

"Smart" meant not getting too emotionally or physically involved with someone before marrying them, choosing not to live together prior to marriage, and fulfilling a successful life plan—including graduation and a good job—prior to marriage and having children. Thus, much of what the *Within My Reach* authors and those of the other healthy marriage programs I studied advocated for being wise about relationships involved making deliberate family-formation decisions that could presumably prevent poverty. Though many instructors and curricula recognized social inequality in a nominal sense—life metaphorically hands some people more red marbles—there was little regard for how economic disadvantage shapes relationship choices and experiences. The classes emphasized that creating a healthy marriage—and the middle-class lifestyle that can better support it—requires having not just the right family values about love and sex, but sufficient relational knowledge and skills to put those values into practice and avoid bad behaviors assumed to perpetuate poverty.

As implicit moral directives for marriage and parenting, these messages about skilled love and healthy relationship behaviors obscured the root causes of family inequality by explaining poverty as a result of differential abilities to make good romantic choices. This is a very meritocratic view of the connection between family and class. Just as many like to believe that the richest individuals are the ones with the strongest work ethic and most valuable job-related skills, healthy marriage education, with its emphasis on developing a relationship work ethic and loving skillfully, also framed relationship success as an earned achievement and skill-based endeavor. Viewed in this way, the marriage gap does not reflect socioeconomic inequality, but is a consequence of a social system that distributes advantages and rewards to individuals on the basis of effort and ability. As with occupational inequality, characterizing family inequality as a meritocracy obscures how work and family success—narrowly defined, respectively, as high-earning, high-status employment and lifelong marriage started before children—depends on access to opportunities and reflects ideological definitions of what success entails.

In addition to teachings on the success sequence, other lessons similarly implied that family-related personal choices are responsible for class inequality and poverty. A common one was that individuals must learn to love skillfully to create and sustain romantic relationships that function as sound long-term economic investments. Though all of the curricula focused to some extent on emotional management techniques, this theme was particularly pronounced in the curricula for youth and low-income individuals and couples. Educators often talked

about "intentionality," especially in discussions of sex, starting relationships, and how to choose good partners that would satisfy the success
sequence. In the workshop for the *Wait Training: It's All About M.E.*
curriculum for youth, the workshop leader emphasized how emotional
self-regulation was vital for success in all areas of life:

> If you look at the social and personal problems people are facing
> in the United States—we're talking drugs and alcohol abuse,
> teen pregnancy, unsafe sex, school failure, shopping problems,
> gambling—the majority of them have self-control failure as
> central to them. . . . Studies show that self-control does predict
> success in life. . . . If we are concerned with raising children to
> be healthy, successful, and happy, forget about self-esteem, con-
> centrate on self-control.

The trainer concluded with the message that if youth can learn to control their emotions and their bodies, "They can learn to control their
life" and will avoid costly decisions such as premarital sex and teenage
pregnancy. Similarly, *Love's Cradle* for low-income families focused on
helping new parents become "emotionally resilient" by teaching them
"to practice habits that manage residue stress" and to "regain control of
their chemistry through relaxation and of their lives by problem solving."[31] Instructors also emphasized the importance of being intentional
when selecting a romantic partner and that one is choosing not only a
potential spouse, but also a future co-earner and co-parent. Part of being
relationally skilled, classes taught, was learning to refocus one's attention
in dating from qualities of fleeting sexual attraction to those that signaled a partner would be a good worker and parent. Exercises like "What
a Baby Wants" from the *Love U2* curriculum for youth required participants to write a mock newspaper ad for an "unborn child looking for a
family" to encourage high-school-aged students to think about what kind
of partner would best help them complete the success sequence.

These lessons described emotional regulation as central to romantic
as well as economic success. People are poor, at least in part, many of the
curricula implied, because they lack appropriate emotional controls, reg-
ulatory habits, and partner-selection criteria. Just as the *Within My Reach*
instructors acknowledged that some people get more "reds" in life than
others who get many more "greens," most of the curricula minimally addressed how social factors, such as money and jobs (or lack thereof), can

affect relationship quality and life opportunities. Yet, they justified the much greater focus on loving skillfully by noting that, whereas people have little control over external factors, including partners' bad behaviors, they could control their internal emotional climate and romantic choices. Though the *PREP* leader's guide recognized that it is more difficult "to make a marriage work when a couple struggles financially,"[32] Stanley noted in the *PREP* training that, "We focus on what matters and what is changeable with training and motivation, not on what we likely can't change." Individual choices and behaviors seem more amenable to change than the inequalities that shape couples' financial struggles.

"Giving Them Hope and Skills": Overcoming Reluctance to Marry

Instructors assumed that couples' apprehension about marriage was especially changeable through relationship skills trainings. Many of the trainers I observed described how low-income individuals are scared of marriage and fear they cannot make it work because they grow up in communities where lasting marriage is uncommon and marriage role models are scarce. Though they share the same hopes for marriage, trainers claimed, they are doubly disadvantaged when it comes to realizing these aspirations: Not only do they encounter more economic obstacles, they are also more likely to lack the knowledge and skills that can help them overcome these challenges. According to the *Connections* workshop leader, relationship skills can bridge the gap between marital aspirations and marital realities: "Ninety-three percent of teens expect that they will get married and 91 percent want children, but 87 percent say that it won't work. The expectations are there, the skills are not. We just need to know how to communicate effectively. . . . Love is a really scary place for most young people." The developers of the *Caring for My Family: Together We Can* curriculum for low-income, unmarried couples also described the various reasons couples do not get married even when they aspire to. Referencing research findings from Edin and Kefalas's *Promises I Can Keep: Why Poor Women Put Motherhood Before Marriage*,[33] one of the trainers noted that before getting married, low-income mothers "wanted their financial concerns resolved . . . and to find a partner that is responsible, holding a job, has enough assets to support a family. . . . They were also worried about fidelity and commitment. They felt their relationship was not strong enough to last." Describing how the curriculum addressed these various challenges, she continued:

> We took this research, and we focused on relationship building, sexual fidelity, trust, commitment, and family processes like conflict resolution, stress management, and communication skills. . . . We wanted to do skill building and help them feel comfortable in their head. We identified ways to increase financial preparation and stability, a whole module just on financial issues and making sure that you're able to provide.

Caring for My Family addressed all these common relationship challenges among low-income couples through instruction in communication, budgeting, and problem-solving skills.

Other curricula similarly emphasized the importance of "transferable" problem-solving skills, which low-income individuals were presumed to lack in matters of love, work, and money. According to the *Love's Cradle* manual:

> If a person can't solve problems, they are unlikely to have much of what they want for themselves or their child in life. . . . If couples can persevere and solve ONE PROBLEM satisfactorily together, it can create powerful change. . . . The conscious application of a repeatable process gives them a new life script. They can take conscious control over their lives.[34]

In a variation on this theme about cooperative problem solving, in the *Mastering the Mysteries of Love* training, Cathy noted that developing the ability to persevere together through problems was the most important skill couples could learn. Keep in mind, she urged, that most relationship struggles, including financial ones, are universal and perpetual. "It doesn't matter if you solve the problems. It only matters that you keep working on them with love, respect, and a sense of security. People often don't need the problem fixed. They just need to be heard."

The speaker for the *Wait Training: It's All About M.E.* workshop described how youth from low-income backgrounds in particular lacked the problem-solving skills and confidence needed for a successful marriage and life because they lacked sufficient marriage role models:

Poor kids and minority kids have the same dreams and hopes. They're just not articulated. . . . Some of our minority kids go to more funerals than weddings. They've never seen a marriage. . . . You have to first get the kids to want to not have sex because if you have nothing to dream about, you're going to go in doors that you normally wouldn't go into. We're giving them hope and skills. We're trying to get them into the right sequence of first comes love, then comes marriage, then comes the baby carriage.

To address this problem, many of the curricula included mentoring activities and speaker panels with long-term married couples, mock wedding ceremonies, wedding planning activities, and marriage simulations. These exercises were intended to help students accomplish their goals for marriage by giving them appropriate marriage role models and by allowing them to vicariously experience the benefits of being married. The *Love's Cradle* curriculum required couples to plan a wedding for $600 for their hypothetical twenty-five-year-old engaged son or daughter. The exercise asked parents to identify what they believed their grown children and their children's fiancés should have in place before they marry and what they should plan to accomplish together after marriage. The *Love's Cradle* workshop leader noted that low-income couples "just don't see the advantages of marriage as being relevant to them. There's this belief that you only get married when you're sure you've entered the middle class and when you're absolutely sure you're going to be true to each other." Exercises like the wedding planning activity aimed to convince participants that one of the reasons marriage was economically beneficial and prevented poverty was because it provided a script for working together as a unified financial team. Accordingly, most of the curricula also offered couples training in how to communicate about and effectively manage their money.

"Doing More with What You Have": Teaching Financial Literacy

A major criticism of welfare policies is that they redistribute income to those in poverty in ways that do not encourage economic self-sufficiency or asset accumulation. In response, the government has created asset-building policy initiatives intended to help low-income families save, become homeowners, and develop financial literacy.[35] The Administration for Children and Families (ACF) included "financial literacy" as one of its advised content areas for healthy marriage programs. According to the ACF's marriage education curriculum guide, financial literacy involves "basic money management skills" related to "budgeting, banking, saving, planning, and investing," "financial responsibility," and "negotiation or communication skills related to the distribution and/or expenditure of financial resources."[36] Conspicuously not included in this definition is access to information about means-tested public benefits, including TANF, Medicaid, subsidized child care, and the Earned Income Tax Credit. Though evaluation research has found that financial literacy programs can improve low-income individuals' knowledge about money matters, there is no evidence that participating in them leads to more economic stability for low-income families.[37] Learning about how to save, invest, and budget does not necessarily translate into having more money, especially if one does not have sufficient money from the start.

The inclusion of financial literacy lessons in healthy marriage curricula reflected research findings that money is one of the most pervasive and recurrent topics of conflict for couples of all socioeconomic backgrounds.[38] Jointly managing finances is a significant symbol of commitment, and money is a primary source of interpersonal stress. Lessons on money, therefore, focused on teaching couples to cooperatively talk about financial issues to reduce the emotional toll of money-related pressures and disagreements. They also pointed to two core assumptions about lower-income couples embedded in healthy marriage curricula: that they, in particular, lack knowledge about how to budget and save and that developing financial literacy skills enables economic self-sufficiency and helps poor couples overcome their reluctance to marry. Without meaningfully acknowledging the social and economic conditions that shape this reluctance, healthy marriage classes presumed that many couples, especially low-income couples, had the wrong psychological orientation to money, one too focused on immediate needs and wants and resulting in poor financial planning and irresponsible spending habits.

Almost all of the curricula explicitly addressed money, some via numerous lessons on financial goal-setting and budgeting, others by teaching couples how to mutually negotiate financial decisions and money-related values and habits. The manual for the FOCCUS (*Facilitating Open*

Couple Communication, Understanding & Study) premarital inventory noted that:

> Shared financial building and planning can be a key marital bonder of trust and a shared life. Financial issues can, on the other hand, cause more problems for couples than any other area of the marital relationship. The problem is usually not so much the actual finances as it is the underlying value orientation on money each partner has.[39]

Similarly, in the *Smart Steps for Stepfamilies* workshop, the trainer explained:

> Both spouses typically have worked and have their own income, maybe assets, so financial issues are especially complicated in step families, [for] your traditions and routines. You wouldn't believe the fights that people get into because of these very different family histories, so teaching each other about those histories is key.

Like *FOCCUS* and *Smart Steps*, many of the curricula stressed the importance of self-awareness and couple compatibility in financial matters. They encouraged participants to ask pertinent questions of themselves and their partners, such as: Are you a "spender" or a "saver"? Are there any concerns about a partner's spending habits, unpaid bills, or outstanding debts? Who has or will have primary responsibility for managing the family's finances? The *Ten Great Dates* guide concluded: "The real concern is not how many bank accounts you have (separate or joint) or even how much money you have, but that you have a realistic and workable financial plan that you both agree on."[40]

Budgeting—with an emphasis on the importance of couples living within their financial means regardless of family income—was the most common financial topic across all the curricula. Like *Ten Great Dates*, many emphasized that the amount of money couples have is not as important for a healthy marriage as how effectively partners negotiate money-related decisions and manage how much they do have. Learning to communicate about and manage money are important relational skills, trainers claimed, because they could help couples cope with economic pressures and create supportive family relationships that are even more important than money. In the *Bringing Baby Home* training, the instructor emphasized that giving children material possessions was much less important than giving them a healthy co-parenting relationship: "You can give your child every toy in the world, but giving them a healthy relationship is so much better."

Many of the curricula taught couples to create a monthly budget or annual savings plan and use their communication and conflict-resolution skills to work through hypothetical financial crises, such as job loss, mortgage foreclosure, and severe illness. They also offered specific tips on how to save, including buying in bulk, saving excess change, learning to distinguish between needs and wants, cutting unnecessary expenses, and avoiding credit cards and all forms of debt. The marital inventory *PREPARE/ENRICH: Building a Strong Marriage Workbook* emphasized that:

> Budgeting doesn't mean having less; it means doing more with what you have. . . . Savings are also important to any financial management plan. . . . By saving a few hundred dollars a month over 30 to 40 years, a person can become a millionaire. It takes some planning and careful budgeting, but the result is financial gain that can help dreams come true. . . . Budgeting is simply the process of allocating expenses on a regular basis . . . and set[ting] financial goals. With a target or goal in sight you'll be more motivated to work together to achieve your goals.[41]

The *Marriage Savers* curriculum also included a budgeting worksheet where each spouse could list their short- and long-term financial goals and how they planned to jointly work toward accomplishing them. The budget guide indicated that a married couple with an annual household income of $15,000 or less should budget 40 percent of their income for housing; 15 percent for food; 4 percent each for clothing, savings, and medical and dental expenses; and 10 percent for tithing.[42] In 2006, when this curriculum was published, $15,000 would have put a couple just above the poverty line of $13,200 for a family of two. Assuming the couple earned $15,000 annually, paid $960 in taxes, and tithed $1,500, this budget allocated a mere $418 a month for housing; $157 for food (or $2.80 per person, per day); and $42 each for clothing, health care, and savings for two people. There was no discussion in the curriculum about the difficulties a couple would face trying to live within these near-poverty means, including severely inadequate amounts for basic necessities of housing, food, and clothing. The curriculum merely emphasized the importance of budgeting and shared financial goals. Like many of the other curricula, *Marriage Savers* stressed that successfully married couples would be more likely to accumulate greater financial resources—and, therefore, be less likely to live in poverty—if they prioritized mutual financial accountability over individual gain:

> For spouses to be able to plan a financially stable marriage, they need to be accountable to one another with an agreed-upon plan of how they will spend and save. . . . The financial goal is sharing resources. Mature married couples think in terms of "ours" as opposed to "mine" and "yours." . . . Couples who cohabit have more financial problems after they marry than do couples who married and never cohabited. Disputes over money appear to be due to their placing value on independence and economic equality. There are arguments over "my money" versus "your money."[43]

Happily married couples' greater tendency to think in terms of joint financial resources was, the curriculum emphasized, one of the primary reasons they were less likely to live in poverty and be better parents. The *Love U2* manual similarly explained that being married and having shared financial goals helps generate greater economic resources: "A married couple is more likely to be financially independent and to have their own apartment or place to live. The median family income for a married-parent household is $62,200 a year. It is $26,550 for a female single-parent-headed household."[44] It also noted that married parents are more likely to give their children numerous financial advantages—"housing in a safe neighborhood with better schools," high-quality child care that is less likely to "hurt a child's development," and health insurance to "provide the health care their child needs."[45] Poverty and single parenthood can also reduce the quality of parenting, *Love U2* explained, because when parents are constantly stressed about money, they have less time and attention to devote to children.

Teaching couples how to work together as a unified financial team within their economic means, regardless of how meager those means are, was a major goal of the healthy marriage classes I studied. Trainers promised that learning to live within a family budget would eliminate many money-related marital problems. The *Connections* curriculum for youth illustrated this by requiring students to randomly select occupations and household incomes ranging from $18,000 to $6,000,000. The occupation cards listed jobs such as secretary, high-school teacher, bank teller, factory worker, auto mechanic, baseball player, and farmer. Once students paired off with their mock spouses and selected occupation and income cards, they had to discuss their money values and spending styles, plan an affordable family vacation, and create a family budget that would allow them to avoid debt and save. Downplaying the importance of the widely varying hypothetical amounts with which couples had to work, the exercise emphasized financial cooperation:

> As in real life, the financial capability to complete this exercise will vary from couple to couple. Less emphasis should be placed on the dollar amount of the resources available to the family and more emphasis placed on using the time together as a way of strengthening the relationships between family members.[46]

Students were supposed to learn that, depending on how relationally skilled couples are, finances can be either divisive or an opportunity for bonding in romantic relationships. The lesson conveyed that whether they collectively earn $18,000 or $6,000,000, no couple is immune from money problems, especially if partners have different spending styles. How couples negotiate financial issues ostensibly matters more for relationship quality than how much money they have to negotiate. As the *Connections* manual explained, when couples disagree about money, "the wife may want new carpeting while the husband may want to take a trip, . . . having a lot of money can be as much of a problem as having too little."[47] Budgeting exercises such as this implied that couples' financial problems are merely interpersonal problems, a result of incompatible spending habits and divergent financial goals. Though fights over money are a universal relationship problem for couples of all economic classes, denying the role of extreme income inequality in shaping these conflicts does little to help couples address them.

Many of the classes did acknowledge that lower-income couples are more likely to struggle with unemployment or low-paying jobs, lack of access to affordable health care and child care, and extra costs associated with being poor, such as high interest rates on payday loans. Yet, even after noting this, instructors and curricula maintained that money mismanagement and the inability to work together are the driving causes of financial problems for all couples. The *Love's Cradle* curriculum noted:

Although the dynamics of money mismanagement in low income couples (impulsive spending, over-spending, inadequate planning) are no different from many middle income couples, the results are often more devastating due to the lack of a societal or a familial "safety net" available to many couples in higher income brackets. . . . Many couples lack basic education or information on how to manage money, specifically: how to get it, how to share it, how to manage it, and how to make it grow. The goal is for couples to leave the experience with confidence in their ability to work as a financial team.[48]

Couples across the class spectrum cite money as one of their most common topics of disagreement. Thus, the problem with this approach is not that the curricula focused on teaching couples how to communicate better and cooperatively manage money. The problem with healthy marriage classes was the omission of any nuance about how budgeting to eat for less than $3 a day and jointly deciding between getting new carpeting or taking a trip are two very different kinds of financial challenges. While the latter situation may be amenable to relationship skills training for couples with middle-class means, the same money management skills are not suited to helping couples simply budget their way out of poverty. Promoting this message, as most of the curricula and trainers did when talking about money, denies how all money problems within marriage are not created equal.

The *African American Relationships, Marriages, and Families* (*AARMF*) curriculum by Patricia Dixon was the one notable exception. Of its ten chapters, only one focused specifically on communication and conflict resolution. It was also the only curriculum I studied that described how structural disadvantage can undermine satisfying and stable romantic relationships. Instead of characterizing unmarried couples and individuals as deficient in skills and abilities, as many of the other curricula did, Dixon explained that:

Those using a deficit approach compare African American marriages and families to the nuclear model of the United States and find them to be deviant, and in some cases "pathological." . . . Those taking an adaptable approach . . . argue that African Americans adapted to their circumstances and their marriages and families have been resilient in the face of tremendous obstacles to their formation and development.[49]

Dixon claimed that educating couples about healthy relationship dynamics necessitates a dual focus on communication and how social factors, such as segregation and racial discrimination, shape couples' abilities to create and sustain lasting love. The *AARMF* curriculum also stressed the importance of budgeting and setting money-related goals, but it did not imply that couples' economic challenges were a direct result of financial mismanagement and being relationally unskilled. It, more than any other curricula, acknowledged that structural factors affect relationship behavior:

> The greatest challenge to African American relationships, marriages, and families has always been and continues to be structural factors stemming from historical and current institutional racism, [including] the economic marginalization and exclusion of African Americans, particularly African American males.[50]

The curriculum also noted that spending on luxury items, often perceived as frivolous, is usually less an issue of bad budgeting skills and often an attempt to gain status for disadvantaged people who have little else. Healthy relationships emerge, the curriculum explained, when couples focus more on family and responsible spending, less on money and material gain. In *AARMF*, Dixon demonstrated how a relationship skills program can contextualize lessons about responsible individual behavior and healthy interpersonal relationship dynamics within discussions about the larger structural factors—racism, poverty, gender inequality—that shape them.

The other curricula only addressed the financial challenges of lower-income couples in cursory ways. Some included information about accessing resources, such as how to qualify for government cash assistance programs and how to claim the Earned Income Tax Credit. The *Active Relationships* curriculum, for example, included two-thirds of a page on "Funding to Assist Families in Need" about how eligible couples could apply for welfare benefits. All the curricula that specifically targeted low-income individuals and couples briefly noted the importance of providing information about other services for families dealing with domestic violence, substance abuse, unemployment, or mental health problems. Alas, none of the lessons in the curricula focused on these topics known to be particularly challenging for low-income couples.

Trainers recognized that couples dealing with serious personal and financial challenges would likely need more support than a relationship skills class could provide. As Stanley explained in the *PREP* training, "If you're in the midst of trauma, this is not a good time to talk about relationship issues. People should not make major relationship decisions when they're under a lot of stress." Instead, trainers advocated distributing handouts with contact information should participants want to follow up about additional services.

Overall, the primary message about finances taught in healthy marriage classes was that learning to love skillfully can help couples avoid economic challenges, including poverty. Trainers and curricula described relationship skills as teachable, generalizable, and transferable abilities that apply equally to love and money. Just as people need to be logical, competent, and controlled to be prosperous in love, classes taught that couples need to develop these same abilities to prosper financially; both relational and financial success depend on the capabilities to develop knowledge, manage desire, work hard, and forego short-term rewards for greater long-term gains. Trainers often noted that low-income individuals share dominant cultural values regarding marriage and work. What they presumably lack are the interpersonal skills necessary to put those values into practice. The *Love's Cradle* workshop leader explained this connection between communication skills in marriage and interpersonal skills in the workplace:

> *Love's Cradle* couples are less likely to have graduated from high school. They are more likely to have minimum wage or working-class jobs, and that translates to the fact that they probably have less [sic] verbal skills. This is a very important thing because verbal skills are directly related to the ability to earn money in the workplace, and it's also directly related to the quality of your relationships and the likelihood that you will not have violence in your relationships because feelings once expressed have done their job. But if you can put words to how you feel, you are likely to put them into action, so the characteristic of being able to communicate is huge in terms of helping the couples have good lives and helping give their children what they would like.

Even in programs specifically intended for lower-income families, educators presented mutual negotiation, rational planning, and self-control as universally beneficial romantic and financial objectives. While the curricula for low-income couples did mention relationship challenges more common among those in poverty—sharing children with multiple partners, trust issues, reluctance to marry for financial reasons— they also stressed, as *Within My Reach* put it, that "Their issues and problems with love are not that different than most people's. . . . Many of us—rich, poor, black, white—are having problems today forming and maintaining quality relationships and marriages. No one, for sure, seems to have a roadmap anymore for how to do things."[51] Paradoxically, like the other curricula, *Within My Reach* stressed that despite the unique relationship challenges of disadvantaged couples, the fundamental relationship problem—lacking a relationship "roadmap" or skills— is the same across all class and racial groups. Accordingly, all twenty marriage education curricula in my sample taught similar lessons about communication, negotiation, and self-control as strategies for managing both love and money.

Love Lives Are Not Equal

Healthy marriage classes taught that skilled love contributes to upward mobility, not only because it allows couples to pool resources and share expenses, but because it provides a conceptual and behavioral framework for responsible relationship and financial choices. By casting family and economic stability as the result of relationship skills and knowledge, the curricula taught that having more money, much like learning to love skillfully, is the result of a cognitive, calculating process. This approach explains intimate inequalities in terms of disparate understandings and practices of love and assumes that couples prosper when they have the ability to regulate emotions and desires more effectively. It also takes for granted middle-class life chances, including educational opportunity, stable, well-paying employment, and available partners with high earning potential. Without accounting for the effects of economic constraints on interpersonal behavior and romantic choices, most instructors and curricula assumed that couples can improve their economic situation by mimicking the relationship patterns more typical of middle-class married couples. Yet, the success sequence is less a recipe for upward mobility than a reflection of inequitable access to education and good jobs.

Many of the programs I studied explained poverty and unstable families as consequences of lower-income individuals' greater tendency to be emotionally and financially unskilled—that is, lacking romantic intentionality and not knowing how to properly sequence life events and prudently manage money. As a neoliberal iteration of the culture of poverty logic that finds the poor's values, behaviors, and abilities deficient, this suggests that their intimate choices and ways of loving are also inadequate. Healthy marriage classes overwhelmingly focused on individuals' abilities to communicate and budget with very little attention paid to how social circumstances make certain romantic and financial choices more or less likely. With the one notable exception of the *African American Relationships, Marriages, and Families* curriculum, there was no scrutiny of the social institutions within which these choices are made—the job market, the educational system, and the family—and the myriad ways they create inequalities among different social groups. As part of a larger trend in poverty policy as described by historian Alice O'Connor, this line of reasoning politically neutralizes and demystifies poverty by framing it as a social problem that can be studied, explained, and prevented using rational behavioral modification techniques, including instruction in skilled communication and financial literacy.[52]

By couching its methods in a seemingly ideological and morally neutral language focused on "relationship skills" rather than "family values," healthy marriage education might seem one step removed from other discourses of cultural deviance and behavioral pathology that are so often used to describe those in poverty. The focus on skills shifts the discourse that pathologizes single parenthood from one about culture and values to one about knowledge and ability. Explaining economic disadvantage in terms of deficient relational knowledge, as many of the healthy marriage education curricula I studied did, conflates skilled love with the ideology of the white, heterosexual, two-parent, married family ideal. It also characterizes poverty as an aberration, a direct result of not making good family and financial choices—"sliding" into bad relationships, having sex and kids too early outside marriage, not budgeting effectively—rather than as a common outcome of social inequality in a capitalist economy. It is prudent to support individuals' abilities to make thoughtful relationship choices that will impact them and their children. But these efforts need not be embedded in messages implying that the solution to poverty is bringing the poor's romantic

choices and family-formation behaviors in line with that of more affluent Americans. Some programs I studied acknowledged that inequality
exists and shapes divergent relationship experiences. This was the intended message of the red and green marble demonstration from the
PREP training. Yet, this admission was merely part of a lesson intended
to teach that those with less need skills even more because disadvantaged families lack a safety net when relationships go awry. The welfare
policy overhaul in 1996 that first earmarked public money for healthy
marriage classes further institutionalized a stingy American welfare
state and exacerbated poverty in the United States. The American poor
do indeed lack a strong social safety net, one for which relationship
skills will never compensate.

Welfare reform and the healthy marriage programs it funded have focused on changing the work and relationship choices of those in poverty
without acknowledging the structural conditions in which those choices
are made. Isabel Sawhill, who coined the "success sequence," has advocated
for programs that promote the sequence by conditioning government
assistance on recipients graduating from high school, marrying before
having children, and working full-time. Because these three behaviors
are the key to upward mobility in American society, Sawhill argued, social inequality will continue to grow the more the behaviors of those in
poverty diverge from the behaviors of the middle class in these three key
areas of social life;[53] policies should, therefore, address the growing class
divide between "drifters" who slide into unplanned parenthood with
"planners" who deliberately prepare for children.[54] However, there is
little empirical support for the claim that those living in poverty have
different values and attitudes about education,[55] marriage,[56] or work.[57]

Though lower-income individuals do exhibit overall different behavioral trends in these domains, it does not mean that they lack the ability
or desire to finish school, work, or marry. Americans stuck on the lower
rungs of the class ladder face significantly more social and economic
obstacles to acting on their values.[58] Teaching skilled love as a route to
upward mobility is based on a limited understanding of what couples
need to improve their relationships and finances. It erroneously assumes that family inequalities operate primarily through differences in
relational knowledge and emotional capacities, while ignoring the role
of resources and opportunities.

The relationships of couples like Dan and Gail and Jason and Nicole
would likely benefit from a more generous social safety net—longer

welfare eligibility and more publicly subsidized child care and housing—and higher wages and jobs with health care benefits. Increasing couples' access to economic resources would lessen their stress and free up some of their emotional resources to work on and improve their relationships. Publicly funded relationship classes could be part of a welfare state that truly supports satisfying and stable family relationships. But in addition to or in lieu of lessons on budgeting, which imply that couples simply need to learn to better manage their resources no matter how meager, why not include lessons on how economic disadvantage can affect romantic experiences? Couples may then come to better understand how romantic and financial choices have behavioral as well as structural causes, which may help them be more empathic as they cope with shared economic challenges.

The vast evidence clearly linking economic insecurity and relationship instability suggests that relationship-strengthening programs for low-income couples are more likely to be effective if they reflect the important connection between love and money. To truly be evidence based, relationships programs should mutually address personal behavior and social context—that love lives are not neutral, but neither are they equal.

We join your friends and family in congratulating you on your anniversary. May the commitment you celebrate and the companionship you share bring you happiness for years to come.

With best wishes, George W. Bush and Laura Bush

4 Intimate Inequalities and Curtailed Commitments

The Marriage Gap in a Middle-Class Marriage Culture

On the date of their fifty-second wedding anniversary in July 2002, my grandparents received this congratulatory note from then President George W. and First Lady Laura Bush as part of the Healthy Marriage Initiative's efforts to recognize long-married American couples.[1] In 1950, my twenty-year-old grandfather, a farmer with a ninth-grade education, met and fell in love with my sixteen-year-old grandmother, who quit school after completing the eighth grade to cook, clean, and help on her family's farm. Both from low-income, rural families, they married a few months after they met in a five-minute civil ceremony at the local courthouse with neither debt nor property to their names and less than $300 in the bank. According to plan, they welcomed their first child eleven months later and another three within five years. Over the next several decades, they built a solidly middle-class life, one founded on hard work, frugality, wise financial investments, and a vow to stay together for richer or poorer—all things that healthy marriage classes taught would lead to prosperity. When I asked my grandfather why he married so young and so soon after meeting my grandmother, he answered as I imagine many of his generation would have: "We were in love, we were grown, and we were ready to start our lives." My grandparents' marriage and economic trajectory exemplified the logic of healthy marriage policy that if couples would get married, stay married, and effectively manage their conflicts and their money, a strong, lasting marriage can be a route to upward mobility.

But their story also points to the flaws of this logic and the vast economic and cultural changes since the mid-twentieth century that have reshaped marital experiences and meanings. My grandparents' abilities to work cooperatively as a financial team and resolve interpersonal conflict likely aided their marital stability and economic ascent. Yet, their financial success was in large part the direct result of several interrelated economic factors that were anomalous during the 1950s in the United States. They married during one of the most prosperous economic boom periods in American history, when the property they eventually inherited and the stocks in which they invested grew exponentially in value. Both white, my grandparents did not encounter racial discrimination when looking for work. Moreover, my grandfather's prime working years coincided with a time period when men without a high-school diploma still had access to well-paying unionized manufacturing and construction jobs that could support a middle-class family.

Couples considering marriage today do not face these same economic circumstances. Nor do they make family-formation choices in the same cultural context. Marriage was the only socially acceptable choice for my grandparents, who wanted to live together and have children. When they argued or felt dissatisfied, divorce never crossed their minds. It would have gone against their religious beliefs and the social mores of their families and community.

My interviews with couples who took Thriving Families classes showed that, in stark contrast to how my grandparents thought about marriage and money, couples are now more likely to believe that marriage requires, rather than creates, a steady economic foundation. The couples I interviewed believed that marriage is something you do only after you accomplish other life goals and become financially secure. For my grandparents' generation, marriage was an important first step in the adult life course and the only route to building a legitimate family life. Now, as sociologist Andrew Cherlin has argued, Americans increasingly view marriage as an achievement and status symbol, a marker of middle-class respectability.[2] My interview with Jennifer and Peter, a couple who graduated from the Thriving Families program, revealed a lot about what had changed since my grandparents took their vows.

Both white and unemployed, Jennifer was twenty-six and Peter was thirty-five. Both were high-school graduates, but neither had gone to college. Together four years, they shared a child, one-year-old Caleb, and Peter was a highly involved stepfather to Jennifer's other child, a six-year-old daughter named Lily. Jennifer's ex-boyfriend and Lily's father, Russell, lived with them, along with Russell's girlfriend, Bethany, and her five-year-old child, Sarah. Conveniently, Bethany was also Jennifer's best friend. Peter had two older children, teenagers with whom he barely spoke. It was a complicated living arrangement, Jennifer told me, but one that worked well because "All our kids kind of have four parents . . . and are very well taken care of." By the time I interviewed them a month after they completed the Thriving Families classes, Jennifer had discovered she was pregnant again. Though Caleb was the result of a planned pregnancy, this baby was not. Still, Jennifer felt that "the pregnancy was a blessing, a surprise that was meant to be."

Peter got laid off around Christmas, three months before I met them in a Thriving Families class. They were just barely making ends meet with welfare assistance and a creative living arrangement of four adults and three, soon to be four, children, all in a 900-square-foot, two-bedroom/one-bathroom apartment. On the recommendation of two friends who had taken the classes and really liked them, they signed up for Thriving Families because, as Peter told me, "We don't get along very well, and sometimes it gets really bad with all the yelling and screaming, just yelling and screaming all over the place. I'll just leave, and she'll follow me." Jennifer was tired of having to follow him out the door when he took off after their arguments, and they had hoped that the classes would help them avoid these screaming matches and Peter's tendency to walk away when things got heated.

When I asked Jennifer and Peter if they anticipated staying together, Jennifer pointed to a tattoo in the shape of a wedding band on the ring finger of her left hand. Peter had a matching tattoo on his left ring finger. Both tattoos were unfinished. Neither Jennifer nor Peter could tolerate more discomfort after the tattoo artist inked the initial outlines of the bands. Jennifer's outlines were starting to fade. They intended to go back eventually, get the lines redrawn, and fill in the quarter-inch bands with solid black ink. After all, Peter told me, "We have to finish because we already have both lines, and people are going to think, 'What kind of marriage is that?'" This gave me the perfect opening in our conversation to ask if they had talked about getting married. Jennifer quickly replied, "Oh yeah, lots, but we're waiting."

I asked why. They lived together. They shared children and had one more on the way. They had even permanently, if only partially, tattooed symbols of their shared commitment on their fingers. One might reasonably think they were ready for marriage. "We're waiting," Jennifer said, "until we can have a proper wedding, . . . not just going to the courthouse and getting hitched, but all planned out, a nice wedding, one where Lily can be the flower girl and Caleb can be the ring bearer." Peter added, "But by the time we get married, Lily's going to be too old to be a flower girl. She'll have to be a bridesmaid." I asked if the "proper wedding" was the only thing holding them back. It was not. Both articulated a strong desire to wait until their emotional and financial problems were resolved. Peter had severe anger and paranoia issues, the result of "being kicked around so much" all his life. Jennifer told me she wanted to regain some of the independence she had lost since getting together with Peter. They had the most to say about the premarital financial goals they shared. Jennifer explained:

> I have a lot of growing to do, too, before we're able to be together. Financially, I'd like for us to be able to get our bills in order, have a place of our own, have jobs, and just not feel like we're at the bottom of the well. Because I wouldn't want to start our new married life in this kind of situation. . . . I'd like to have all my debts paid off and even just be able to start at zero instead of where we are now. I'd just like to be able to afford a house with a yard and have to tell the kids "Stop playing with the dog in the house. I told you to put the cats outside. Quit chasing the chickens!"

Peter interjected, "And with me not having worked for a few months, my self-esteem is so low. I feel like I'm dead weight in the water. I want to be worth something." Jennifer lovingly replied, "I don't feel like that at all about him. We've gone through periods of not working before, . . . but he holds a lot of worth in what he does and what he gets back from it. But that's not all that makes you worth something."

I came to understand their unfinished ring tattoos as hauntingly symbolic of Jennifer and Peter's shared aspirations and challenges. Both sincerely wanted to commit to each other and had the outlines of a married life in place—living together, deep affection, shared financial goals, children—but the thought of filling in the marital picture by making it official was too unsettling and uncomfortable. For now, the gap between what they had and what they hoped for was just too great.

The other Thriving Families couples I interviewed described their plans for marriage with the same mix of optimism and despair. Couple after couple told me they just "can't afford marriage." As in Jennifer and Peter's case, not being able to afford marriage meant not having the means to pay for the wedding they had dreamed of and not feeling fully prepared to get married until they finished school, got out of debt, found good jobs, and could buy a house. Being married, much like being employed, meant you are, to use both Jennifer's and Peter's aptly chosen words, "worth something," both as a person and a financial asset.

This phenomenon—what I call curtailed commitment—is founded on the belief that if they cannot live up to middle-class ideas of family life, including college degrees, stable, well-paying jobs, and single-family homes, low-income couples are not equipped for marriage. In this chapter, I explain how curtailed commitment is deeply rooted in growing social inequality, changing cultural views of family, and ideological understandings of the necessary economic underpinnings of a healthy marriage.

As illustrated in the previous three chapters, the legislative intent of healthy marriage policy was to encourage high-quality, lasting marriages by teaching relational and financial skills. When targeting low-income families, healthy marriage policy sought to remove barriers to marriage and improve families' economic position and their children's life chances. To a point, couples like Jennifer and Peter and pro-marriage policymakers shared a similar view of marriage as something that represents a happy family life and economic well-being. But the unfulfilled longings for a more financially secure marital life that shaped Jennifer and Peter's relationship story revealed a telling contradiction between the lived experiences of low-income, unmarried families and the legislative intent of healthy marriage policy.

The marital aspirations of couples living in poverty often go unrealized in the face of unmet ambitions of economic security. Policies and programs that encourage marriage as a route to a more secure financial future reinforce the association disadvantaged couples already make between marriage and prosperity without addressing the economic constraints that underlie curtailed commitment. To fully grasp why, it is important to understand the economic and cultural changes associated with marriage that transpired in the sixty years between when my grandparents married and when I interviewed Jennifer and Peter.

The Changing Economics and Culture of Marriage

Throughout the twentieth century, shifting cultural norms of marriage intersected with changing economic trends to significantly reshape Americans' relationship experiences and marital choices. Marriage historically functioned to pool resources from large extended kin networks during times of scarcity and to govern all aspects of economic life, including labor and the ownership and transfer of property. This institutional view of marriage was the dominant understanding of American marriage until the end of the nineteenth century.[3] In the early 1900s, the first of two major shifts in marriage deemphasized its role as a social and economic institution and accentuated the emotional and sexual bonds between spouses. During this companionate era of marriage, women were expected to be full-time homemakers, while men were supposed to work for pay and bring home the money. Economic cooperation through this starkly gendered division of labor was still understood as foundational to marriage. But the social unit deemed responsible for meeting a family's economic needs shrank from a large extended kin network to a mere two-person partnership. Understood primarily as an expressive, private relationship, marriage was increasingly sentimentalized throughout the twentieth century and assumed the financial self-sufficiency of the married couple.

Class differences in marriage rates—what is often called the *marriage gap*—have been associated with economic inequality since the late 1800s. As sociologist Andrew Cherlin has shown, marriage rates plummeted during periods of growing economic inequality and the loss of stable employment opportunities for low-income workers.[4] Strong pro-marriage cultural norms and civic institutions tempered inequality's effects on nonmarital childbearing rates for most of the twentieth century. The social stigma attached to single parenthood and living together while not married prevented most people from having children together outside marriage despite the economic hardship many faced. Cohabitation was rare and few children were born to unmarried parents during the Great Depression, when economic deprivation and unemployment were especially high; families could not afford, socially or economically, to have children outside marriage. Social pressure and economic constraint stabilized family life despite high inequality in this marriage-only culture, but there was an underside to this stability. Unmarried and divorced mothers were socially ostracized; unhappy couples were pressured to stay married; and spouses, wives in particular, often did not have the economic means to leave abusive relationships.[5]

More Americans married and at younger ages during the unprecedented economic prosperity of the post–World War II decades. In the 1950s, American marriage was nearly universal, with 95 percent of whites and 88 percent of African Americans eventually taking at least one trip down the aisle.[6] During the countercultural era of the 1960s, alternatives to marriage became more socially acceptable, paving the way for greater cultural acceptance of family diversity. Couples experienced more relationship transitions, and family instability increased. Americans postponed marriage until later in life, cohabitation became increasingly common, divorce rates accelerated, and more children were born to unmarried parents.[7] Before the late twentieth century, a strong marriage-only culture mitigated the effects of economic hardship on family stability. Couples faced less stigma if they had children while not married during subsequent eras of high unemployment and inequality. This cultural shift led to a retreat from marriage, which has continued unabated, even during periods of strong economic recovery and growth.[8]

According to Cherlin, all these changes ushered in a new era of individualized marriage.[9] Unlike mid-century brides and grooms, including my grandparents, who married early, young, and in droves during the relatively prosperous postwar period, people began to delay marriage until after they accomplished other major life goals and felt financially secure. This reflected a twofold transformation in norms of family life pointing to the synergistic effects of economic and cultural change: the decline of a marriage-only culture and a concomitant rise of a middle-class marriage culture. Rather than the foundation of adult life that it used to represent, marriage came to symbolize the capstone of the transition to full adulthood.[10] Getting married and having children used to be the primary routes to a socially acceptable adult status. Now, people are much more likely to develop a sense of themselves as adults by finishing college, pursuing a career, and exploring different identity options through dating and living with multiple partners before they settle down as spouses and parents. These changing cultural norms of being ready for marriage are fraught with significant challenges for economically disadvantaged couples.

Many of the new prerequisites for marriage—a college degree, a stable career, and financial independence—are not just symbols of adulthood. They are also markers of middle-class affluence. Marriageability, or readiness for marriage, has become a status symbol that two people have made it, complete with all the accoutrements of a middle-class lifestyle. Because these marital prerequisites all assume a certain level of economic stability and privilege, this shift has also ushered in a new era of intimate inequalities.

Twentieth-century changes in cohabitation, marriage, and divorce rates have altered marriage and family life for Americans largely along lines of class. At mid-century, when companionate marriage was approaching its end, all women married at roughly the same rates, regardless of class, and the least educated were the most likely to marry.[11] As the number and proportion of women attending and graduating from college started to rise, the marriage rates of college-educated women also rose until 1980, when marriage rates began to fall for all women. By the mid-1980s, women living in poverty were only 75 percent as likely to marry as those who were not poor, a pattern strongly correlated with whether they had a college education.[12] In the following decades, education and its effect on social class via job and marriage opportunities significantly stratified the marriage market in ways that pushed many disadvantaged individuals out of it entirely.[13] Couples, like Jennifer and Peter, with only high-school diplomas who live below the poverty line are significantly less likely to marry and stay married than their college-educated peers.[14]

Those who are the most economically disadvantaged in terms of income and education are also the most likely to become single parents.[15] The concentration of single parenthood among low-income American families is another significant class-based trend that emerged throughout the latter half of the twentieth century. The two in five American children who are now born to unmarried parents are significantly more likely to grow up in poverty.[16] Like Jennifer and Peter, while many low-income, unmarried couples who share children are romantically involved and living together when their children are born, they are less likely to stay together than married parents.[17] This can have profound social and economic consequences. Being and staying married helps parents combine their resources, at least when parents have resources to combine, which they can then invest in their children. Despite the focus on individual satisfaction and emotional fulfillment within marriage, one of its most important contemporary institutional features is how it structures resource-pooling in families. This has become a primary mechanism of social and economic inequality in modern social life.[18]

Marriage is associated with economic benefits, but not primarily for the reasons taught in the healthy marriage classes I studied. Managing money and loving skillfully do not necessarily promote economic stability. Rather, in a middle-class marriage culture where the most affluent marry, stay married, and continuously consolidate resources, middle-class stability best supports marriage.

Marriage, the Middle Class, and the Real "Success Sequence"

Some have feared that women's gains in higher education and the labor market since the 1950s undermined marriage as an institution founded on a gendered division of labor that assigned women to the home.[19] On the contrary, these changes actually fortified marriage for the middle and upper classes. When couples like my grandparents married in the 1950s, most wives were not primary or co-breadwinners. Out of necessity, single-mother and low-income families—especially families of color that faced race-based wage discrimination—often had to rely on women's (and sometimes children's) earnings just to survive.[20] Still, husbands did not expect that getting married would considerably increase their household income. Discriminatory norms and policies in higher education kept most women out of college, and when they did work, they were paid a fraction of what men earned. Since then, two important social and economic trends have collided to change this: women's gains in higher education and the job market and growing income and wealth disparities between those with and those without a college degree.

Education increases more than just earning potential. It also increases the economic benefits one gains by getting married and splitting expenses and pooling resources with an equally advantaged spouse.[21] More women than men now earn college degrees.[22] Women have not yet reached full income parity with men; they still only make $0.81 on the dollar.[23] Yet, women's earning potential is increasing significantly faster than that of men's, which has stagnated in recent decades and even regressed for men without a college degree. Women, who now comprise almost half of all paid workers, are closing the earnings gap. From 1970 to 2007, women's earnings grew 44 percent, compared to only 6 percent for men's.[24] This is largely due to the fact that women's earnings started out much lower than those of men, but it does not diminish the importance of the gains, especially as they relate to marriage.

As women have outpaced men in higher education and as they approach more equitable earnings, marriage increases the gains made by highly educated, higher-income individuals. Through what is called marital endogamy or assortative mating, people tend to choose spouses with similar social characteristics, such as education, class, race, and religion. Education has been a particularly strong and consistent form of marital endogamy throughout American history.[25] Yet, for previous generations, women's earnings did not always correlate well with how much education they had. Because wealthier women were more likely to go to college and marry wealthier men, they could afford and were expected to stop working when they married or had children. This is one reason college-educated women were less likely to marry than women with less education throughout much of the twentieth century.

This is no longer the case. Women with more education are now more likely to marry and continue working after they have children,[26] and college-educated women are the only social group with higher marriage rates than at any point in the 1950s.[27] Moreover, both unmarried men and unmarried women have fared less well in the labor market since 1970 compared with their married counterparts. Unmarried men without a college education lost the most ground between the 1970s and 2000s. As their real earnings decreased, many did not have a wage-earning wife to compensate for the decline. On its face, this would seem to lend support to the antipoverty logic of healthy marriage policy. But this does not account for the powerful role of marital endogamy in stratifying the marriage market and shaping social inequality. Because people tend to marry within their own economic class, when poor and low-income individuals do get married, they do not tend to "marry up" economically. They most often marry others who are also living in poverty or make low wages.[28] They therefore have fewer assets to pool and struggle just to cover rising living expenses, much less to save or invest.[29] Middle-class spouses are also more likely to have jobs that come with employer-provided benefits, such as health insurance, that cover their spouses and allow them to directly profit from marriage.

Ultimately, college-educated Americans have made the largest income gains since 1970, when individualized and middle-class ideas of marriage started to emerge. As importantly, they have further strengthened their economic advantage over Americans with less education due to their greater likelihood of getting and staying married to similar spouses with college degrees and high earnings.[30] Much like the traditional wedding portrait showcasing a couple's new wedding bands, certain socioeconomic advantages related to marriage now go hand-in-hand. Those who are financially secure tend to be people who are fortunate enough to get a college degree, acquire a well-paying job, and find an equally educated spouse who can buffer them against any occupational or financial setbacks.

Moderately educated Americans—those with some college but without the degree—also tend to struggle in ways that reflect their precarious position in the middle of this hierarchy. They are more likely to marry and have children within marriage than couples in poverty, but they are significantly more likely to divorce than couples with a college education. White individuals with some college have the most turnover in cohabiting relationships and marriages.[31] In a middle-class marriage culture, a lasting marriage is a luxury that seems out of reach for those in poverty and attainable but harder to hold onto for the working class.

The main reason the "success sequence" of graduation and work before marriage and children—a prescription for economic success taught in healthy marriage classes and described in chapter 3—predicts living above the poverty line is not because marriage prevents poverty, but because education is associated with both earnings and marriage. Education, one of the most important factors that influence someone's position on the economic class ladder, is also now one of the most reliable predictors of one's chances of getting married, staying married, and staying happily married.[32] Money may not buy love, but it can help a couple create and sustain a happy marriage. More important than affording an expensive, "proper" wedding, economic resources afford a college degree that will likely keep someone out of poverty, drastically improve their marital odds, and minimize the stress of economic deprivation that can take a huge emotional toll on marriage.

Due to these shifts in the economic underpinnings of intimate life, marriage is increasingly associated, both practically and symbolically, with already being middle class. Most couples no longer marry assuming, as my grandparents did, that marriage will allow them to accomplish their financial goals for upward mobility. As described by Jennifer and Peter, having already met these goals is what makes couples feel ready for marriage in the first place. Thus, instead of thinking that marriage can prevent poverty, the sociological research on why those living in poverty marry less urges us to consider how poverty prevents marriage. Put another way, the absence or poor timing of marriage is not what tends to undermine the success sequence. In a culture where marriage means you are already economically worth something, the absence of educational and occupational opportunity does.

There are two primary ways that economic inequality, particularly inequities in income, prevents marriage. First, couples in poverty find it increasingly difficult to reach the marriage bar, the standard of living people are expected to meet before they are considered ready for marriage.[33] Second, low-income men who suffer the most from growing wage inequality find it increasingly difficult to realize the financial expectations embedded in the still-dominant male breadwinner norm.[34] Risk-averse, low-income women are reasonably reluctant to take on the financial burden of low-income men who may be a drain on, rather than a contributor to, their economic resources.[35]

The marriage bar is not an absolute standard that stays stationary, but a relative one that fluctuates. As median income rises, forced upward mostly by high-earning, college-educated individuals who tend to marry other high-earning, college-educated individuals, so too does the marriage bar. This makes it increasingly difficult for those with less education and fewer well-paying job prospects to ever feel as though they are financially equipped for marriage.[36] Money is often the primary reason low-income, unmarried couples indefinitely delay their plans to marry.[37] Similarly, couples who are not solidly middle class cite wanting to be more economically stable to explain why they defer or avoid marriage.[38] Based on their interviews with cohabiting couples, sociologists Pamela Smock, Wendy Manning, and Meredith Porter found that marriage signifies overcoming economic struggles. Couples first wanted to complete the middle-class "respectability package," which includes getting out of debt, finishing school, acquiring a well-paying, stable job, and owning a nice car and house.[39]

Because the large white wedding has come to symbolize that two people have made it, couples also postpone marriage until they can afford more than just a simple civil ceremony at the local courthouse as my grandparents had. Even when couples share children and sincerely want to get married, there is often an insurmountable gap between their relational and financial aspirations and their actual experiences with love and money.[40] Missing pieces of the middle-class package ultimately keep many low-income couples from the altar altogether,[41] especially now that living in a nonmarried family is less stigmatized than it once was during the marriage-only era.

Social inequality also prevents marriage through its impact on low-income men's economic opportunities. Both men and women have high expectations that men need to have good jobs and be successful financial providers to be husband material. Sociologist William Julius Wilson has called this the "marriageable men" problem.[42] Despite women's gains in education and employment, gendered norms of masculinity that hold men responsible as primary breadwinners remain strong.[43] Growing inequality in men's wages—especially the increasing gap between the earnings of men with a college degree and those without one—accounts for much of the overall decline in marriage rates in recent decades. Couples in which men earn less are more likely to delay marriage and have trouble reaching the economic marriage bar. As income inequality increases, those men lower down the socioeconomic ladder who are most likely to be unemployed or poorly paid are viewed as the least desirable husbands, especially compared with middle- and upper-class men who have benefited most from the concentration of income and wealth at the top of the ladder.[44]

Racism contributes to these intimate inequalities independently of class differences. African American and Latino men in particular are further disadvantaged by how racial discrimination contributes to dwindling job opportunities, earlier death, and high incarceration rates and the lasting stigma of having a criminal record. When men of color do have college degrees and well-paying jobs, they are more likely to marry women of other races. African American women are especially disadvantaged in the marriage market and more likely to be single parents at every level of education and income.[45] Moreover, economic resources seem to be even more influential for relationship stability among couples of color who tend to have significantly less wealth and lower earnings than white couples because of the myriad effects of institutional racism.[46]

These numerous and overlapping class, gender, and race inequalities intersect in a middle-class marriage culture, as reflected in low-income, unmarried parents' high, though often unrealized, marital aspirations. Sociologists Kathryn Edin and Maria Kefalas set out to understand why women in poverty marry less and have children they must struggle to support.[47] They found that poor, single mothers valued and aspired to marriage as much as their middle-class, married counterparts. Yet, they differed when it came to their chances of actually finding a partner who could meet the high financial and emotional standards regarding marriage that women across class lines share. Low-income, unmarried mothers often refused to marry their children's poorly paid or unemployed fathers, who seemed like risky long-term marriage prospects. Ultimately, though low-income and middle-class women tend to share similar marital values and aspirations, socioeconomic circumstances make it harder for disadvantaged couples to live up to the middle-class norms of family life that couples of all classes now associate with marriage.

As discussed in chapter 3, low-income couples also disproportionately face noneconomic relationship challenges. Interpersonal dynamics, especially supportiveness and trust, predict if a couple will eventually marry. Low-income women often choose not to marry their children's fathers because they do not fully trust them to be sexually faithful, avoid alcohol, drugs, and crime, get and keep a job, and be involved dads.[48] Low-income fathers also often struggle with trusting their children's mothers.[49] Trust and support are particularly challenging when one or both partners have children from other relationships, a situation more common among low-income couples and a major source of ongoing conflict because of the jealousy it can provoke.[50] Couples are less likely to marry when partners maintain ties to their exes, even if only because of the kids.[51] Living arrangements of the kind Jennifer and Peter created to minimize living expenses and maximize child care rarely work out well.

Understood in light of these larger economic, cultural, and social trends, Jennifer and Peter's decision to wait for marriage and hold off on finishing those tattoos made a lot of sense. Peter's unemployment and anger issues, Jennifer's desire for greater financial and emotional independence, and their family's uncertain economic future did not bode well for realizing their dream of a middle-class married life complete with a house and kids running around in a backyard large enough to chase chickens. Ironically, by teaching low-income couples to mimic the relationship choices of middle-class couples in the absence of middle-class resources, healthy marriage classes reinforced aspirations of middle-class family life while largely ignoring the social inequalities that undermine them. Framing marriage as an income-producing institution based on the assumption that it encourages spouses to love more skillfully, work harder, and save more money ignores how marriage is an inherently unequal social institution that selects the most privileged and stratifies access to economic resources, social opportunities, and legal rights.

Stories I heard from other low-income parents who took Thriving Families classes revealed that Jennifer and Peter's experience with curtailed commitment was common among couples who found their way to a government-supported healthy marriage class. They struggled with the choice to marry in a culture where marriage means you are worth something at the same time that growing inequality increasingly undermines that sense of worth for low-income couples.

Jessica and Mitch

Jessica, twenty-two, and Mitch, twenty-six, both white, met through mutual friends about two years before they took Thriving Families classes. Neither had graduated from high school. Jessica was working part-time as an in-home health aide, but Mitch had not had a job for almost a year. A month after meeting them in class, I interviewed them when their newborn daughter, Nevaeh—*heaven* spelled backwards—was just five days old.[52] Nevaeh was Mitch's first child and the second for Jessica, who also had a four-year-old son named Patrick. Patrick had been living with Jessica's uncles ever since she lost custody about a year before our interview because of a severe drug problem. Patrick did not yet know that he had a new baby sister because Jessica was not allowed to see him, and they rarely talked on the phone.

Nevaeh's arrival was timely, Jessica and Mitch told me, because they had both been off drugs and alcohol for a while and had just settled into a new apartment only a few weeks before her birth. "It's a decent place," Jessica said, "only a small problem with roaches and some neighbors who are meth heads." Before she got pregnant and throughout her first trimester, Jessica and Mitch had been homeless, alternating among community shelters, local tent communities, and the occasional motel room when they could scrape together enough money. Once Jessica was in her second trimester, they decided that she needed to live with her grandmother for the safety and health of the baby, while Mitch contin- ued to sleep in a shelter known as "the mission." Child Protective Ser- vices required Jessica to take a parenting class to keep custody of Nevaeh. Her caseworker informed her that Thriving Families would fulfill the requirement. Mitch grudgingly agreed because, as he told me, "They pay you, and we really needed the money."

Jessica and Mitch emphasized how strong their relationship was and how all their problems—being homeless, Jessica's drug use and brief incarceration for writing fraudulent checks, and struggles to create a stable home for Nevaeh—had made them a stronger couple. Jessica explained, "I was writing checks to the store, writing checks to the hotel, making sure that we were all taken care of, which is noble, but still illegal. . . . I thought it was the right thing to do at the time. My morals and ethics were in the right place. My brain might not have been." When I asked Jessica and Mitch if Nevaeh was a "surprise," they imme- diately corrected me:

JESSICA: No, no, it was all planned. . . . I don't know how it came up, just one night we decided we wanted her and nine months later there she was. . . . She's just so perfect. It's like she knows how much she's wanted and how much she's loved.

MITCH: She makes us a complete family.

JESSICA: She's the little missing piece of our family. I'm so proud of me and Mitch because we always make sure she has what she needs first. It's like if they turn my cable off, so what, I want to make sure my daughter has diapers.

MITCH: It makes our sobriety even better. I don't want to drink or do drugs or stuff like that.

JESSICA: We only did drugs because we were depressed. You know, we had nothing, and now we have her. She depends on us.

MITCH: And we ain't got no money to do drugs anyway.

JESSICA: Welcome to the world of parenting. We will never see money again unless we walk down the street and find a $100 bill, which we'll end up spending on her. . . . It just comes naturally. We wanted her that bad.

Even though they had planned the pregnancy, Mitch initially wanted Jessica to have an abortion because they were still struggling to find a place to live. Nevaeh was conceived while they were homeless, most likely, Jessica and Mitch guessed, during one of their nightly stays in the mission. When I asked them if they had considered getting married, they told me they had discussed it many times. Jessica said, "I feel bad for my daughter because her parents aren't married." Mitch quickly interjected: "But what's a piece of paper supposed to say about being a family. . . . It doesn't mean we're bad parents, and I doubt we're less committed to each other than married people." "Well," Jessica sighed, "we'll probably end up getting married, but not today. I can barely pay to keep our lives going. I can't pay to go get married."

Chelsea and Simon

Both white, Chelsea, thirty-two, and her boyfriend of eight years, Simon, thirty-four, were living together and enjoying their two-week-old son, Collin, when I interviewed them. Chelsea had an associate's degree. Simon had not graduated from high school. They were doing better financially than most of the couples I interviewed. Chelsea was working part-time, and though Simon was between construction jobs, he had a good lead on a new one. Chelsea was slowly adjusting to first-time motherhood, a task made difficult by Collin's constant colic and high-pitched screaming. Collin was unplanned, and Chelsea had seriously considered getting an abortion in her first trimester. When I asked her why she contemplated ending the pregnancy, she told me while sobbing:

Truthfully, I had a rough childhood. I'm ashamed to say that I thought I couldn't keep him. My head said, "No, you can't do this for lots of reasons." I'm a drug addict, up until that moment when I found out I was pregnant. I'm an alcoholic. But I stopped drinking that second. Simon doesn't have his GED. He doesn't have a license. Both of my cars are total buckets, both two-seaters, too. We're talking '81 and '85 [year models]. But the drug history was a big thing because I don't feel that I should put that on anyone else. Simon is an adult. He has a choice to walk out and leave. The baby doesn't have a choice, and that's not fair. I was abandoned by my mom and dad, and it really bothers me when I don't see kids taken care of. I guess I didn't think I could be good enough to be better. . . . In the end, I told myself, even though we're screw-ups, we love each other. If we don't have a house, a nice car, an education, really, we do love each other, and we try, and that's what we're going to do for our baby. . . . He's my miracle because I have purpose now.

Chelsea and Simon were about to get another addition to their household. Simon's eleven-year-old son, Bradley, was preparing to come live with them full-time after his mother, Simon's ex-girlfriend, had to relinquish custody of all four of her children. Though Simon had been out of work for a while, Chelsea was currently employed as a part-time surgical tech. Happy to at least have a job, her commute was 100 miles each way, and because she "was lowest on the totem pole at work," she had to take the on-call shifts that often got canceled because there were no patients. This situation left Chelsea and Simon questioning how much money would come in every month. Thus far, she told me, "We're not broke, so we can still pay the bills."

They signed up for Thriving Families after Chelsea learned about the program through her WIC (Women, Infants, and Children nutrition program) case manager. "I thought it would be good to start building our teamwork before the baby got here, and then they mentioned all the amenities. How could I say no if you're going to give me gas money, feed me, take care of the baby, and then the money? I saw nothing but positives."

When I asked Simon if he and Chelsea had considered getting married, he told me very matter-of-factly, "Yeah, but we can't afford it." When I asked him what they could not afford, he explained: "We'd like to get married. We just can't afford it. I'm like 'Let's go to Reno and do it, it's fine.' But she wants the wedding. That'll probably be my only wedding, so if she wants to do it that way, that's fine." I had earlier asked Chelsea the same question, and her initial answer was exactly the same, "We can't afford it." Yet, when I asked her what she meant by that, it had nothing to do with dreams of a big, expensive wedding. According to Chelsea, it was because they could not afford to pay the fines Simon had accrued from traffic tickets. Because they had a new baby and would soon have two kids to support, she did not want to marry Simon until he had a legal driver's license. He needed it to drive to work and stay out of jail. She explained:

My mom has been married three times, so when I was growing up, I didn't believe in marriage. I thought, "What's the point?!" So, I've never been married. . . . I didn't dream about getting married, but now that I'm getting older and having babies, now I feel like [Collin's] mom and dad should be married, but I want Simon to have his license first. . . . That's one of the biggest problems in our relationship, well, not in our relationship, but in our life because that just makes for more problems. I told him, "I won't marry you without a license." . . . It's so much money. We pay what we can, but he has to drive when he actually works, and he gets pulled over again and gets another ticket. It's a vicious cycle.

For the last ticket he got, the traffic court judge sentenced Simon to two days in a correctional center because he had not yet paid off his more than $5,000 in combined traffic fines. Chelsea told him that he had to serve his time before she was due to give birth. He went in on a Thursday, planning to get out the following Saturday, but Chelsea called from the hospital on Friday morning—in labor. Luckily, he was able to get to the hospital in time for Collin's arrival. Chelsea understood, but it was just one more problem the license issue caused for their relationship. Chelsea made it clear that she was not giving Simon an ultimatum that he needed to have a high-paying job before she would marry him. She just wanted him to be employable. Though Chelsea was willing to pay off his $5,000 if and when she had the money, Simon seemed like too much of a risk to marry until those traffic fines were paid off.

Elise and Matthew

A little over a year before I met them, Elise, thirty-eight, and Matthew, thirty-four, both white, met and fell in love in an online chat room and quickly decided they wanted to marry. After getting to know one another over long, late-night phone calls for about six months, Matthew decided to move from the Midwest to be with Elise and her children in California. When they began dating, Elise was pregnant with her third child, Julia, and had a nineteen-year-old daughter and a thirteen-year old son, Jack. Both Elise and Matthew had finished high school, but neither had been employed for many months. Matthew received a small monthly disability stipend because of a back injury that kept him from working the manual labor jobs he could get with only a high-school education. When I interviewed them, Elise, Matthew, Julia, and Jack were all living with Andrew—Elise's ex-boyfriend and Jack's father—in a one-bedroom/one-bathroom, 500-square-foot apartment. Julia had just turned eight months old, and Matthew was proud to claim her as his own. Elise learned about the Thriving Families program through her food stamps coordinator and wanted to take the classes to learn how to:

> Communicate in a rational and positive manner without trying to hurt the other person and open up more. I used to be closed like a clam, and you could take the strongest pliers and my wall was not budging. I really looked forward to going to the class and just meeting other people going through the same thing, just knowing that you're not the only one.

Matthew had officially proposed the previous Christmas with a modest, yet beautiful diamond ring. Elise joyfully accepted. Though both dreamed of their wedding day, their lives had just taken an unfortunate turn. On a tip from Jack's teacher who reported that Jack was complaining about ten people sleeping in their small apartment at night, Child Protective Services put him and Julia in foster care. The social workers cited the filthy condition of the apartment, lack of food in the kitchen, and orange drink mix in Julia's bottle as reasons why the home was unfit. I interviewed Elise and Matthew three days later as they were preparing to go to court for both a custody hearing to get Jack and Julia out of foster care and a paternity hearing filed by Julia's biological father.

Distraught over the loss of her children, Elise still perked up when talking about how much she adored Matthew. After Elise told me that she and Matthew got "fake married" in the online chat room where they first met and were proud of their fake marriage license, I asked Elise why they had not made it official. She told me:

> He asked me to marry him in December, so we've been engaged three months now, but we're taking our time because we want to get married outside. We want our friends to be able to come down and be a part of it, . . . and we're waiting because I want to be able to make it as affordable as possible. I'm not one for extravagance. I'm a very simple person. It doesn't take too much to make me happy.

Yet, later during the interview, she admitted that the tough economic times were taking a toll on their relationship, and she wanted to wait until she was sure that it would last this time. She had been married briefly once before, and she would be Matthew's fourth wife. "I'm not going to have Matthew and I become a statistic. The divorce rate, I'm sure, has skyrocketed compared to what it was before because of the economy. You know, everyone is feeling the stress."

Matthew told me he was trying to remain strong in front of Elise about the kids being taken away, but described to me in detail how difficult it was for him, too:

> I've been happy in my relationship with [Elise]. It's just the situation we've been in with bouncing around and everything else. It just takes its toll on both of us. . . . Sometimes I get upset because I feel like I'm not doing enough for her even though I'm bringing in a little money. . . . She keeps assuring me that there's no problem because I do enough when we did have the kids, . . . but to me, just taking care of the kids isn't enough. I get upset because I don't have the extra income so we can afford more. That's one of the reasons why we're here because we can't even afford a place ourselves. It's a lot of stress, especially when you have multiple families living in a one-room apartment. . . . At one point, it got bad enough that we had to take stuff to a pawn shop just to get diapers because we'd run out of money. . . . We had to put on loan the ring I got her, the ring I asked her to marry me with. I look at it as, yeah, it's a bad thing she had to give up our ring, but then again, it's stuff we need. . . . I have nothing left I could even try to pawn.

Matthew wanted to do whatever he could to keep the family together, even if that meant living with Elise's ex-boyfriend and two kids in a one-bedroom apartment for a while longer so they could avoid homelessness. For now, they were focused on the overwhelming task of working with the child welfare system to be reunited with Jack and Julia. They were going to have to figure out some way to address the problems cited by the social worker—cleaning up the place, getting food in the kitchen, buying expensive formula for Julia—and stretch Elise's $800 monthly welfare check a little further. After all, Matthew told me a second time, they did not even have Elise's engagement ring to pawn anymore. That outdoor wedding ceremony would have to wait a little longer. For now, they had more pressing things on their minds.

Middle-Class Marriage Culture: Affording Marriage and Costly Choices

Most of the parents I interviewed told me they wanted to get married. Some even had tentative wedding dates and plans for a ceremony. But they were either struggling with more immediate concerns or had strong reservations because of long-terms problems with unemployment, housing, and unresolved emotional issues. Consequently, they believed they could not afford marriage. This meant that they understood marriage, not as a means to a better life or a stronger family, but rather as something you do when that better life—complete with a job, a house, or even just a balance sheet in the black—had already been realized. To them, marriage was symbolic of a strong, loving relationship supported by a middle-class lifestyle of which they could only dream. Without this, couples understood marriage alone to be "expensive" or "just a piece of paper that wouldn't change anything" about the circumstances of their daily lives as they struggled to make ends meets and raise their children. Though they wanted their children to have officially committed, married parents, they knew marriage would not put food on their tables or keep a roof over their heads. When parents like Jessica told me they could not afford marriage, they literally meant that it would be an economic hardship for them to pay the fee for a marriage license, which was $60 at the time. This expense was small compared to the cost of a big wedding many of the couples wanted. But even $60 would have been a lot for couples who struggled to buy formula and diapers day to day.

This points to how cultural norms of marriage and social inequality intersect to shape distinct marital cost–benefit calculations. For middle-class couples, marriage does tend to be an economic asset, a key step in the "success sequence" of fortifying and reproducing socio-economic privilege. For couples like Jennifer and Peter who have reservations about perpetual struggles with trust, anger, money, and jobs, marriage seems like a long-term liability. For others who, to paraphrase Jessica, can barely keep their lives going, much less pay to marry, marriage seems like just another short-term expense they simply cannot afford. The $60 they would need to scrape together for the license alone would have paid for a week's groceries or a month's electric bill. It would have been just enough for Matthew to get Elise's engagement ring out of the pawn shop. Marriage had, therefore, become a symbol of a lifestyle they merely fantasized about, rather than a relationship step that would improve their economic situation.

Couples made decisions about having children differently. Parents viewed children as an opportunity to drastically change their lives for the better, as evidenced by couples like Jessica and Mitch who deliberately chose to conceive their daughter Nevaeh while homeless, broke, and struggling with drug addiction. They "wanted her that bad" even if the expenses associated with raising a child would make their financial situation more complicated and would certainly cost more than a marriage license. Even when children were unplanned, as with Chelsea and Simon, parents decided to continue the pregnancies and rationalized the costs of raising a child as worth the joy and purpose that children would bring to their lives. They assumed they would figure it out along the way.[53] Marriage was different. It had receded in importance in couple's lives, not because they devalued it nor because they feared they could not make it work. The struggles of their daily lives—feeding their children, finding and keeping jobs, maintaining a place to live, addiction, uncertain trust—pushed marriage way down to the bottom of their priority list. In these circumstances, waiting to marry seemed like the rational choice.

These unmarried couples raising children in poverty viewed marriage differently than the healthy marriage educators I observed who taught about skilled love and marriage as ways to craft a better, more prosperous family life. Instructors and parents also had very disparate understandings of costly relationship choices. Though the healthy marriage education curricula taught that falling in love with the wrong person or having sex and children before marriage were costly choices because they could compromise the success sequence, the couples I interviewed viewed marriage amid economic struggle as the costly choice. Parents often attributed their decisions to hold off on marriage to their partners' behaviors, emotional issues, and inability to provide financially. But they were just as likely to blame their own struggles in these areas as reasons why waiting on marriage was the prudent choice. They were actually making the kinds of skilled romantic decisions advocated by healthy marriage programs. But, ultimately, these choices resulted in curtailed commitment and reflected how low-income couples' lives and views of marriage starkly contrasted with the middle-class assumptions of healthy marriage policy.

When the Healthy Marriage Initiative was created in 2002, the Department of Health and Human Services adopted psychiatrist Jerry

Lewis and psychologist John Gossett's definition of a healthy marriage to guide marriage education programs. It included the following eight "essential characteristics of a healthy marriage":

1. Both partners participate in the definition of the relationship.
2. There is a strong marital bond characterized by levels of both closeness and autonomy.
3. The spouses are interested in each other's thoughts and feelings.
4. The expression of feelings is encouraged.
5. The inevitable conflicts that do occur do not escalate or lead to despair.
6. Problem-solving skills are well developed.
7. Most basic values are shared.
8. The ability to deal with change and stress is well developed.[54]

None of these eight "essential characteristics" mentioned financial resources, a sense of economic security, employability, or any of the other economic prerequisites that shaped the marital decisions of the couples I interviewed. Marriages in poverty can certainly be strong and happy, as many are. Conversely, many affluent couples have dissatisfying marriages that do not last. Money alone rarely makes or breaks a marriage. Yet, a policy focused on supporting healthy marriages should take into account how intimate inequalities lead to curtailed commitments for disadvantaged families.

Social inequality, high unemployment, and the growing low-wage sector of the labor market are key drivers of family instability and the marriage gap. But they are not the only factors. Growing social acceptance of having children outside marriage combined with rising cultural expectations of marital prosperity ideologically drive low-income parents' decisions to hold off on marriage until they meet certain economic standards. As inequality grows, more families find it difficult to reach the level of economic stability that all Americans, regardless of class, now associate with marriage. High-earning couples push the economic marriage bar higher as low-income couples lose financial ground. This reinforces the strong cultural association between marriageability and being middle class. While marriage was once considered a companionate financial partnership, most people now view it as a primarily emotional relationship. Yet, it is still an economic union that is most likely to survive and thrive among those who live and love with the advantages of middle-class affluence.

Healthy marriage policy sought to stabilize families by turning back the clock to a marriage-only culture. This ignored the most important cultural change regarding marriage that transpired in the latter part of the twentieth century. Growing social inequality in the absence of marriage-only cultural norms has created new economic incentives—and increasingly, disincentives—to marry. This has fundamentally reshaped the meanings people attach to marriage, including when people feel ready to marry, when they believe marriage is valuable, and what they value in a potential spouse. Both economic and cultural changes are driving the class-based marriage gap. Alas, healthy marriage policy did not seriously contend with middle-class marriage culture and how resources and values are mutually constitutive in shaping marital choices and experiences. Gone are the favorable economic conditions that supported my grandparents' ability to marry in near poverty and ascend the class ladder with little education. Consequently, couples like Jennifer and Peter and their classmates are not the likely recipients of presidential notes congratulating them on a long and prosperous marriage. So often, these couples pawn away more than the engagement rings that best symbolize their hopes for marriage. Intimate inequalities that lead to curtailed commitment cause them to sacrifice their hopes, too.

5   The Missing "M Word"

Promoting Committed Co-Parenting

"Hard times will not destroy you if you're committed," proclaimed José, the instructor, to the nine couples who had gathered for a
Thriving Families class on an early fall Saturday morning. As we drank
the juice and ate the pastries and fruit provided by the program, José, a
manager for a waste treatment facility, continued his introduction. "We
talk about loving each other, but love isn't a feeling, it's a commitment.
When you tell someone you love them, it should mean that you're
committed to them." Reading from the Thriving Families instructor's
manual, José explained how research had shown that one of the main
characteristics of a strong family is "an ability to cope. Strong families
draw strength from each other when problems arise. If you don't have
your families, you really don't have anything." Gesturing to Susan, his
wife of thirteen years and Thriving Families co-instructor, he said, "I
know that if I have her I can do anything. If for some reason you can't
cope with your problems, ask yourself why. Why aren't you committed?
These are things you can learn."

José then asked the group to describe their families' strengths. An
African American mother in her twenties replied that her family was
"there for each other when we need it, even when we need money." A
Latina mom in her early twenties added that her family provided "spiri-

tual comfort" and prayed for each other during tough times. An African American dad in his late teens said that he and his family took turns watching the kids. Another father, Timothy, African American and in his twenties, explained that his family, especially his unborn child, was the inspiration he needed to turn away from a life of crime and drugs. Timothy found out about his girlfriend's pregnancy while incarcerated. Upon discovering that he was going to become a father, he vowed to "clean himself up and straighten out."

Susan was currently unemployed after being laid off from her job as a bill processer at an electric company. She thanked the parents for sharing and added that "being committed was particularly important nowadays because of the recession." Wanting to emphasize how important committed relationships are, especially given the couples' financial difficulties, she added:

> The jobs may not be there, the kids may be screaming, but you've still got each other. You can have all the money in the world and still be miserable. The most important things in the world are the person sitting next to you and that little bundle of joy you're holding in your arms or carrying in your belly. Relationships are what really matters, through the good times and the bad. Just knowing that person is going to be there for you is what counts, and the tough times will only make you stronger.

José concluded the morning's introductory lesson by echoing Susan and adding: "You see, it doesn't take spending money to create a healthy, strong family."

The couples in attendance that day were struggling with more than their fair share of relationship and economic challenges. None of the couples were married. All were either expecting a baby or had a newborn. Most were on welfare and unemployed. A few were homeless. As evidenced by parents' enthusiastic nods, José and Susan's message that we should view love, not as an emotion, but as a secure, committed relationship fell on receptive ears and hearts. The point that was so convincing to parents—that real love is about commitment and that strong families do not require a lot of money—was the very idea that made the larger political context of this conversation so controversial. Healthy marriage policy has been most strongly critiqued for codifying the idea that marriage can prevent poverty. Funded directly by a federal Healthy

Marriage Initiative grant, Thriving Families' main goals were to help low-income, unmarried couples improve their co-parenting relationships and encourage them to think about marriage as a way to strengthen their families both emotionally and financially.

Yet, José and Susan did not once mention the word "marriage" in class that morning. Instead, they talked about "commitment," "strong families," and "relationships." Ironically, "marriage" was conspicuously absent in most of the Thriving Families classes I attended. Staff and instructors frequently referred to it as the "m word," highlighting its controversial connotation both for the couples targeted by the program and in national debates over healthy marriage policy and same-sex marriage. Most of my research in the Thriving Families program took place in the latter half of 2008 and throughout 2009. Proposition 8—the California ballot proposition that created a state constitutional amendment defining marriage as only that between a man and a woman—passed only a few weeks after I observed that Saturday morning class taught by José and Susan.[1] I soon discovered that just as marriage was one of the most controversial issues in larger political debates over family and welfare policies in America, it had become equally controversial in the Thriving Families classroom.

Street-Level Strategizing: Promoting Parental Responsibility through Marital Habitus

As I described in chapter 3, healthy marriage programs taught that marriage would directly benefit families' economic circumstances. This reflected an instrumental understanding of marriage as a relationship that helps couples manage financial risk and attain economic security. Yet, as illustrated in chapter 4, couples who attended Thriving Families classes wanted to get married only after their relationships and economic circumstances improved. To them, marriage symbolized having already met major financial goals, being able to focus on more than daily survival, and finding a partner who was not a financial liability. Influenced by living in a middle-class marriage culture and their experiences of economic stress, Thriving Families couples believed that marriage is a consequence of prosperity, not a route out of poverty. Parents had little reason to believe that marriage would directly improve their finances or their lives. This contrasted sharply with the views of

Thriving Families instructors and staff, whose pro-marriage moral beliefs, training in healthy marriage curricula, and simplistic interpretations of social scientific evidence motivated them to teach that marriage prevents poverty.

These incompatible understandings of the connection between marriage and financial well-being created an implementation challenge for translating healthy marriage policy into practice. Without directly improving parents' economic circumstances, how did Thriving Families classes encourage marriage for couples who eschewed it for economic reasons? The answer reveals a lot about political ideologies of parental responsibility and inequality embedded in healthy marriage policy. Thriving Families staff and instructors acknowledged the financial hardship that shaped parents' lives and choices about marriage. Yet, they also believed their mission as healthy marriage educators was to help parents overcome the insecurity they associated with the "m word" and to teach them to see committed co-parenting, preferably via marriage, as a social and economic safety net for their children.

Political scientist Michael Lipsky's theory of street-level bureaucracy helps explain why staff and instructors turned to this strategy.[2] Lipsky argued that those who actually implement policies on the ground—what he called *street-level bureaucrats*—are an integral part of the policy-making process and exercise immense political power. As policy scholars Steven Maynard-Moody and Michael Musheno have argued in extending Lipsky's theory, street-level bureaucrats do more than just implement policy. In the process of service delivery, policy takes shape as street-level bureaucrats' perceptions and moral judgments interact with official policy guidelines.[3] Lower-level bureaucrats and service providers like Thriving Families staff and instructors play a particularly important political role in the translation from written legislation to implementation, especially when policies are characterized by uncertainty, contestation, and conflicting objectives. Healthy marriage education is an illustrative case of how policy at the point of delivery is often fraught with tensions among legislative objectives and clients' views and circumstances.

My goal in studying Thriving Families was to do a street-level analysis that went beyond policy rhetoric and administrative measures to examine how policy reaches into everyday life. This is what policy scholar Evelyn Brodkin called "deep dish" policy analysis.[4] To this end, this chapter focuses on how Thriving Families staff and instructors strategized as street-level bureaucrats when their ultimate policy goal of encouraging marriage was at odds with the lived experiences and view-points of low-income, unmarried parents living in a middle-class marriage culture. Recognizing that parents in poverty often delay or avoid marriage because of economic insecurity, and assuming that low-income couples are less likely to value marriage as an end in itself, those who ran the Thriving Families program deliberately avoided talking about marriage. Instead, they tried to convince couples that strengthening their romantic relationships was paramount to fulfilling their responsibilities as parents who should strive to bolster their children's life chances. This analysis of street-level strategizing is akin to other studies that have investigated how street-level bureaucrats, in the words of sociologist Celeste Watkins-Hayes, "help bridge the divide between agencies' missions and the needs of constituents."[5] The Thriving Families case is distinct, however, because the central concern for staff and instructors was not how to best meet the needs of low-income families as parents understood them. Rather, staff and instructors sought to reshape parents' understandings of their own needs and priorities in line with the policy's mission to encourage marriage.

The program promised that parental commitment could disrupt the intergenerational transmission of poverty to children. Poverty is often experienced as a chronic problem within families across generations. Largely due to differences in family income and the long-term effects of lower-quality nutrition, health care, education, housing, and other missed opportunities, parents who live in poverty are more likely to have children who also grow up to be poor.[6] The intergenerational transmission of poverty is particularly high in the United States compared with other developed countries because of high rates of income inequality and the American tendency to devote fewer public resources to early childhood education, health, and care.[7] Yet, there was no reference in any of the classes I observed to how inequality and the divestment of public resources in social programs like welfare shape children's life chances. Instead, Thriving Families, like healthy marriage programs generally, promoted the idea that children's opportunities for upward mobility depend on parental responsibility, especially parents' abilities to make skilled romantic and co-parenting choices. For parents, marriage was a concept fraught with connotations of economic risk and unmet financial goals. The program, therefore, strategically emphasized parents' skilled relationship behaviors as more important than money for children's life chances. As discussed in previous chapters, children significantly benefit when their parents get along and have a stable relationship—married, cohabiting, or cooperatively co-parenting—that supports both parents' sustained emotional and financial contributions to their lives. This is an important message for any parenting class. But promoting the distinct message that children's opportunities for escaping poverty rest squarely on their parents' relationship behaviors and choices was yet another way that healthy marriage classes obscured the root causes of family inequality.

Social theorist Pierre Bourdieu's concept of *habitus* is useful for elucidating the logic of this marriage promotion strategy linking relationship skills and the cycle of poverty. Habitus refers to a class-based set of dispositions, values, and expectations that individuals acquire through their social experiences anchored in the family.[8] Through habitus—a mental framework that organizes how we think, feel, and act—we internalize and embody cultural sensibilities shaped by our socioeconomic class. Social inequality is reproduced from one generation to the next, Bourdieu argued, because, in addition to economic assets, parents pass along socially and economically useful cultural values and skills. Rather than marriage, per se, Thriving Families classes promoted committed co-parenting as a way to develop what I call *marital habitus*—a set of pro-marriage values and skills—that would presumably allow parents to enhance their children's economic futures.

From a street-level perspective, the moral judgment that most shaped how Thriving Families instructors implemented healthy marriage policy was the belief that low-income parents lack a marital habitus. According to staff and instructors, low-income parents were less likely to develop relationship skills in their youth because many of their own parents were not married and because living in poverty requires a focus on daily survival. They believed that coming from families where marriage is uncommon generates fear of marriage and an inability to plan with long-term marital goals in mind, two tendencies that fuel a cycle of single parenthood and poverty. Staff and instructors assumed that low-income parents avoid marriage and are reluctant to talk about it because they lack the confidence that comes from having marriage-related skills and role models—that is, from their own parents' inability to pass along a marital habitus.

Healthy marriage programs like Thriving Families endorsed marriage as more than just a relationship status. They taught that organizing one's life for marriage and developing the ability to love and parent

skillfully requires a particular marital worldview that shapes goals, motivates behaviors, and supports greater financial stability. This assumed
that the ability to form a healthy marriage is a learned aptitude typically
developed in the family of origin and depends on adopting the right
cultural values and skillful relationship behaviors. This perspective
took for granted that one learns how to value and be married much like
one learns a language, through socialization and modeling by parents
and peers—and, if necessary, formal instruction.

The main problem with this strategy was that it assumed poverty is
reproduced from one generation to the next, not because of inequitable
access to social and economic opportunities, but because low-income
families do not transmit the right marital values and abilities necessary
to create healthy marriages and strong families. Healthy marriage programs sought to disrupt the intergenerational transmission of poverty
by teaching parents to adopt pro-marriage values and the relationship,
goal-setting, and budgeting skills that constitute a marital habitus. The
ultimate hope was that parents would then pass these values and skills
on to their children who would, in turn, have healthier relationships that
generate greater prosperity. Even though the "m word" was often missing
in Thriving Families classes, I show in this chapter how staff and instructors tried to circumvent couples' reluctance to marry for financial
reasons by encouraging commitment and a marital habitus for the sake
of what parents valued most—their children and the better lives they so
desperately wanted to give them.

Co-Parenting and the Commitments of
Couples in Poverty

The parents I interviewed agreed that there was only a minimal emphasis on marriage and a much greater focus on co-parenting in
Thriving Families classes. Chelsea, a thirty-two-year-old, white mother
told me: "They really only talked about relationships. We saw a video on
how these people got married and how they were going through rough
times and how they made it through, but the class is mostly on the kids
and the partner." Similarly, Mason, twenty-four and white, said: "They
didn't talk too much about marriage. They just really made it a point to
work on the relationship and be a good figure for your kids." Giovana,
Mason's fiancée, also twenty-four and white, agreed:

They weren't promoting marriage saying, "You have to get married, you have to get married." I know some other people feel very strong in that aspect, and they mentioned it, but in the end their biggest thing was to try to build up the relationship when you can. You get married or you don't. "Even if you don't get married," they told us, "the father needs to have a relationship with the mother so both parents are still involved even if the relationship doesn't work out."

This downplaying of the marriage message was very important for helping parents feel comfortable in the classes. Peter, a thirty-five-year-old white father, commented: "It was more about staying together for the sake of the kids. They didn't make us feel like sinners because we're not married." Most of the parents echoed Peter's feelings, noting that no one associated with the program made them feel immoral or otherwise bad because they were not married.

Without my prompting, few parents discussed the likelihood they would marry or their plans for marriage. When I asked them directly, many told me they wanted to marry, though few had a clear sense of when or how they would do it. What participants did discuss at length was how they hoped the classes would help them be better partners and especially better parents. Class messages about committed co-parenting as a way to enhance children's opportunities were particularly salient to parents who otherwise felt they had not met their economic and emotional standards for marriage. This reflected how low-income couples tend to think about the economic consequences of marriage and parenting differently.

Scholars have found that marriage and the upward mobility it symbolizes seem increasingly elusive for those in poverty, while being a good parent and raising a child that can escape the same socioeconomic fate seem possible. This was reflected in the interviews I conducted with Thriving Families parents who told me they "couldn't afford marriage" but prioritized parenting despite the greater financial costs associated with having children. Policy scholar Christina Gibson-Davis found support for this dual understanding of marriage and parenthood among low-income couples.[9] Though higher earnings and income were directly associated with a greater likelihood of getting married among the couples she studied, neither earnings nor income affected their childbearing decisions. Because having children is often viewed as a necessary part of life, parents were more likely to make decisions about having kids independently of financial circumstances. This contrasted sharply with how couples felt that they must meet a certain economic standard before marriage.

Research on low-income parents has also found that parenting takes on a unique meaning for those in poverty. Sociologists Kathryn Edin and Maria Kefalas found that low-income, single mothers viewed marriage as a luxury, something that was unlikely given their own economic circumstances and those of their children's fathers, who were just as likely to be poor.[10] Conversely, single mothers viewed children as central to their happiness; parenting imbued their otherwise difficult lives with joy and purpose. The mothers chose to have children while unmarried instead of risking marriage to the wrong person and getting a divorce, or worse yet, jeopardizing their chances of having children altogether if they waited for the right partner to come along first.

As for low-income, unmarried fathers, although some research has found that they actively try to avoid responsibility for paternity and parenting,[11] other research has revealed that they readily acknowledge and embrace it.[12] Many studies have found that men were happy to learn about girlfriends' pregnancies and, in some cases, deliberately tried to have children.[13] Though fathers' relationships with their children were once largely contingent on their relationships with their children's mothers—what is often called the "package deal" of fatherhood and marriage—low-income men increasingly view bonds with their children as central to a meaningful life, while ties to mothers seem peripheral.[14] Sociologists Kathryn Edin and Timothy Nelson's study of low-income fathers revealed that, for many disadvantaged couples, the path to parenthood is haphazard and rarely the result of deliberate planning in an already committed relationship.[15] Nevertheless, the low-income dads they studied often greeted unexpected fatherhood with optimism; it motivated them to get their lives together and become the fathers they believed their children deserved.

Both low-income mothers and fathers tend to believe that children bring a redemptive quality to an otherwise impoverished life. Kids represent one of parents' few chances at a certain kind of upward mobility, even if that mobility is only experienced vicariously through their children. Like Timothy articulated in the Thriving Families class I described at the beginning of this chapter, children are often parents' ultimate motivation to straighten out and become the kind of person they deem worthy of being a parent. As role models or even just cautionary tales, children provide low-income parents opportunities to feel valued in ways that other parts of their lives—especially low-wage, low-status jobs and precarious romantic relationships—do not.

Yet, as Edin and Nelson concluded, shared commitments to children do not always translate into strong desires among parents to commit to one another.[16] Mothers and fathers living in poverty tend to share similarly high standards for marriage that, combined with shaky romantic foundations prior to becoming parents, make for weak couple bonds. Fragile connections based first and foremost on kids are more likely to lead to break-ups than lasting marriages. "For these couples," Edin and Nelson found, "children aren't the expression of commitment; they are the source."[17] Eighty percent of unmarried parents are together in a romantic relationship when their children are born.[18] More than half of these relationships end before the children turn five, and most parents find it difficult to successfully co-parent after a break-up.[19] Having a child while not married is also associated with a lower likelihood that low-income parents will marry after the child is born.[20] Still, there is some evidence of the "package deal" effect. How committed unmarried fathers are to their children and their children's mothers even before the children are born tends to predict how involved dads will be as the children get older.[21] Married or not, how well parents cooperate when it comes to shared parenting decisions strongly influences how active dads are in their children's lives as the kids grow up.[22] Co-parenting is thus becoming increasingly central to partnering as marriage wanes as the primary expression of commitment in low-income couples' intimate attachments.[23] Regardless of marital status or income, children benefit in many ways when their parents get along—an important message Thriving Families and the other healthy marriage programs I studied strongly emphasized.[24]

These trends help us understand why Thriving Families staff and instructors deliberately downplayed the marriage message while simultaneously emphasizing the importance of committed co-parenting as central to their children's life chances. Staff and instructors knew that focusing on commitments to—and through—children better resonated with parents. This strategy also aligned with couples' tendency to prioritize parenting due to their limited opportunities for meeting the high financial and emotional expectations of marriage. This was an attempt to reconcile the contradiction between the antipoverty logic of healthy marriage policy and low-income parents' view of marriage as unaffordable and inconsequential for their own economic well-being. Instructors quickly learned that talking about marriage explicitly, especially when they implied that marriage could improve couples' financial circumstances, would be met with strong resistance.

"Just Trying to Get to Tomorrow": Problems with Promoting the "M Word"

Instructors tried to influence parents' views of marriage by referencing social scientific research showing that married families experience more emotional, economic, and health benefits. Parents often challenged instructors when they talked about these "benefits" of marriage, especially when instructors claimed that marriage generated more money. This message did not align with parents' experiences of childhood, romantic relationships, or finances.

Pursuant to federal funding, healthy marriage grantees were required to teach about the benefits of marriage and to encourage unmarried couples to think about marriage as part of their families' futures. Thriving Families instructors used a true/false quiz from the program curriculum to teach this lesson. Some instructors read each question from the "Rate Your Knowledge about Healthy Marriage" quiz aloud and asked everyone to announce their answers. Others had parents take the quiz on their own and then read the answers to the group to see how many they answered correctly. Parents got more answers wrong than right.

Mark, a white instructor in his early twenties and a college senior majoring in psychology at a local university, always led this lesson when he and his teaching partner, Deborah, an African American social worker in her fifties, taught classes together. During one class that included the marriage quiz, Mark asked if it was true or false that "A healthy marriage has more benefits for women than men." Most answered "false," which Mark satisfactorily told them was correct. Per the prompting of the instructor manual, he then quoted a statistic on marriage and heart disease: "Compared to singles, the chances of developing heart disease drop 20 percent for married men, but only 4 percent for married women." Next, Mark asked if it was true or false that "People who are in healthy marriages tend to be happier and have lower stress levels." The sixteen parents in the room offered a confident "false" in unison. "No, actually, that one's true," Mark told us. "Three, true or false, married people tend to help each other make healthier choices." Again with steady confidence, the whole class offered a resounding "false." "That one is actually true as well," Mark said. One mother immediately challenged him: "You don't have to be married to help each other make healthier choices!" "But what about compared to married couples?" Mark asked. Neither the mother nor I understood this as a response to her claim. Mark quickly moved on to the next question. "Unmarried people who love each other and live together enjoy the same health benefits as married people." Having lost all confidence to answer at all or perhaps as a result of questioning the quiz's validity after the previous questions, only a third of the class answered "true." "Nope, that one's false," said Mark. He continued, "Finally, what about this one: Married people tend to weigh more and suffer from obesity more than people who have never gotten married." "Oh, that's definitely true," said one of the fathers. "That's correct," said Mark, "but why, do you think?" The father quickly quipped: "Because being married is part of being comfortable, and you let yourself get fat." "And, married people have more kids, and they make you fat, too" added another dad.

In an alternate version of the quiz, instructors asked parents: "Married couples make more money than unmarried couples, true or false?" Given their belief that marriage should follow financial security, parents were much more likely to answer this question correctly by stating "true." Instructors never once mentioned selection effects—the greater tendency for people who make more money to marry and stay married—and simply implied that marriage itself directly causes couples to make more.

On one occasion, a tense conflict erupted when José and Susan used the quiz exercise. One of the mothers, Claudia, stood up in irritation after the fourth question about "unmarried people who love each other." She complained, "This quiz is wrong because it makes married people sound better than everyone else. My parents weren't married, and I'm not married. I turned out okay, and my kids are going to turn out okay." Obviously uncomfortable, José tentatively responded: "Well, I'm not saying this is true. This is just what the research says about people overall, not one person specifically." Although Claudia did not seem satisfied with his answer, she begrudgingly sat down and said nothing more about it. But she, along with some of the other parents, made comments to me suggesting that they understandably interpreted this message as a negative value judgment about their relationships, the quality of their parenting, and, in many cases, their own upbringings as children of single parents.

Like José, when challenged, staff and instructors often justified their pro-marriage stance by vaguely referring to "science" and "research" on all the reasons marriage is good for adults, children, and society. The statistics that instructors cited in class were taken mostly from a Mayo Clinic review of studies entitled, "Healthy Marriage: Why Love Is Good for You," that admittedly could only speculate about the relationship between marriage and physical health.[25] The Thriving Families curriculum advised instructors to tell parents that:

> While [the benefits of marriage] are clear, it is not clear *why* married people lead healthier lives. Many experts believe that people benefit from living together, having greater financial stability, and having social support. But the most likely reason has to do with stress management. . . . Researchers believe that married couples work better together as a team to handle stress. For example, they may share the tasks of running a household, earning money, and raising children. With two people, you have two times as many resources. On the other hand, a single parent has to handle these demands on his or her own. . . . There is more money in a married household. People pool their incomes and are able to build up more resources over their lifetime. Financial stability has been shown to improve people's health [emphasis in original].[26]

Instructors often paraphrased this lecture script by emphasizing that marriage is beneficial because, as the instructor Susan often told classes, "Two parents working together is better than one." Many instructors also emphasized that being married encourages people to make better choices and be more responsible out of respect for their partner.

These messages were at odds with parents' lived experiences. Most of the couples were already living together and pooling their meager resources and avoided getting married in part because one or both partners were unemployed. The assumption that marriage automatically translates into more resources—and twice as many at that—did not ring true. Abigail, a twenty-one-year-old Latina, told me that she desperately wanted to marry her daughter's father, James, but not until she could find a job and help financially support their daughter Nevaeh. "I want to get married with him right now, but it's really hard. It hurts me to see [James] go work and support us all by himself. I want to get a job before anything." James, twenty years old and Latino, agreed: "We want to make sure we have the right money and the right time before we get married. If I had money a long time ago, we would have done it then. We broke up when I lost my job, but we moved back in together when I made enough money and could get this apartment." It was unclear how marriage could help fix their major problems, especially having too little money and the need for consistent work.

Though parents tended to agree with instructors that marriage and two-parent families were better for kids, their understanding of the direct benefits of marriage was more narrowly focused on spouses' legal rights. As Jamie, twenty years old and white, told me about her view of the benefits of marriage: "I want to wait to have a nice wedding, which we can't afford now. If we do get married, and we got in a car crash, and he was alright and I was messed up, he wouldn't be able to say anything if we weren't properly married. So, that's a benefit. It's a stronger bond, and no one can deny him the power of attorney."

Not only did class exercises like the marriage quiz not resonate with parents' views of and experiences with marriage, they often demeaned them. Instructors were trained to teach the curriculum over a mere two days and were motivated to teach for a variety of reasons, including religious values, a belief in the power of educational approaches to modifying human behavior, and a sincere desire to help those they considered less fortunate. They were not, however, particularly well versed in the specificities of marital research, much less equipped to handle challenges to the claims they were espousing. Aware of this disconnect, but hesitant to discuss it openly with parents for fear of sparking conflict, instructors avoided talking about marriage.

There were many instances during classes when instructors accidentally said "marriage," only to quickly correct themselves and replace it with "relationship" or "commitment." This happened during the following conversation between José and Susan and a white father in his twenties named Michael:

JOSÉ: I want to thank you guys for coming out to the Thriving Marriages class.

MICHAEL: Wait, I don't know what you guys got going on here.

JOSÉ: Well, the program goes by a lot of different names.

MICHAEL: That was a good comeback there, man!

SUSAN: This is the Thriving *Families* class, though it's put on by an organization called Healthy Marriages. None of the couples who take these classes are married.

JOSÉ: Well, we just want to thank you for coming out. Basically, we're—even we as the instructors—are just trying to learn the skills that will help us be better parents, to nurture our children, to help them grow. We want our children to be better than we were, to be better than we are.

MICHAEL: (Nodding satisfyingly in agreement) Ok, then.

As this exchange revealed, some parents were concerned about how much the classes would focus on encouraging couples to marry. Assuring them that this was not going to be a class that was "out just to get them married," José added that some of the parents who took the classes eventually got married and that many couples had that as a goal. However, he emphasized, this was not the main goal of the program.

Beginning with recruitment, circumventing talk of marriage was strategic. Recruitment staff intentionally downplayed the marriage message to avoid intimidating couples from enrolling. They believed talking about marriage would conjure up anxiety about parents' relationships and misrepresent the goals of the Healthy Marriages organization. From their perspective, the program's purpose was to encourage and support all healthy relationships, including co-parenting among couples who were no longer romantically involved. They emphasized that marriage was the ultimate goal only in best-case scenarios.

Emilio, a Latino staff person in his forties, recruited for Thriving Families in mandatory parenting classes for women receiving WIC (Women, Infants, and Children nutrition program). I observed several iterations of his fifteen-minute presentation about the program's purpose and benefits. He stressed that the program was for anyone who cared about their kids and that improving their relationships, married or not, was one of the best things they could do for their children. When I interviewed him after one of these recruitment sessions, I asked how he explained the inclusion of the word "marriage" in all the informational brochures he distributed to parents. He replied:

Sometimes in my speech I say, "This is not a session to get people married. That's not our job." If it happens, it happens after the class, but that's not our purpose. Our purpose is to help people acquire skills that will help their relationships become healthy. . . . They don't like to talk about long-term goals because some live one day at a time. They don't even know if they're going to make it to the following week. So to talk to them about things for the future, it's not very appealing to them for themselves, but this is the time for them to think about their baby. "If I could not make it, my baby might make it." I plant that seed in their mind, to think, "I couldn't make it going to college, but maybe my baby will do it, and I'll do the best I can to support that."

Emilio learned in the Thriving Families instructor training that prospective participants were in a daily survival mode that prevented focusing on long-term goals like marriage.

Other staff and instructors similarly described how the two-day training taught them that low-income, unmarried couples often avoid marriage because they fear they cannot make it work and because they are struggling financially. Instructors learned to expect that their pro-marriage message might conflict with parents' relational and economic insecurities. This tension also pointed to the middle-class perspective and stereotypical beliefs about those in poverty shared by many of the staff and instructors. Sonia, the program's coordinator, twenty-seven and white, described what she learned from the instructor training:

I was surprised that people tried to get pregnant when they weren't connected with the guy, that the commitment of having a baby is less than having a commitment to being married to somebody, and those two things don't necessarily need to go together. I think it was also interesting to see the generations of single moms and women on welfare and just really realize that people's goals a lot of times are created by what is around them. . . . There could be a single mom on the block who gets her alimony checks, so a goal is to become like her, not necessarily to go to school, get married, and then have a kid. . . . It taught me to treat it like it was just a different culture than what I'm used to and not to assume any reason that would get people in those situations. They have a lot to deal with.

Another staff person, a thirty-year-old Latina named Maria, worked directly with Thriving Families couples to arrange class meetings, transportation, and incentives. Unlike Sonia who told me she had to learn to see participants as coming from a "different culture," Maria empathized with their reluctance to marry. Maria was a low-income, single mother of two young sons and worked for the Healthy Marriages organization in conjunction with the state's welfare-to-work program. Though she was engaged to be married and supported the organization's marriage promotion goals, she was particularly sensitive to the concern that classes might seem coercive about marriage. Like Emilio, she worried that explicitly talking about marriage would prevent couples from signing up:

> I don't think they're ready for marriage. I think they're barely struggling with being together for right now, and when you talk about being together forever, they'd probably be like, "I don't want that right now." It's not even in their mind. You know, to be honest with you, I don't even use the word "marriage" because I feel like I might lose them in the recruitment process ... because they're probably thinking, "Marriage, oh no, I don't want to go to a class that's going to get me married." They are scared of that word.

Justine, a forty-year-old, African American single mother who also worked for the organization as part of the state's welfare program, rounded out the Thriving Families recruitment staff. She, too, believed that most parents were too consumed with getting by day-to-day to make concerted plans for their long-term future. She praised the program's curriculum for encouraging parents to be goal oriented, but thought that talking about marriage would be overwhelming and unhelpful given parents' more immediate needs:

> Some don't even have their goals set. I find that really valuable in our curriculum because it gets you thinking about what you're going to do. Where do you see yourself? And then you talk about marriage. But, right now, it's not even in the picture. They're just trying to get to tomorrow. How can they even think about the future if tomorrow is even bigger? . . . I've been poor all my life, . . . so I know how they feel. . . . I have a lot of people just asking how they can get their electric bill paid.

To a point, class background shaped how staff and instructors interpreted couples' reluctance to marry as either a cultural or economic issue. Though all recognized that the couples were struggling financially, staff from lower-income backgrounds were more likely to explain parents' reluctance as a matter of, as Justine put it, "just trying to get to tomorrow." There was, however, general agreement that parents feared or felt unequipped for marriage and did not fully comprehend how beneficial it would be for their families. When staff and instructors told me that they believed couples were unprepared for marriage, they often meant that couples lacked marriage role models and relationship skills that generate confidence in the ability to make marriage work. When I asked the program's creator and director, Cynthia, a white marriage and family therapist in her fifties, if the program intentionally avoided talking about marriage, she told me:

> Yes, it's intentional. . . . It isn't that these people don't believe in marriage, it's that they don't believe they can do a good job. They also believe they have to have all the accoutrements before they get married, like a house. . . . They are not choosing to not do it; they are just afraid they can't do it well. They need to build confidence in their ability to do a relationship well, and when that is in place, the marriage will follow. . . . They just never got support to do something different.

From the perspective of staff and instructors, the problem was not that parents devalued marriage. Promoting marriage was, therefore, not about getting couples to hold marriage in higher regard. Rather, classes focused on addressing the fear and myths about marriage that staff and instructors believed most undermined marital commitment among low-income parents. Mark described learning about this in the Thriving Families instructor training:

> The thing I remember most is that it's not that they don't value marriage, it's that they value marriage so much. It's so important to people who don't have as much monetarily that they don't want to risk it on something that could fail. They see so many relationships failing in the world around them, and they don't want to end up like that. . . . We're not there to just push marriage. We're there to give them tools to have a healthy relationship and teach them why it's beneficial. . . . A lot of people in our class have been married and divorced, so I don't know if throwing the term

"marriage" out there is going to help them if they don't have the skills. Marriage is already the goal.

Susan agreed, noting that disadvantaged couples avoid marriage because of fear, lack of confidence, and not having adequate marriage role models: "I think most of them are just scared. I don't think that they don't want to. I think that they come from broken homes and they think, 'Oh, our parents come from broken homes, and it doesn't work. I don't even want to bother with it.'"

This shared belief among staff and instructors that couples feared marriage because many came from "broken homes" and "never got support to do something different" indicated another underlying assumption of healthy marriage programs: Poor couples avoid marriage because they are deficient in the relationship and life skills that long-term marital commitment requires. According to this logic, parents in poverty avoid marriage because they lack knowledge about how to set goals and make decisions with a lifelong outlook in mind. Thriving Families couples presumably needed more than encouragement to think about marriage as part of their families' futures; they needed to learn how to start thinking about any future at all. As Cynthia talked about why she chose the curriculum used by the program, she said:

When you have been traumatized, you don't look into the future because there is no future. . . . Most of them will tell you they never thought they would make it to their twenties. So when you think this way, then you live day-to-day, you don't set goals, and you don't create a plan for your life. . . . First they are going to be taught decision-making skills, and then they're going to be taught envisioning a future, and another exercise has a life timeline, which says, "Look, I've overcome obstacles, I can do this." This is about building self-confidence, empowering them, and . . . making them smart.

Street-level bureaucrats implement policy based on their understandings of the constraints their clients face and their own moral judgments of those they serve.[27] This was evident in the Thriving Families program. Staff and instructors experienced a conflict between wanting to teach that marriage would greatly improve families' lives and the need to frame their pro-marriage message in ways that were salient to how parents prioritized children and getting by over marriage. To resolve this conflict, they mostly avoided talk of marriage. Instead, they focused on teaching couples how to develop the skills they believed comprised the marital habitus—how to set goals, think in terms of the future, and communicate more effectively—to overcome parents' reluctance about marriage. Central to this strategy was highlighting parents' commitments to one another for the sake of their children, a lesson intended to reorient parents' focus to the future and disrupt the cycle of "broken homes" instructors presumed shaped fears of marriage among those in poverty.

"Breaking the Chain": Promoting Committed Co-Parenting as a Socioeconomic Resource

Thriving Families classes taught participants that commitment to their children's other parent would help them realize all the dreams they had for their families. They characterized committed co-parenting as a socioeconomic good that could disrupt the intergenerational transmission of poverty. Instructors used catchphrases that referred to parents' own childhoods and strategically tapped into how they desperately wanted something better for their children. For Katherine and Karl, a married African American couple in their fifties who taught the classes, the phrase "break the chain" best encapsulated the overarching goals of the program as they understood and taught them. Getting couples to think about how their relationships could support their children's social and economic opportunities was the goal of the family web exercise, the first activity of every series of Thriving Families classes.

In one representative instance, Karl and Katherine initiated the exercise with Katherine's enthusiastic promise that, "In this class, you'll get to know yourselves better and learn how to create a network of support for your children. Both of you must be involved in your child's life, whether you're with other people or if only one of you has custody." She then told everyone to sit in the middle of the room in a close circle. Some of the parents grumbled, but everyone eventually cooperated.

We took turns answering Katherine and Karl's questions as we threw a ball of yarn across the circle. If someone caught the ball, they had to answer next. For the first round of the exercise, we said our names. For the second, we told everyone how many children we had. For the third and final round, everyone shared their hopes for their children. Some parents were specific, expressing that they wanted their children to "always have enough to eat and clean clothes," "graduate from high school," and "go to college." Others were more general, sharing that they wanted their children to be "happy and successful." A few phrased their hopes in terms of what they did not want for their children: "to turn out like me" or "get pregnant or knock someone up when they're in high school." One particularly poignant answer came from a young African American father who said he wanted to raise a daughter with "a lot of self-esteem because she's surely going to need it in this world that just tries to put Black women down."

By tossing the ball of yarn around the circle during all three rounds while each person held their several pieces of yarn taut, we ultimately created a web of yarn meant to symbolically represent the collective dreams parents had for their children. "Look," said Katherine, "much like this web, if you create a strong network of support for your kids through a healthy co-parenting relationship, it will take care of your child." Karl then took out a beach ball, told the parents that it represented their children, and threw it in the middle of the circle onto the yarn web. He described how the web was a metaphor for co-parenting: "If our relationships with our partners are strong enough, it can keep our children from falling through the cracks and help them achieve all the things we hope for them."

Next, Katherine pulled out a pair of scissors and cut one of the strands of yarn. She told us: "This is what happens when partners don't support one another, when they don't communicate effectively, or when they don't resolve conflict in a healthy way." She continued to cut pieces of the yarn until the web could no longer support the beach ball, and it fell to the floor. "This is what this class is about," she emphasized, "how your child needs a good web of support that is your co-parenting relationship." Karl interjected: "If you don't give that to your kids, if you're not there to shape them, then someone else—society at large, their peers, or television—will in your place." Katherine added: "This is about you, both of you, for you to break the chain, break the cycle. You don't have to become the parents you were raised by. You can do things differently, and that means making a commitment to your child and each other every day." The take-home message was clear: Parents' abilities to give their kids what they hoped for depended on how committed they were to being responsible parents who got along with one another.

Instructors believed that lessons about "breaking the chain" deeply resonated with parents' own childhood experiences of poverty and parental absence. My interviews with parents suggested they were right. Though some parents found the web exercise silly, most liked it because it symbolized how they wanted to ensure their children's lives were better than their own. Because of this, instructors assumed that promoting co-parenting commitments was more salient to couples than encouraging them to marry; it shifted parents' perspectives from focusing on their own deprivation in the present to the anticipation of their children's socioeconomic security in the future. As Karl told me during our interview:

> We always tell them "break the chain, break the chain." We emphasize how much they teach their children, and then the children grow up to be like the parents, and it just goes on generation after generation, and it's sad. It's getting them to understand, and they've all experienced it. That's why when we do the yarn network with the beach ball and we say, "What do you want to change?" they say, "I want to be there because my father wasn't," and "I want to do this because I didn't have it." So I say, "Yes, what are you doing to make that difference?"

The lesson that followed the web activity taught couples that, to accomplish the goals they had for their children, they needed to develop specific parenting habits. Instructors emphasized the importance of spending time with kids, helping them with their homework, and boosting their self-esteem through positive affirmations. Sonia, the program coordinator, described how Thriving Families focused on teaching couples parenting behaviors that best promote children's social and economic success:

> On the first day of class, we'll ask them what they want for their kids. They want their child to have a better life than they've had, they want their child to not worry about money, and they want their child to have an education, to be happy. The basic desire is there. They just don't know how to put that into action. So these parents that desperately want their kid to attend college just haven't been taught that, "Okay, well just help them with their homework on a day-to-day basis." . . . I was fortunate enough to be taught that

stuff at home. And some people don't have that, and that's what we're teaching people, just things that if people were from healthy families everybody would know this, and we wouldn't need our classes. But that's not the case.

Like Karl and Sonia, most of the other staff and instructors described to me how parents could directly improve their children's life chances and break the cycle of poverty by learning specific parenting and relationship skills that poor parents presumably lacked. These skills would be even more effective, they reasoned, if both parents would commit to one another and work on learning and implementing them together.

Ultimately, classes taught parents that children's upward mobility was dependent not on what they have, but on what they do for their partners and children. Although parents' economic circumstances may be tenuous, instructors noted, couples' relationships could be stronger— not in spite of this difficulty, but because of it. Staff and instructors also emphasized that it was imperative to make co-parenting relationships work because they are the best resource parents in poverty have to give their children better lives. Like other healthy marriage curricula I studied, many Thriving Families class lessons emphasized that good, strong relationships are more important than money when it comes to happiness and well-being. As Katherine told me during our interview:

> It's not about how much money you make. . . . In my experience, people who had the most money had the most problems. And that's not to say that you can't have money and still be happy. There's nothing wrong with having things, but things break down. We have so much materialism and an economic system that's failing. You could have all the money in the world, or you could have nothing. The most important thing in reality is having family, having that love between you. That's what's going to pull you through.

Katherine's teaching philosophy that love is what pulls you through, even if you have nothing, was similar to José and Susan's appeal to parents that "Hard times will not destroy you if you're committed." From this perspective, love and commitment among poor parents are not just more important than money and other resources, they *are* economic resources. This message was particularly salient to parents. Unlike access to education, well-paying jobs, and other opportunities parents were lacking, committed co-parenting was framed as a more secure basis of social and economic support for kids that parents could control. The implication was that parents could give their children every-thing they never had if only they were willing to learn and adopt good relationship and parenting behaviors—and especially if they were willing to commit to and skillfully love one another for the sake of their children.

Staff found that appealing to parents' commitments to their children was particularly effective for encouraging couples to sign up. Focusing on committed co-parenting rather than marriage allowed staff and in-structors to circumvent parents' resistance to marriage as something that symbolized out-of-reach economic prosperity; it simultaneously tapped into how children are central to parents' hopes for a vicarious upward mobility. As Emilio told me:

> I appeal through their kids because they're their priority. That's why we work so hard. . . . I say, "You came to this country looking for opportunities. You sacrificed a lot to come here, so don't you want to give them the opportunity of having this great relation-ship for your kids?" Sometimes I use some research. I say, "You know what, it's been proven that parents who have good commu-nication, their kids have better grades in school. And the better grades they have, the prouder you'll be of them."

Pessimistic that he could recruit couples with a hopeful message about their own futures, Emilio emphasized how the classes "planted a seed" of optimism for couples' children: "Many of them come from very bad neigh-borhoods, and they don't know if they're going to survive the next day. . . . These are people who cannot see a future in their lives. When you start planting seeds about their kids, they think, 'Maybe there's something here for me.'" Similarly, Maria described how she appealed to mothers and their desire to increase fathers' involvement in children's lives:

> I want to stress that we are about family unity. We also teach dads that it's very important to be in a baby's life regardless of the rela-tionship with the mother. . . . I want these women to understand, "Come to our class, and we'll teach your man how to be in your baby's life regardless of your guys' future." . . . We teach that your children are your priority.

Other staff commented on how deemphasizing marriage was a po-litically strategic decision, one they did not fully support. The program's educational director, Nathan, white and in his fifties, was the staff per-son most critical of downplaying marriage:

> There isn't enough money in the universe to address all of the social needs that have arisen out of broken relationships. Any place of disruption, dysfunction, anxiety, or suffering you can trace it to broken relationships . . . , and while we have to be com-passionate towards dysfunction, I don't think we have to tolerate it in a sense of normalizing it. This is no longer coming from the realm of tradition or opinion. Now we have a research base to say it is better for a child to grow up with its biological mother and father or at least a mother and a father. Why not strive for the ideal without making somebody feel bad because they're outside of the ideal? I don't see those two as being in conflict at all. They wanted to make sure we didn't put too much emphasis on marriage because marriage has become a bad word for a growing number of people. Even internally, in the last year we say "marriage and rela-tionship education" just so we don't have to squirt water on that fire.

Nathan's comment here from an interview conducted in late 2009 anticipated an important shift deemphasizing marriage in government-supported relationship skills programs. Many of the earlier state and community programs funded by the federal Healthy Marriage Initiative included the word "marriage" in their organizational titles. Up until 2010, this was the case with the organization that coordinated Thriving Fami-lies. That year, the leadership staff decided to rename the organization and allowed those on their organizational electronic email list to vote on a new name that would reflect their goal of improving all relationships, re-gardless of marital status. Of the new name options offered to voters, not one included the controversial "m word." After voters weighed in, the or-ganization went by a new moniker highlighting "relationship skills."

Despite differences of opinion about how much the classes should explicitly promote marriage, all the staff and instructors agreed that it was important for couples to know about the benefits of marriage, to develop the skills presumably needed for marriage, and to learn how to cooperatively co-parent whether they were married or not. The instruc-tor Deborah explained to me how parents themselves were in the best position to judge their readiness for marriage and that her role was to ensure couples had the information they needed should they choose to get married:

> I'm not living in their homes with them. They are the experts of their own relationships. I'm just here to educate and guide them in a direction where they can hopefully come to some sort of agreement. We're not here to persuade someone to become married, but to try to get them to understand that being married has its benefits. Through understanding and problem solving, conflict management, and discussing, at the end, you might want to make a more committed relationship with that person. Getting married is not for us to say. We're just here to say, "Here are the things you can do to stay together."

Sonia also described how she believed the program should focus more on teaching parents to work together for the sake of children than encouraging them to marry:

> Two people working together are better than one, and two people working well together are much better than two people trying to work together and failing at it. . . . Parents leave for two main reasons. One of them is that parents are scared of their responsibility or think they can't do a very good job providing, and so they think it's better for them to take off. . . . The second is that they're just not getting along with the other parent and so they take off. Our classes address those two issues, showing parents that they can provide for their child and make a huge difference in their lives, and secondly, they don't have to continue to be in a romantic relationship with the other parent. If they learn to work together for the betterment of the child, then that's okay. It's not about pushing people into loving each other. It's about having people work together because they decided to have a child together.

Yet, staff and instructors assumed that parents were in ongoing romantic relationships and frequently underscored how taking shared responsibility for their children could buoy their romantic commitment to one another. Despite talk of marriage being rare in the classes, there was clear intent to promote it by parlaying shared commitments to children into overcoming parents' reluctance to marry. The primary message that their relationships could be stepping-stones to a better life for their children was intended to build confidence so that, in Cynthia's words, "the marriage will follow." As José explained to me, "I teach that love is not a feeling, it's a commitment. Because if you're going to be committed to that person, why not marry them? Why not make it the best relationship so that your child can benefit? It's not all about you. It's about your children who are going to prosper from your relationship."

Converting Poverty into Prosperity through Committed Co-Parenting

Children do indeed benefit when their parents get along, regardless of the parents' marital status.[28] But as beneficial as cooperative co-parenting relationships can be, they cannot offset the various social and economic inequalities that prevent many parents from realizing the hopes they have for their children. Teaching that skilled love and shared commitments to and through children can transform poverty into prosperity does a disservice to poor parents. Reminiscent of the love-can-conquer-all ideology, this misguided message belies how social and economic disadvantages often undermine rather than bolster romantic commitment. No matter how strong or skilled, neither parental nor romantic love can compensate for economic deprivation. Shaping parents' behaviors with the intent to help them develop a marital habitus will not guarantee their families' economic success or break the cycle of poverty.

Parents mentioned repeatedly in classes and interviews that they struggled with unemployment, paying bills, finding affordable housing, and other financial problems. Yet, though they discussed parents' economic challenges in interviews with me, instructors rarely addressed in the classes how poverty can undercut romantic commitment. The curriculum acknowledged these challenges only in a limited way. For example, one exercise that was supposed to help couples decide if they were ready for marriage featured "Diane" and "Kevin," a fictional couple who were thinking about getting married. They had a newborn daughter, and Kevin really wanted to marry Diane and live with her and the baby. But he could not afford it because he only worked part-time as a clerk in a convenience store. Diane lived with her mother and the baby in Section 8 housing and hoped to graduate from high school soon, but she worried that she had fallen too far behind during her difficult pregnancy.

Two other versions of Diane and Kevin's story presented couples with even more challenges to consider: Kevin's children from previous relationships and divorce-related financial problems; Kevin's lack of job skills, alcohol abuse, and possible physical abuse of Diane; and Diane's infidelity and criminal record for shoplifting. When I observed instructors teach this lesson, parents quickly identified numerous reasons Diane and Kevin should delay marriage—too little money, lack of trust, few job prospects, abuse, cheating—and they empathized with the fictional couple's obstacles. Afterward, the instructors were understandably at a loss to explain to parents how they might overcome the same challenges in their own lives given their limited means. With the caveat that abuse was unacceptable in any form, instructors resorted to vague generalizations that at least the couples had each other and that a strong family draws on good coping and stress management skills.

As part of another class lesson on "Managing My Stress," instructors asked participants to rate from one to five how significant various sources of stress were for them and their relationships. Stressors listed in the workbook included "detention in jail," "no health insurance," "finding transportation," "feeling unsafe in neighborhood due to crime," "can't find a job," "not having enough money to pay bills," and "finding and paying for child care." When I observed couples do this exercise in class, unemployment and not having enough money topped parents' lists of stressful problems. Regardless of which stressors came up, instructors generically encouraged parents to find ways to manage their stress for the health of their relationships and families, such as by setting and working toward achievable goals, doing breathing exercises, and finding a relaxing place to spend downtime with their partners.

Instructors did not blame parents for these problems and occasionally acknowledged the larger economic and political context of their stressors, including high levels of unemployment during a recession and the prohibitively high cost of health and child care for those on an extremely limited income. Couples also appreciated the message that love and relationships are more important than money; it gave them hope about otherwise desperate family and financial situations. But neither the curriculum nor instructors discussed how couples' stressors, both relational and financial, can weaken the kind of commitment the program promoted to help parents manage their money problems.

The United States is often described as a child-friendly society that protects and promotes the best interests of children. Yet public investment in social programs that directly increase children's opportunities and access to resources is waning.[29] Healthy marriage policy was premised on the assumption that children and their life chances are best served by growing up in two-parent, married households. However, there is no evidence to suggest that when children are born into poverty, marriage between their parents directly improves their chances of long-term economic success.[30] To its credit, the Thriving Families program mostly avoided promoting the dubious message that marriage will solve poor families' economic problems.

Instead, the program promoted responsible parenting and commitment through children as a foundation for developing a marital habitus that would presumably allow couples to enhance their children's life chances. By promoting marriage in this way, healthy marriage classes reinforced the American ethos of individual parental responsibility—the idea that family should be a private, self-sufficient economic domain in which parents are solely responsible for meeting children's needs and providing them with opportunities for social and economic advancement.[31] When there is little political will for and social investment in policies and programs that equalize access to resources, children's opportunities are circumscribed by what their parents can afford. This political philosophy does not bode well for children growing up in poor families. The solution is not to teach parents who have little else that their commitment to one another is the greatest resource they have to promote their children's upward mobility. Doing so only justifies and reinforces the intergenerational transmission of poverty.

Recall the yarn web exercise. The web we collectively created was meant to symbolically represent parents' hopes for their children and how couples' co-parenting relationships would allow parents to realize those aspirations. More often than not during the activity, either the beach ball was partially deflated or there were gaps in our web large enough for the ball to easily fall through. When this happened and the instructor threw the ball on the web, it fell to the floor. Despite repeated attempts by the group to hold our yarn more tightly, the web could rarely support the ball without one of the instructors holding it in place. Even if they are raised in two-parent, married households, children who grow up in poverty have less access to all the things they will ultimately need to accomplish what their parents wish for them. Just as the ball fell through our web, their deflated life chances and the highly unequal society in which they live leave many children on the socioeconomic floor, despite the love or commitment their parents share. Each time I observed the ball fall, it was a poignant reminder that strong relationships—both romantic and co-parenting ones—thrive most within the context of social and economic support. No love or commitment is great enough to convert poverty into prosperity.

I came to understand the importance of fatherhood through its absence—both in my life and in the lives of others. . . . The hole a man leaves when he abandons his responsibility to his children is one that no government can fill. We can do everything possible to provide good jobs and good schools and safe streets for our kids, but it will never be enough to fully make up the difference. That is why we need fathers to step up, to realize that their job does not end at conception; that what makes you a man is not the ability to have a child but the courage to raise one.

Barack Obama[1]

6 Men, Money, and Marriageability

Promoting Responsible Fatherhood through Marital Masculinity

In honor of the 100th anniversary of Father's Day, President Obama issued this statement in *Parade* magazine describing a real man as someone who accepts his fathering responsibilities by actively raising a child.[2] This had become a familiar message to me during the 18 months I spent studying the Thriving Families healthy marriage program for low-income, unmarried parents. Along with lessons about the benefits of marriage, lessons on the importance of fathers were a major component of the Thriving Families curricula. Instructors congratulated and thanked men who showed up for their willingness to take a class about relationships and parenting. Cynthia, the program's executive director, noted that fathers' participation should be specially commended because men are reluctant to talk about "touchy, feely stuff like relationships" and do not always see themselves as valuable to children and families.

I attended numerous Thriving Families classes in June 2009, the same month President Obama wrote about the limits of government in filling the holes left by paternal absence. For one of those classes, parents, instructors, and I all had to unexpectedly caravan to a new class site because the building manager did not show up to unlock the door for us. Cynthia arrived exasperated about an hour after the class was supposed to begin, thanking everyone for waiting patiently and accommodating the last-minute location change. She directed her gratitude at the men there that day. Their presence, she passionately claimed, was a clear indication of responsibility and being committed to their children. As the instructors Mark and Deborah indicated that it was time for class to begin, Cynthia left us with these parting words: "Men, congratulations! Thank you for taking the time to attend a class like this and hanging in there with your kids and partners! It's so important in this time of so much family breakdown."

That morning's class focused on fathers. Mark and Deborah described how dads play a unique and irreplaceable role in their children's lives for which no one else, not even the best mothers, can fully compensate. Deborah showed a video from the *Bringing Baby Home* curriculum for new parents. In it, renowned couples researcher John Gottman discussed how important fathers are for various childhood outcomes, including academic achievement and avoiding juvenile crime.[3] Gottman emphasized findings from studies about how fathers and mothers tend to play differently with kids. Fathers, he noted, encourage independence, risk-taking, and confidence in children; they are less likely than mothers to be overly gentle in play for fear of children getting hurt. Gottman concluded the video segment by bemoaning how fathers are made fun of as oblivious goofs and viewed as secondary helpers or babysitters who are unequipped to be primary caregivers. Mothers in particular, he noted, often discount fathers and see them as incompetent when it comes to kids.

In the class discussion that followed, Deborah told us that fathers are essential and contribute to children's lives in ways that mothers simply cannot, ways that have nothing to do with money. Mark critiqued media portrayals of fathers and the tendency for men to be relegated to the sidelines when it comes to caring for children: "The media tell us that dad isn't contributing. He's a lot of jokes on sitcoms, the guy who doesn't know how to take care of kids. Dad can be secluded from childrearing, and mom needs to realize he's important for the children's academic, social, self-esteem, and all sort of successes in life."

Caleb, twenty-three and Latino, was in class that day. When I interviewed him, he explained how these messages significantly influenced his understanding of fatherhood:

We watched this video on why dads are so important, and I never thought about it that way. I figured a dad's place was he's just there, he works, and then he comes home. You know that's pretty much how my stepdad was. He was the protector, the provider, and the disciplinarian. Then Mom was the one you had fun with. In that video it talked about how kids enjoy playing with their dads more than their mothers because dads are more spontaneous, and we're more worried about fun. Mom's worried about what's beneficial to the kid's learning. Ever since then I look at the kids, and it's cool. Junior does come to me more than her because I play with him a lot. . . . Dads are really important when they're involved. They're not just off in the background. It actually has a major effect on the kid's psyche.

Like Caleb, several of the other fathers told me they appreciated how the Gottman video and lessons on the importance of fathers validated the uniquely valuable role they played in their children's lives. Caleb could not tell me if he did more for Junior since taking the classes—for example, changing his son's diapers, a chore he avoided because Junior's mom was "better at it anyway"—but the classes did give new meaning to his and Junior's playtime. They also fundamentally changed the way Caleb saw himself as a father. This was one of the Thriving Families program's main objectives. The hope was that men like Caleb would identify more with being dads and parlay this stronger paternal identity into a commitment to marry their children's mothers. The ultimate goal was to encourage Caleb to be a responsible and productive husband who would earn more and prevent Junior from growing up in poverty.

Responsible Fatherhood, the Marriage Premium, and the "Package Deal"

The Thriving Families program's emphasis on the unique role of fathers reflected how fatherhood—namely, "responsible" fatherhood—has become central to U.S. family politics since welfare reform in the mid-1990s.[4] The Personal Responsibility and Work Opportunity Reconciliation Act of 1996 sent a clear message that all parents, regardless of gender, are responsible for financially supporting their children. The law instituted time limits on cash assistance and implemented work requirements for custodial parents, who are more likely to be mothers.

It also mandated that mothers establish paternity and required parents who do not live with their children—nonresidential parents who are more likely to be fathers—to comply with child support orders.

A major goal of marriage and relationship education programs first funded via welfare reform was to increase the number of two-parent, married families by teaching fathers how to be more responsible dads and have better relationships with moms. Along with $100 million annually for marriage promotion activities, the 1996 welfare reform law earmarked $50 million a year for programs and services that promote responsible fatherhood. These provisions encouraging fathers to be more active in children's lives were geared toward getting families off welfare and allowing kids to benefit from the money, time, and care that two parents can provide. Programs like Thriving Families that were supported by the Bush administration's Healthy Marriage Initiative created in 2002 prioritized marriage and relationship education to increase fatherhood involvement. More recently, President Obama's 2011 Fatherhood, Marriage, and Families Innovation Fund continued the federal funding for fatherhood programs that combine marriage education, parenting skills training, and employment services. This initiative led to the Pathways to Responsible Fatherhood grants starting in 2012.[5]

Family policies focused on promoting healthy marriage and responsible fatherhood reflected and reinforced normative ideals of how family members should behave and politically defined the key attributes of good parents and spouses.[6] Welfare reform defined work, marriage, and responsible fatherhood as mutually constitutive; the policy assumed that work encourages marriage and that marriage encourages men to be responsible partners and fathers, which in turn inspires men to work harder. Accordingly, healthy marriage programs taught that higher productivity and earnings among men is one of marriage's best benefits.

There is an empirical basis for this claim. Research has for decades found that marriage is associated with higher wages for men.[7] Yet, while it is undisputed that husbands on average make more, it is still a matter of debate why. It is, therefore, unclear if marriage actually causes men to earn more or if other factors explain this "marriage premium." There are three dominant explanations: selection, treatment effects, and discrimination. The selection effect hypothesis suggests that husbands make more because characteristics that predict success in the labor market, such as education, also make men more likely to marry. That is, more productive men, at least in terms of paid employment and earnings, are selected into marriage. For example, if Caleb, Junior's father quoted earlier, was married and had a college degree, the selection effect hypothesis would predict that he would make higher wages, not because of marriage, but because higher education makes him both more employable and more marriageable. Because men typically get married during a time in their lives when their earnings are also rapidly rising—in their twenties and thirties—this association may also be a matter of age. That is, husbands' earnings may rise, not because they married or changed their behavior in anticipation of marriage, but because they delayed marriage until they were earning more.

The second major explanation, treatment effects, suggests that marriage increases men's productivity by changing their work behavior. One type of marital treatment effect is known as "specialization," the tendency for husbands to focus on breadwinning and wives to do more of the housework and child care.[8] This explanation predicts that if Caleb married Junior's mother, he would work for pay and earn more because his wife would do a much greater share of the unpaid family labor. Another treatment effect explanation suggests that marriage directly changes men's behavior because they more strongly identify with the social responsibilities associated with being a husband.[9] This would predict that, if Caleb married, he would earn more directly as a result of working harder and longer to fulfill the gendered role expectations associated with the male family breadwinner. Caleb may also work harder if his wife monitors his productivity.[10]

The third major explanation for the marriage premium is discrimination. Employers may judge married men to be more responsible and worthy of higher wages because of gender and family stereotypes. If married, Caleb might make more than his unmarried counterparts if his boss assumes that he is a more productive worker and deserving of a higher salary because he is a husband, irrespective of any actual differences in work effort or skill.

Fathers also earn more on average—the "fatherhood premium" or "daddy bonus"—regardless of their marital status. Marriage and fatherhood premiums interact such that married fathers tend to make more than unmarried fathers,[11] and married fathers receive a larger daddy bonus when they live with their children and the children are biologically related to them.[12] The earnings bonus for being a father persists even when researchers control for hours worked and effort. Lending support to the discrimination thesis, this suggests that positive stereo-types of marriage and fatherhood lead employers to view married dads as harder, more dependable workers.[13] However, marriage and father-hood bonuses do not benefit all men equally. Privileged men—specifically, white, married, college-educated professionals—receive the largest fatherhood premium.[14] Fathers like Caleb—non-white and without a de-gree, job, or wife—stand to gain less from the daddy bonus. Are healthy marriage classes wrong, then, to teach them that they could gain finan-cially from getting married?

Because researchers cannot directly observe all the factors that ex-plain the marriage premium—men's productivity at work before and after marriage, how marriage and fatherhood shape men's identities and behaviors, and how employer biases influence hiring and salary decisions—these explanations remain speculative. Nevertheless, though the premium is decreasing,[15] getting married does tend to be associ-ated with more hours worked by men,[16] and a combination of selection and treatment likely causes this. Thus, healthy marriage classes are correct, at least in part, when they teach fathers like Caleb that getting married is associated with more work and higher earnings. Yet, if classes are to be truly evidence based, it is just as important to teach other things we know about the marriage premium. The marriage premium often exists prior to when men marry,[17] suggesting that greater work effort, which assumes employment opportunities, makes men more marriageable. Therefore, increasing men's employability through train-ing and education may be a more effective way to promote marriage than teaching about hypothetical benefits that do not equally apply to all men. Moreover, there is little evidence to support the specialization thesis that husbands earn more at work because their wives do more at home.[18] Promoting a traditional gender division of family labor, which is associ-ated with less marital stability,[19] would therefore likely undermine rather than promote happy, stable marriages.[20]

Ultimately, given what we know about low-income couples' tendency to delay marriage until they are more financially stable, promoting mar-riage by teaching men that it will increase their productivity and allow them to fulfill masculine expectations of family behavior may have negative unintended consequences for family stability. It could rein-force the tendency for low-income men who struggle with low earnings and unemployment to avoid marriage because they do not believe they appropriately perform the male breadwinner role.

The reason for this is that men tend to understand their experiences as fathers at the nexus of work and marriage. Research on fatherhood has found that men view well-paid work, marriage, and parenthood as interrelated achievements necessary for being masculine and reaching full adult status—that is, for being *real* men.[21] Sociologist Nicholas Townsend found that men measure their success and evaluate their masculinity in terms of four deeply intertwined elements of father-hood: children, marriage, employment, and homeownership.[22] This "package deal" is a dominant cultural norm of men's proper family re-sponsibilities; it assumes a middle-class standard of living supported by a man's secure, high-paying job from which he earns enough to be the main, if not sole, provider for an entire family.

Understanding fathers' responsibilities in terms of the package deal often has negative repercussions for low-income families. Sociologists Frank Furstenberg and Andrew Cherlin first coined the "package deal" to refer to how fathers' commitments to children are frequently con-tingent on their relationships with their children's mothers.[23] Dads themselves and others often see men as failed husbands and fathers if they do not make enough money to financially support their partners and children. If men are not viewed as marriageable by their children's mothers, it can prevent fathers' involvement with their kids.

How does a policy intended to encourage marriage and responsible fatherhood for unmarried men in poverty circumvent the middle-class breadwinner norm central to the package deal? The answer is that it teaches men and their partners to think about the package deal in a fundamentally different way to take advantage of the marriage pre-mium. In this chapter, I show how Thriving Families classes tried to reconcile the tension between the ideology of male breadwinning as a prerequisite for marriage and the economic constraints of low-income fathers like Caleb. Classes challenged the idea that only men with secure, well-paying jobs were husband material. Instead, they promoted another definition of marriageability that assumed commitment and marriage come before, rather than after, financial success in low-income families.

Thriving Families lessons on the importance of fathers encouraged parents to value what I call *marital masculinity*, the idea that marriage provides the best incentive for low-income men to work hard, earn money, and create masculine identities as responsible fathers and breadwinners. Instructors decoupled what it means to be a real man from a middle-class salary. They taught parents that a good prospective husband and father need not have a consistent track record of breadwinning, but rather contributes to his family in any way, including through housework, child care, and emotional affection and support. Central to this strategy was masculinizing certain kinds of care, including teaching fathers like Caleb to think of playtime as uniquely valuable for their children's development and well-being. Thriving Families staff and instructors hoped that couples would ultimately come to understand that, despite fathers' limited employment prospects, men could initially demonstrate their commitment to their families by substituting unpaid care for paid employment. Once committed, preferably via marriage, fathers would presumably be even more invested in seeking and securing a job that allowed them to make significant financial contributions to their families.

In encouraging marital masculinity, the program taught parents to think of marriage as what sociologist Steven Nock called a "template of masculinity," a social context in which men can develop, sustain, and reinforce a masculine identity as responsible husbands and fathers through paid work.[24] The promotion of marital masculinity assumed that marriage modifies men's behavior by binding them to a set of social expectations that encourage them to work harder and earn more money as husbands responsible for women and children, rather than as single men who are only accountable to themselves. This strategy attempted to modify low-income couples' views of the economic bar to marriage by severing the strong ideological link between male breadwinning, middle-class financial security, and marriageability. Like other marriage promotion strategies used in healthy marriage classes—rationalizing romance, teaching skilled love as a tool for upward economic mobility, and encouraging parents to adopt a marital habitus to improve their children's life chances—instructors' efforts to encourage marital masculinity assumed that skilled relationship choices would allow couples to overcome economic constraints. It too discounted how inequality shapes family experiences.

How Poverty Undermines the "Package Deal"

Children who grow up with fathers who can support them both socially and financially tend to have better academic, emotional, and economic outcomes, including a lower likelihood of growing up in poverty.[25]

Men living in long-term poverty face many obstacles to providing the resources children need to thrive and to being practically (changing diapers, feeding) and emotionally (talking, hugging) involved in their children's lives. There are two dominant theories of why unmarried, low-income men have overall lower levels of fatherhood involvement: the deficit model and the family systems model.[26] The deficit model, widely propagated in political discussions of family decline and responsible fatherhood, attributes "fatherlessness" to bad family values and men's deliberate unwillingness to sustain relationships with their children.[27] The family systems model posits that a combination of economic, social, and psychological factors—including access to financial resources, social support outside the immediate family, and mental health—significantly influence how much fathers can be and are involved in their children's lives. Though much of the political commentary on responsible fatherhood reflects the deficit theory, research on low-income, unmarried fathers increasingly supports the family systems model that emphasizes the importance of economic and social factors.

Dads are more likely to stay involved if they have education and well-paying jobs,[28] if they stay on good terms with mothers,[29] and if they have a strong paternal identity.[30] Since the 1960s, men with little education have experienced declining earnings, rising rates of unemployment and incarceration, and fewer prospects in labor and marriage markets.[31] Even in families where parents are still together, being poor and in need of welfare tends to negatively affect how involved fathers are in the daily lives of their children.[32] Family and policy scholars Katherine Magnuson and Christina Gibson-Davis found that both fathers and mothers cited incarceration, unemployment, and lack of resources as the main reasons low-income, unmarried men did not provide more economic support for their children.[33] Rather than "deadbeat" dads who deliberately choose not to take responsibility for their children as the invective suggests, many low-income fathers are "dead broke."

The occupational, relational, and residential instability that accompanies poverty negatively affects how involved fathers are in numerous ways. Fathers who make little money because of unemployment or low-wage work struggle to financially support their children.[34] They are also less likely to live with and have regular contact with their children because they are less likely to stay together with and marry their children's mothers.[35] Low-income, unmarried couples are also more likely to have children with more than one partner, which is often a source of ongoing conflict in couples' romantic relationships. Creating blended families among low-income couples who share children with others tends to involve numerous trade-offs for fatherhood involvement. Fertility expert Lindsey Monte found that low-income couples are more likely to marry when their children's other parents from previous relationships are no longer involved in the children's lives.[36] Because a father's time and money are finite, what residential children gain from their dad's often comes with a reciprocal loss for the children with whom he does not live.

When low-income men cannot live up to the dominant cultural ideal that they must be successful breadwinners to be good fathers and potential husbands, they have fewer opportunities to develop strong identities as worthy dads who have value independently of their ability to provide. By prioritizing fathers' responsibilities as wage earners and payers of child support, American welfare policies have historically reinforced this narrow understanding of men's paternal obligations that depend on access to economic resources fathers in poverty are less likely to have.[37] These gender norms built into the welfare system disadvantage all low-income parents. They reinforce traditionally gendered notions of parental responsibility that create a double burden for mothers to both care and provide, while reducing fathers' perceived parental role to only that of breadwinner.

Welfare reform's healthy marriage and responsible fatherhood provisions similarly reflected a gendered understanding of parental responsibility, one that assumed a close relationship among work, marriage, and proper fatherhood. Legislative debates over including these provisions in welfare legislation prioritized work and money as central to definitions of responsible fathering.[38] In a representative passage from congressional hearings about welfare reform, Stephen Martin, state senator from Virginia testifying at a meeting of the House Committee on Ways and Means in January 1995, argued: "Work is essential to achieve financial security and move upward, but having a job provides a person more than just a paycheck. It gives *him* a sense of purpose and responsibility. It makes *him* a role model for *his* family and compels *him* to contribute in their enhancement and their success" (emphasis added).[39] Welfare reform institutionalized the idea that marriage is best for men who want to be responsible fathers. According to a report prepared on behalf of the U.S. Department of Health and Human Services: "Responsible fathering means establishing paternity, being present in the child's life (even if divorced or unmarried), sharing economic support, and being personally involved in the child's life in collaboration with the mother" preferably within "a caring, committed, and collaborative marriage," which is the "optimal environment in contemporary U.S. society for the father/child relationship."[40]

This logic echoes claims made by pro-marriage fatherhood advocates, such as sociologist David Popenoe, who have argued that, to stay involved with their children, men need "cultural pressure" via marriage to convert their voluntary paternal investments into legal, social, and economic obligations to families.[41] Sociologist Steven Nock likewise argued that husbands work longer and harder because only within marriage do men fully accept their responsibility for women and children.[42] From this perspective, marriage can help alleviate poverty and promote upward economic mobility for families because it obligates men to adopt and enact ostensibly middle-class values of hard work, achievement, and smart financial planning. Marriage is the most important part of the package deal in this view because it civilizes and motivates men to achieve all the other key elements of the package by providing the incentive they need to hold down a job and earn enough to buy a home and financially support children. That is, marriage presumably has the unique ability to compel them to be hardworking, respectable, middle-class men and responsible fathers.

As revealed by research on low-income families, including my interviews with Thriving Families parents, couples in poverty often delay or forego marriage because they believe that, other than children, the rest of the package deal should remain intact. Money is essential for accomplishing the life goals most couples believe they should achieve before marriage, including finishing school, getting off public assistance, and affording a home.[43] Stable, well-paying employment is important for the marriageability of both men and women, but because of gender norms that still hold men more responsible for being primary family breadwinners, this expectation is even stronger for men. Fathers who face limited opportunities for well-paid, stable work often find that the package deal is out of their reach. This is yet another way that intimate inequalities lead to curtailed commitments.

The promotion of healthy marriage and responsible fatherhood as interrelated antipoverty policy goals makes sense when understood through the lenses of the package deal, marital masculinity, and curtailed commitment. Fatherhood scholars William Marsiglio and Kevin Roy coined the term *conditional commitment* to describe when a father's relational and legal commitment to his children's mother is necessary to reinforce an emotional and financial commitment to his children.[44] Implicit in the logic of marital masculinity is the idea that conditional commitment can help low-income couples overcome curtailed commitment.

Thriving Families instructors masculinized caregiving and subverted the male breadwinner ethic for fathers in poverty because economic disadvantage prevented dads from achieving three of the key components of the package deal: employment, marriage, and homeownership. Promoting marital masculinity strategically repackaged the package deal by redefining marriageability for low-income men in a way that downplayed work and earnings and prioritized masculine forms of care believed to help improve relationships with children's mothers. Once committed, the benefits of marriage—especially the marriage premium in earnings—would presumably enable men to put together the rest of the package.

Teaching Marriage as a Template of Middle-Class Masculinity

Thriving Families staff and instructors believed that marriage best motivates men to become responsible fathers because it directs their behavior toward being hard workers and successful financial providers. Thriving Families classes redefined marriageability for fathers in poverty by challenging the idea that they must first earn a middle-class salary and reach the economic bar to marriage to be good prospective husbands. This strategy assumed that committed men would ultimately be an economic asset, rather than a liability, for their families because marriage is an incentive for fathers to work hard and pull their families out of poverty. This took for granted that a man's ability to earn money is dependent on the development of a proper masculine gender identity that motivates him to be a good employee, husband, and father, rather than the economic opportunities that allow him to act on that motivation.

Staff and instructors presupposed that men's desire to parent is culturally shaped, specifically through marriage's ability to harness and constrain men's natural tendency for irresponsible behavior. In interviews, they told me that, once committed, men would be even more invested in seeking and securing a job that allows them to make significant financial contributions to their families. As Cynthia, the executive director, reasoned:

> We know that marriage has a civilizing influence on men. . . . The research shows that men do not commit to being faithful until they propose. Women make that decision much earlier on, but men don't make that decision until they commit. And once they commit, they do all kinds of things differently. It's as if they make a decision to grow up. They go out, they make more money, they're healthier. What marriage does is that it gives meaning to a man's life. I mean why are you going to work? Why are you doing something you don't really want to do all day long? . . . Now why on earth would a man do that? He would do it for his family. Would a single man do that? Not on your life. He would just do what he needed to do to get along. But men are willing to do things like this to take care of their family, and that's what comes out of this.

According to Cynthia, marriage has the power to alleviate poverty because it imbues a man's—and, ultimately, a dutiful employee's—life with meaning and purpose, the inspiration he needs to work hard day after day. In committing to his family, a man adopts a particular worldview that empowers him to work harder, earn more money, and most importantly, bring his behavior and values in line with the middle-class breadwinner ethic of responsibility. Fundamentally, Cynthia reasoned, marriage socializes men as responsible workers and committed fathers.

Cynthia also told me that if we want to ensure that fathers remain involved in the lives of their children, we need to focus on improving their relationships with their children's mothers. Too often, she claimed, fathers are not active dads even when they genuinely want to be because they do not get along with moms. Cynthia and other staff believed that women are the glue of family life, the medium through which men's connections to and responsibilities for their children are negotiated and maintained. Mark, an instructor, also talked about this in describing his view of the main purpose of the classes:

> I think the whole point is to get dad involved. I mean scientifically they say the father has voluntary investment in the children where the mother has obligatory investment. She has to carry the child for nine months. She has to keep the child alive. That's how they

explain it in evolutionary psychology. The whole point of the class is to keep the dad in a relationship with [mom].

Like Cynthia, Mark believed that fathers' involvement with children was contingent on having committed relationships with their children's mothers. Staff and instructors shared an underlying belief that fatherhood, much like masculinity, is precarious for low-income, unmarried men; commitments to mothers, preferably via marriage, would provide the social context through which fathers could reinforce their voluntary investment in children and partners.

For this reason, the curriculum and instructors taught that marriage is optimal for raising children. In the lesson on "What Is a Healthy Marriage?" instructors told parents that "Kids develop best when their parents marry and stay married," a message that many believed was particularly important for fathers who were more likely to be irresponsible and self-centered. This is why José, the instructor, believed that the classes were particularly important for men:

> The guys think, "It's all about me." ... Guys have to be able to break their selfishness, because when you're used to being single, you want to hang out with your friends. Then you meet this girl, and she wants to change your whole life. That's where guys struggle. Once you're committed, you say, "Okay, now I'm going to have to get my finances together because I have to support my children." It's something guys have to learn to care about.

Like Cynthia and Mark, José believed that, whereas women are naturally inclined to stay involved with children, parenting is something men need "to learn to care about" through external pressure—namely, marriage. Similarly, Nathan, the program's educational director, was particularly worried about fathers who "seem to be so broken, so testosterone challenged. . . . We need to take them from where they are in their cultural dysfunction . . . their irresponsibility, their 'I'm 30 years old and I'm never going to grow up' kind of mindset to move them into responsible fatherhood." Justine, one of the program recruiters, also stressed how the classes provided the cultural pressure men needed to stay involved because they "bring fathers to the plate and make them responsible and accept the responsibilities of having a child."

Staff and instructors believed that marriage could solve the problems of both "dead beat" and "dead broke" dads. They told me that marriage uniquely influences men's identities and behaviors in ways that keep them connected to women and motivate them to be responsible fathers who work hard to financially support their partners and kids. Because marriage is associated with specific gendered expectations that men are supposed to be family breadwinners, they presumed that it provides the social context in which fathers constantly reinforce a valued masculine identity based on providing and investments in partners and children.

This understanding of the relationship between marriage and parenting pointed to several key gendered assumptions embedded in healthy marriage and responsible fatherhood policy about how marriage serves distinct social and economic purposes for mothers and fathers: It institutionalizes women's economic dependence on men and, in turn, civilizes men to want to accept this obligation to financially support women and children. Unlike fathers who ostensibly need social and political pressure to stay committed to families, women were presumed to naturally feel an obligation to care for their children. Promoting fathers' involvement, therefore, necessitates direct intervention and explicit messages about the "importance of fathers," while mothers apparently need no similar encouragement to stay involved because they feel innately compelled to parent due to their biology and gender identity.

What mothers needed encouragement to do, staff and instructors believed, was value men more for their nonfinancial contributions and future ability to provide—that is, to learn see their low-income partners as a potential economic asset, even in the absence of prevailing evidence that men could financially support them. In strategically promoting marital masculinity, the classes challenged the expectation that men were marriageable only if they were already stably employed and earning good wages. Instructors even refuted the idea that fathers were "real" men if all they did was provide a paycheck; good fathers, they taught, were more than mere providers. Despite their limited employment prospects, staff and instructors reasoned, low-income fathers could initially demonstrate their commitment to their families by compensating unpaid care for paid employment. Promoting masculine forms of care—namely, physical play and male role-modeling—was intended to encourage fathers to become more involved in their children's lives and develop a stronger paternal identity. The hope was that this would compel fathers to stay invested in their families en route to marriage, leading to more work, higher wages, and less poverty.

"It Takes a Real Man to Be a Daddy"

In downplaying middle-class employment as an essential component of successful fatherhood, classes challenged the idea that breadwinning alone is what makes someone a good man, husband, and father. The instructor Deborah once began a class by insisting that we should "think of fathering differently, that a man doesn't need to bring home a big paycheck to be a worthy partner and father. As long as he's pitching in somehow, whether it's by keeping the house clean or taking care of the kids while she's at work, that's being a real man." According to instructors and many of the parents, the best fathers—and men—are those who do more than just provide a paycheck; they recognize that being a good dad and a real man means being emotionally and physically present, not merely a provider.

One of the fathers, Clark, a thirty-two-year-old African American, told me that the classes taught him to think differently about being a good father and partner and what he called the "male role belief system":

> It's the belief that the man is in control, . . . that he's the dad instead of being a partner. . . . Me not helping around the house came up in [the classes], too. I help out around the house more now. I help cook more, clean up more, just so she doesn't have to do as much. . . . I'm learning that paying all the bills ain't enough, no matter how much money you make. . . . I felt that as long as I paid the bills and kept money in the pocket, that's enough. I should be able to go out and drink with the buddies or do what I want. I learned that don't matter, that that ain't love. I want finances to be comfortable and not have to worry about it, but I learned over time that I didn't know how to love.

As discussed by many of the other fathers I interviewed, the classes taught Clark that being a good dad and truly loving his girlfriend meant doing more than paying the bills. It meant "helping out" around the house and spending quality time with their kids.

When instructors did admonish fathers for not doing enough as parents, it was almost always in reference to fathers of previous generations who were either absent or just breadwinners. Though they most strongly criticized men who did not stick around for their kids at all, instructors also disparaged fathers who simply worked and paid the bills without playing a significant emotional role in their children's lives. The married instructor team of Katherine and Karl often discussed how becoming the fathers most of the men themselves did not have as they grew up had little, if anything, to do with money. It was really about "sticking in there" with moms and kids; learning to love better and talk through hard times; and using financial challenges to strengthen families, not fracture them. Karl frequently referenced the famous "Cat's in the Cradle" song by Harry Chapin as a cautionary tale about a father so preoccupied with work and paying bills that he misses watching his son grow into a man. "Anyone can be a father," Karl told us, "but it takes a real man to be a daddy." This was an ironic message given that working too much was generally not a problem for the fathers in the classes. Only five of the twenty-two fathers I interviewed were employed. They struggled more with getting enough hours at work to support their families.

Nevertheless, this message resonated with parents, especially the men, who talked about growing up and knowing who their fathers were, but the fathers "weren't around." As one of the men in class said, "I know who my father is, but he's not really 'Daddy' to me." Instructors and participants were quick to distinguish between a *father*, who simply got a woman pregnant, and a *daddy* or *dad*, someone who, regardless of biological relationship, loved their children and proved that love by being an ongoing part of their lives. Though David, twenty-eight and African American, reversed the meaning of the father/daddy dichotomy, he, too, made a clear distinction between a biological father and a "true man" who accepts his responsibilities:

> My father was around maybe twice a year until I was seven and then he disappeared. . . . I really had no father, and I know a lot of my disappointment is not having one. . . . Being a father means I have to provide for it. I have to care for it. . . . It's easy to be a dad. All you have to do is get someone pregnant, and you're a dad. But to be a father, to handle responsibility and your actions for that child, that's amazing. I can never call myself a true man until I have that responsibility.

Mothers also distinguished between real dads, those who were actively involved in their children's lives, and fathers, who were just "sperm donors" and a name on a birth certificate. As Gwen, twenty-four and African American, told me about her son's father, Isaiah, also twenty-four and African American:

> He used the class as an opportunity to talk about his father who wasn't really around and his childhood. I can see opportunity for him to be an amazing father to [Joshua] and for him to really know him. You know anybody can be his father on a piece of paper, but it's another thing to really spend time with him and know that he can shape and mold him.

Parents and program staff and instructors agreed that a real father was a man who accepted and fulfilled his parenting responsibilities through unremitting involvement in his children's daily lives. A biological link and a legal proclamation of paternity via a birth certificate were both deemed meaningless without this kind of involvement.

The message that "real men" were there for kids and partners in nonfinancial ways did not necessarily entail promoting equal responsibility for child care and housework. Instructors praised men for doing anything at all and often blamed mothers for not letting them do more. When teaching parents to rethink the scope of fathers' responsibilities to include both money and care, instructors often directed their message at women, suggesting it was mothers who primarily perpetuated the idea that men needed to be breadwinners to be worthy fathers and husbands. Many instructors explicitly critiqued mothers for "gatekeeping," being overly critical and letting men help with the kids only when under constant surveillance. Katherine often told couples that it "doesn't matter what the diaper looks like if dad changes it; as long as it stays on, don't criticize him, or he might never want to do it again." Much of the problem, instructors implied, was that women valued men's wage-earning activities more than their parenting and emotional support. This assumption faulted women's gendered expectations of men's behavior for fathers' inability to feel masculine in the face of economic hardship. As Mark the instructor told me:

> We tell them, "Women, you know you really need to be kind to your husband, or to your partner, when he's out of work because

he really doesn't feel as manly." . . . A lot of them have to define themselves in other ways than just employment . . . such as someone who is helping out around the house. He could care for a child. . . . Both mom and dad need to talk to each other and realize they're both equally important. Dad needs to realize he's important to the kids so he feels valued in the relationship and he feels like he should be there, he's contributing, he's a good person. And mom needs to feel that he's contributing something.

Instructors warned mothers not to make fathers feel like they were less important when they were unable to contribute much money to the household because of unemployment or low-wage work. They told women that good men, even when unemployed, do what they can to "pitch in" by listening to them at the end of a hard day, picking up things around the house, and watching the kids while mothers worked. According to this directive, women needed to ensure they were not complicit in fathers' low involvement with children. They could do this by helping fathers feel manly and valued by recognizing and praising any contribution men made. Yet, as sociologist Kathryn Linnenberg found, gatekeeping among mothers in low-income, unmarried families typically resulted from lack of trust in the couple relationship, not because women devalued fathers as caregivers or believed they must be tested or micromanaged.[45]

Thriving Families staff and instructors also believed that different racial and ethnic groups had distinct views of which family responsibilities men and women could acceptably perform. Recounting a presentation she gave to a community organization for African American families, Cynthia, the executive director, described how she told the group:

Men need to provide in order to be okay. When I do a survey of the women in my [Thriving Families] classes, I ask, "If you went to work, and you're the one who had the job, and the house was clean, and the groceries had been shopped for, and the kids had been taken really good care of all day long, would that be enough?" And they said, "You better believe it." . . . The research shows that Black families have more flexibility in their roles than most families do, and this is one of those strengths that we can build on. Men do not have to be superstars and make super amounts of money. What they need to be is a loving presence for their woman on a day-in, day-out basis, and they can have a great family. Over time, they will figure out how to make an income. It might not be clear from the start, but there are ways they can contribute and be a valuable part of their family.

What Cynthia saw as a strength of African American families others saw as a challenge for Latino men. Lourdes, Latina and in her thirties, was one of the instructors for the Spanish Thriving Families classes and talked at length about how Latino men were especially negatively affected by the male breadwinner norm. She believed their exaggerated sense of machismo interfered with their ability to feel masculine if they were not making a lot of money.

Interviews with fathers revealed that this was a challenge for most of the men who took the classes, regardless of race or ethnicity. Many dads who believed they were doing an equitable share or more of the housework and child care still felt inadequate and emasculated if they were not earning enough money to pull their families out of poverty, especially if mothers were working and earning more. Matthew, a thirty-four-year-old white father, struggled with debilitating health issues and received some money via his disability check; nevertheless, he still felt guilty that he could not find some way to earn more to support Elise, his white, thirty-eight-year-old fiancée, and her two young children from previous relationships. Elise brought in only slightly more money per month through welfare. She described how she saw Matthew as her daughter's real father because he cared and provided what he could for her: "In my eyes, that is [my daughter's] father. He takes care of her. He buys diapers and formula for her. He gets up at night so I can sleep. He helps out so much." But she also described how Matthew felt like less of a man and an inadequate father and future husband because he did not make more through work: "He beats himself up a lot because he wants to be able to provide more, to have a job. He tells me, 'It should be me working, not you. I don't care what I do as long as I can make money and provide for my family with much more than I make now.'" Many of the parents shared both Matthew's concerns and Elise's understanding of a "real" dad. They told me that, whether or not fathers had a biological connection to their children, a good man and real dad is someone who figures out, despite any obstacles, how to provide the resources his children need. Many described this as the defining quality of a responsible dad and respectable man; being a good partner and prospective husband entailed taking at least most, if not all, of the financial burden off of mothers.

Both mothers and fathers also emphasized how working hard and providing financially was the ultimate sign of men's commitments to their families, especially because men could spend their money else-where. This was especially important for couples, like Elise and Matthew, for whom at least one of the mother's children was not biologically related to the father. Another example was Ashley, white and twenty-four, and her fiancé Saul, Latino and thirty-five. They were raising their shared biological daughter and her son, Garrett, from a previous relationship:

> Thank God I have this man who takes care of my son, who treats him like his own. He's never done anything bad to that boy. He's been like a father to him. . . . When I had [Garrett] in diapers and his biological dad wouldn't buy diapers, Saul would bring me dia-pers, and I didn't even have to ask him. He'd be like, "Oh, we have to buy diapers this paycheck. As soon as it's payday, what does my baby need?" If she needs diapers, if she needs wipes, he's on it. . . .
> If it wasn't for him, who knows where we would be. He works, he brings the money home, the food. He's our everything.

According to Ashley, Saul best demonstrated his commitment to her by working hard, earning a "decent living" as a landscaper, and making the children's needs his first priority. Even though they rarely had any money left at the end of each month and lived in what Ashley called "the ghetto," she told me through tears that she "felt rich" because she had a man who loved her and her children enough to work hard for them.

Other parents held less gendered views about who was most respon-sible for providing financially, especially because when either parent was working, they usually made so little that it was not enough to keep their families out of poverty. Brooks, a fifty-one-year-old African Ameri-can father, best summed up this perspective when he told me that it did not matter whether a parent was a man or a woman, both needed to work to make ends meet: "People don't live like Ward and June Cleaver anymore. As far as economics are concerned, you can't live that way now-adays. You got to get every single penny you can into the house." Other parents like Gina, a thirty-six-year-old African American mother, be-lieved that everyone, men and women alike, should protect themselves and "be prepared to always be the number-one provider" because relationships and even "marriages were never a guarantee" of emotional or financial support.

Thriving Families classes strongly emphasized the importance of fathers' varied contributions to their families and taught mothers to value any contribution they made. However, this strategy did not assuage deep-seated feelings of guilt or insecurity on the part of the men who felt inferior as partners and parents if they were unemployed or made low wages. Though no one said taking the classes significantly affected how much housework or child care fathers did, many parents, including several mothers, told me the classes did seem to increase men's willingness to "help out" or "chip in" more around the house.

Pedro, a thirty-five-year-old Latino father, said the classes taught him that he could show love to his fiancée, Diane, twenty-nine and Latina, by helping her do dishes and laundry. Diane cared less about how the classes taught men to merely pitch in than she did about how Pedro was willing to do anything around the house at all. Both agreed the change had significantly improved their relationship. Instead of encouraging men's equitable contributions to housework and child care, classes emphasized housework and child care as manly tasks and ways to enact a masculine identity, especially until fathers could find well-paying jobs. Rather than promoting degendered, fully shared parenting responsibilities, classes taught parents that fathers play a uniquely gendered and irreplaceable role in children's lives because of their innate maleness.

Dad as a "Big Toy" and Role Model of Masculinity

To encourage men to become more actively involved fathers, Thriving Families classes masculinized child care in two primary ways. Instructors taught parents that children need their fathers as male role models for proper development; only fathers can teach their sons how to be men and their daughters how to feel secure and demand self-respect in relationships with other men. They also promoted the idea that fathers play a unique role in children's lives because of men's greater tendency to play with children in ways that encourage independence and confidence.

The curriculum, staff, and instructors repeatedly emphasized that fathers are an irreplaceable influence in children's lives, one for which no one else, not even mothers, can fully compensate. Classes taught that children benefit when they have access to diverse gendered styles of parenting that result from mothers' and fathers' naturally distinct tendencies to interact differently with children. One workbook activity for a lesson on the importance of fathers instructed parents to fill out a chart comprised of two columns—one each for mothers and fathers—indicating how they could be involved with their kids throughout the different stages of childhood.

Using separate columns was indicative of the program's dichotomous and gendered characterization of parental involvement, as was the practice of having one man and one woman as instructor pairs, preferably married, to model heterosexual communication in class. Conveying the idea that successful parenting relies on gender complementarity, Lourdes, an instructor, told me: "Talking about the difference between mom and dad is my favorite topic. I tell them that, 'Between the two of you, you are giving that balance to the baby. She is teaching the baby some things, and he is teaching the baby other things, and between the two of you, you're giving your baby the best.'" Lourdes was referring to the lesson in the class workbook that taught parents how children benefit when both their mothers and fathers are involved because women and men parent differently. The curriculum explained:

> Fathers and mothers both do important things, and researchers think they parent in different ways. Sometimes this means they don't understand each other. It's often easy to become angry with each other when it seems one parent is not putting in equal effort. . . . Mothers are more likely to focus on nurturing tasks, like physical care of babies, emotional nurturance, and encouraging language development. Fathers might be more likely to do well at setting disciplinary boundaries and encouraging motor (muscle) development. The more kinds of parenting a child has, the stronger he or she will become.[46]

From this perspective, having two heterosexual parents is essential for a child's well-being, but not just because the child stands to benefit from the time, care, and money that two parents potentially provide. Rather, having two parents of different genders is equally important because mothers and fathers presumably care for children in distinct ways and teach children different skills due to essential, sex-based gender differences. By promoting what sociologist Anna Gavanas termed the "parenting equation," classes taught couples to think that nurturing care from mom plus discipline and physical play with dad equaled the best form of parenting kids could have.[47]

Instructors never explicitly said that kids thrive most when they are raised by a heterosexual couple. Alas, teaching about the importance of fathers based on the logic of the parenting equation strongly suggested that having two heterosexual parents was essential for proper child development. Instructors assumed that all parents taking the classes were heterosexual, as indicated by the exclusive use of *she/he* and *her/his* pronouns to describe couples and hypothetical conflict situations. All the couples portrayed in the curriculum's images and case studies were heterosexual.

There was one instance during my fieldwork when a lesbian couple—Delia and Shantelle, both African American and in their twenties—attended a Thriving Families class. The instructors, Deborah and Mark, and most of the other fourteen parents in class that day readily included them without note. However, their presence clearly drew attention to the program's heteronormative assumptions that kids benefit most from having two different-gender parents. Shantelle had just given birth to a baby girl, Camille, two days before. At the beginning of class that morning, Deborah asked both Shantelle and Delia to stand up so the entire group could congratulate them on the very recent birth of their daughter. "How much did the baby weigh? How long was she?" Deborah excitedly inquired, looking at Shantelle who immediately looked to Delia. Delia replied, "Our baby girl was a healthy seven pounds and twenty-one inches long." Two of the men in the class blurted out simultaneously, "*Our* baby?!" Deborah did not acknowledge the comments as she quickly started to talk about the next lesson on communication and trust. For the first five minutes after Delia and Shantelle's introduction, Deborah very conscientiously used the words "partner" and "co-parent" instead of "boyfriend" and "father."

Though when it came time to divide the parents into two groups for what Deborah called "the fishbowl," it became more obvious how a same-sex couple challenged the program's core assumptions about relationships and parenting. Deborah told all the men to pull their chairs to the center of the room, while she instructed all the women to sit at the edge of the room, be quiet, and just listen. All eight men, including Mark, formed a circle between the tables. Deborah then motioned for Delia to join the men in the circle. Delia complied. Deborah continued, "As men and fathers, it's important we talk about trust. As you were growing up, what did you learn from fathers, male family members, or other men in your life about trusting women?" One of the fathers corrected her as he sternly sat up in his chair: "Come on now, we ain't all men and fathers here!" Delia responded with a definitive wave of her hand, "Come on man, you know I'm with you guys in all this. [Camille's] my kid, and I love her mom." "Alright, then," the man simply said as he sat back down. Delia's retort that she was a parent and partner too and that she loved Camille and Shantelle seemed to diffuse the palpable tension in the room. Though Deborah could have just as easily asked Delia to wait to participate in the women's group, the dominant part of Delia's identity for the purpose of participating in class exercises was as a co-parent, specifically a father-like figure who was committed to loving both the baby and the baby's birth mother as part of a package deal.

Deborah and Mark both later told me during interviews that they welcomed Delia in class because she clearly loved the baby and that it is always a good thing when any adult is committed to caring and providing for a child. Yet, Deborah's choice to include Delia in the fishbowl exercise as part of the fathers' group—the discussion for which focused on how to trust and respect women—revealed how norms of gender and heterosexuality shaped class messages and exercises. It implied that any set of parents must be made to fit the gendered parenting equation.

Despite this one instance of a same-sex couple being welcomed in class, all lessons on the importance of fathers focused on how children benefit most when they have access to feminine and masculine styles of parenting, which ostensibly entails having both a mother and father present in their lives. Instructors taught that children's social and economic opportunities depended on having involved fathers, not just because it meant more adults are committed to children's well-being, but specifically because dads are indispensable as role models of masculinity. Staff, instructors, and many of the parents strongly believed that having a father around during childhood to model strength, respect, and responsibility protected children from catastrophic life and relationship outcomes. This assumed that fathers' parental involvement—just "being there" as many of my interviewees said—directly shaped children's financial prospects, regardless of the amount of economic resources fathers could provide for their children.

Based on a strikingly essentialist understanding of masculinity, class lessons on parenting conveyed that only fathers could bequeath security, certain emotional skills, and advantageous life chances to their children. Rochelle, an instructor, described in detail all the negative ramifications she understood to be directly related to absent fathers, especially the problems rooted in children's inabilities to develop self-esteem without male role models. Rochelle also taught parents that father absence has different gendered consequences for girls and boys. She told me that daughters need fathers to develop healthy relationships with other men:

> Self-esteem has to be learned early on when you're a kid. This is why you get a lot of women who get into abusive relationships. They don't feel good about themselves, and then if they didn't have a great foundation of two parents, whether they're married or not, and they don't get the love and attention from a dad, they'll take any type of relationship because they don't understand first and foremost that they're important. If you don't have that you'll just go into a destructive relationship, and it doesn't matter, you'll stay in that relationship.

Rochelle also told me that boys need fathers to model being a good, moral man who respects women:

> A lot of African American men are in prison because they didn't have a father in the home, they didn't have a person to model, and they had a hole in their heart. . . . When you talk to them you can still see that little boy who longs for their parent. . . . It's very difficult to make changes in a person if they came from a family where there's no dad, and their self-esteem and self-confidence are low.

Another instructor, José, also described how he believed that fathers play a unique role in the parenting equation as irreplaceable role models of masculinity:

> There are certain things that a father brings and certain things that a mother brings. [JR: What does a father bring?] Self-esteem for a young girl, especially. I think a father makes a little girl

understand who she is. For a boy, it's rough-and-tumble, just going to the games, just learning how to be a man, how to treat a lady because you know the man should be teaching their children all these things throughout life.

Similarly, the instructor's manual for the program noted that:

Children are more likely to have problems when one parent, often the father, is not in contact with them. They are more likely to drop out of school and get involved with drugs or alcohol. Girls are more likely to get pregnant while teens, and boys are more likely to commit crimes and/or violent acts. Overall, children with only one parent are more likely to live in poverty.[48]

Just as instructors did, the curriculum explained negative childhood outcomes as a direct result of fathers' absence without any reference to how all of them—lower academic achievement, drug use, teenage pregnancy, and criminal activity—are also strongly correlated with growing up in poverty, regardless of family form.

Instructors often framed these messages about the importance of fathers and male role modeling by referencing what the men in class themselves had missed by not having constant, reliable father figures in their lives as children. The men were presumably disadvantaged as both fathers and potential husbands because they did not have adequate male role models to teach and demonstrate what being a good man involved. Emilio, the program recruiter, told me that many of the fathers who attended the classes were not well-prepared to be engaged fathers because "Many Hispanic men did not grow up with their dads, so they don't know how to be a real man. For many Hispanic guys, being a real man means making a bunch of kids and having sex with a bunch of girls, go and drink and spend time with their buddies." The instructors Katherine and Karl also described how father absence was a major obstacle for "breaking the chain" of family dysfunction. Staff, instructors, and parents all agreed that disrupting the cycle of absentee fatherhood and the social problems it created would require dads to "step up" for their kids by being real men and daddies, despite the pain and disadvantages they inherited from their own childhoods without adequate male role models.

Parents appreciated these messages about masculinity, male role modeling, and the importance of fathers. Mothers especially commended their partners for "being there" and "sticking around" to teach their sons to be men, especially when those men were not the children's biological fathers. This was the main reason Marcy, a twenty-one-year-old white mother of two young sons, tried to remain amicable with her eldest son's father. She told me:

> I wanted my son to have a male figure to look up to instead of me having to play both roles, which isn't fair to the child. It's not fair to me either because I have to take 100 percent responsibility. I have to show him what it's like to grow up and be a man, . . . and that's not fair because he should be getting that from his father.

Marcy's current boyfriend and youngest son's father, Thomas, twenty and African American, had become, according to both of them, "more his father than his real father." When I asked why, Marcy answered, because "He has that man connection with him. . . . It's so funny, he'll come over and play a videogame, and he'll sleep right next to him playing the game. . . . Even if his dad isn't good enough, he still has someone to be a man." Marcy's comment echoed what instructors taught in class about how responsible fatherhood and demonstrating manliness only required men to be involved in a limited way, typically by playing with children and being physically present around them.

Several parents also described how it was important that fathers teach their sons racialized forms of masculinity. Lewis, a fifty-seven-year-old African American father, had twenty-five biological children from previous relationships, but told me he was most proud of being actively involved as a social father to his girlfriend Veronica's two young sons. Saying that he "met his responsibility" when he fell in love with Veronica, African American and thirty, Lewis stressed how he taught "his sons as young Black men that the first and only thing we have is our word and there's nothing wrong with being a strong, honest individual." Veronica also told me that this was one of the things that most endeared her to Lewis:

> He's the only one that has been a solid father figure to either one of them. . . . He listens to them, he talks to them, and he takes them through the stages of being young, Black boys going to manhood. He talks to him about stuff like that, things I can't give

them. He opens their mind to the manly things you know, and they open up to him about things they never talk to me about.

Neither parents nor instructors were able to explain what exclusively enabled men to teach boys about being men or girls how to successfully relate to them. The one exception was staff and instructors' emphasis on fathers' tendency to play with children differently than mothers. As Cynthia, the executive director, told me, dads are particularly important as "big toys" for their children because they play with children in distinctly masculine, physical ways that encourage risk-taking and the development of self-confidence and autonomy. The instructor José told parents that fathers "play a unique role in the lives of their children; they foster independence." He stressed that moms and dads "tend to differ most in their forms of play. Moms tend to play more visual and verbal games, while dads are physical and tactile." In our interview, José also described how dads are often minimized in representations of family life:

> We need to change the images of dads in this culture. Your kids just want to spend time with you, to learn your values. You can do so many things to be a caring dad: hug your child, spend quality time with your child, praise your child. Even if you just go to the grocery store and give the change back if a cashier overpays you, be an example for your kids. Little things, like being honest, are important.

This message that fathers' mere presence bequeathed advantages to children reinforced the gendered division of child care, both in degree and kind. More than anything, Thriving Families classes urged fathers to have fun and play with their children, rather than do an equal share of the more laborious tasks of feeding and changing them. Parents already strongly adhered to this pattern. Though fathers held and played with babies as often as mothers during classes, mothers were more likely to feed babies, change diapers, and soothe them when crying. Mothers were almost always the ones to leave class to attend to children in the nursery.

There was a tacit, unequivocal consensus among staff, instructors, and parents that some essential personal quality of men was necessary to raise well-adjusted and successful children of either gender. This message that masculinity is an essential quality of all responsible fathers and has the power to enhance children's life chances in ways that mothers alone cannot was a persuasive message for the low-income parents targeted by the program. It validated fathers for their mere presence without resorting to definitions of masculinity and responsible fatherhood that were contingent on employment, breadwinning, or even doing an equitable share of housework and child care. Ultimately, instructors encouraged fathers to play with children and help out more around the house, while they urged mothers to value them more for doing so, despite low or no earnings. This message was a means to the greater end of subverting the gendered, middle-class expectations that require men to be stable providers prior to marriage.

Repackaging the "Package Deal" for Fathers in Poverty

The fathers I interviewed could not complete the full package deal because they struggled with unemployment and low wages. Thriving Families staff and instructors, therefore, redefined marriageability for poor fathers by emphasizing how men could prove their commitment to their families in ways that did not require money. Once committed, marriage would presumably enable them to realize the rest of the package and help pull their families out of poverty by reshaping their masculine identities into that of middle-class breadwinners who are more responsible, work harder, and make more money.

The program also strategically employed gendered and heteronormative ideas of parenting to promote fathers' limited care of children. Rather than suggesting that successful—and, hence, marriageable—men must be secure financial providers before marriage, classes focused on low-income men's capacities to be caring co-parents and partners. Claiming that men have a specifically masculine orientation to parenting and are uniquely important for child development, family prosperity, and social order, classes taught that fathers play a role in children's lives that only men can fulfill. In doing so, they emphasized that mothers and fathers are essentially different, have naturally different parenting styles, and are compelled to parent for different reasons.[49] Though the classes advocated that children need both mothers and fathers to lead success-ful lives, research on parenting does not support the claim that some essential masculine quality of fathers is necessary for children's well-being or healthy development.[50] The heterosexual parenting equation is an ideological view of proper families that lacks empirical support. Children raised by same-sex parents fare equally well academically, socially, and emotionally as children raised by heterosexual parents.[51]

Men in all financial situations and family types—including low-income, unmarried, and gay dads—increasingly view caring for their children as central to their responsibilities as fathers.[52] By promoting a limited version of gender flexibility in parenting, household labor, and paid work, Thriving Families classes highlighted the importance of fathers' abilities to both care and provide financially for their children. Yet, by endorsing the idea that children and commitment, preferably via marriage, are necessary to get low-income fathers seriously invested in the breadwinner ethic, the program merely repackaged the package deal by promoting the idea that children and marriage can best support men's commitments to work and upward economic mobility. This reinforced the long-standing social norm that well-paid work, heterosexual marriage, and fatherhood are the trifecta of modern manhood.

It also implied that men's sustained involvement with their children depends on having the right gender and sexual identities that motivate them to get and keep a job. Like other strategies that instructors used to encourage couples to marry, this approach ignored how fathers need resources to enact parental commitments, including education and jobs that pay decent wages that allow them to contribute emotionally and financially to their children. Men's involvement in children's lives and their likelihood of getting and staying married to their children's other parents are greater when these opportunities are available.

The promotion of marital masculinity was informed by a selective interpretation of research on the marriage premium, one that ignored how intimate inequalities push the package deal out of reach for fathers in poverty. Evidence of a marital treatment effect suggests that marriage can support economic success and middle-class stability when it is part of a larger package of stable employment and earnings. However, evidence also points to selection effects, which means not all men benefit equally from the marriage bonus, especially those who do not have access to jobs that provide opportunities for more work hours, higher wages, and occupational advancement. Marital masculinity ultimately reinforces the stereotype of the hardworking married father who is worthy of higher wages and promotion because of his gendered family responsibilities; this perpetuates the discriminatory ideas underlying the marriage premium and the tendency for more privileged men to capitalize on it. It is a matter of ongoing research and debate whether treatment, selection, or discrimination plays the largest role in shaping the marriage premium. In any case, Thriving Families fathers and the millions of men like them—those who are unmarried, have little education, and struggle with low wages and precarious work—are the least likely to benefit from it.

Promoting greater gender flexibility, rather than marital masculinity, would likely help low-income parents more. As sociologist Jennifer Sherman found in her study of low-income rural families, gender flexibility allows couples to avoid many of the relationship problems typically associated with unemployment and low wages among men.[53] Couples who were able to reframe a husband's masculinity in terms of active fathering experienced less conflict and more long-term family stability. Other studies of low-income fathers have similarly found that being a highly involved dad can compensate for the toll that unemployment and low wages often take on men's masculine identities.[54] Government relationship programs that have focused on encouraging fathers to be directly engaged with children without promoting marriage have had positive effects on parents' relationship quality, parenting stress, and children's behavioral problems.[55] These results are hopeful.

Thriving Families' emphasis on fathers' employment and marital status without truly equal regard for their ability to provide care reflected welfare reform's focus on promoting work and marriage for both mothers and fathers. Though fathers of all class backgrounds have expressed diverse and multifaceted definitions of good fathering that include care, policymakers still tend to assess good or "responsible" fatherhood according to standards of the package deal and conditional commitment rather than the direct nurturance of their children.[56] Programs that encourage fathers to believe that their relationships with their children are dependent on their relationships with their children's mothers will not likely bode well for father–child relationships when moms and dads cannot make commitment work. Attempts to repackage the package deal by promoting marital masculinity—attempts that focus on shaping gendered parental identities and practices—reinforce deficit understandings of fatherhood and the privatization of support for poor families. As another marriage promotion strategy that focuses on an individual-level solution for managing social problems, marital masculinity frames family poverty as a result of faulty gender identity and a weak work ethic.

Thriving Families classes taught fathers that they are real men when they care for their kids, albeit in masculine ways, and that they are important in their children's lives. This was a crucial message. But, ultimately, teaching that marriage is a private safety net held together by fathers' interrelated commitments to work, mothers, and children ignored intimate inequalities and excluded unemployed and poor men from definitions of successful fatherhood.

7   "It's Not Just Us"

Relationship Skills and Poverty's
Perpetual Problems

The most commonly cited relationship statistic I heard during the more than 300 hours of marriage education I observed for this book was credited to John Gottman and his research on communication within stable marriages.[1] Several of the Thriving Families instructors told parents that 69 percent of the issues happily married couples argue about—including those involving kids, in-laws, housework, and money—are never resolved. Gottman called these issues "perpetual problems." He argued that, while perpetual problems do not necessarily have solutions, how couples talk through them profoundly influences how happy they are and whether they stay together. Though it did not misrepresent Gottman's main conclusion, this claim that 69 percent of relationship troubles are perpetual problems was based on a slight misinterpretation of his findings. Gottman wrote in *The Marriage Clinic: A Scientifically-Based Marital Therapy*:

Our research has revealed that an overwhelming majority (69%) of couples experience perpetual problems—issues with no resolutions that the couple has been dealing with for many years. . . . For most perpetual conflicts in marriages, what matters is not the resolution of the conflict, because it will never generally get re-solved, but the *affect* around which the conflict is not resolved.[2]

Many couples stay together and happy despite persistent challenges, Gottman found, not because they resolve the problems that threaten to undermine their relationships, but because they are able to sustain feelings of love and connection as they cooperatively confront their shared challenges. Like many of the instructors for the healthy marriage education curricula I studied, Thriving Families instructors emphasized that how couples communicate about their problems has a bigger impact on relationship satisfaction and family stability than the problems themselves.

Specifically, Thriving Families instructors taught parents that active listening—being attentive to a partner's feelings, resisting defensiveness, and seeking the underlying meaning of spoken words—is the hallmark of being a good communicator who can better manage perpetual relationship problems. Katherine and Karl often taught about the importance of using active listening to cope with perpetual problems by acting out the "toilet seat dilemma." Katherine pretended to confront Karl about hurting herself because she fell into the toilet in the middle of the night after he used it and did not put the seat down. Katherine first modeled being a "defensive" communicator by yelling at Karl, accusing him of being deliberately careless, and rolling her eyes at him. Demonstrating a more empathic active listening style of communication, Karl sweetly acknowledged Katherine's frustration, apologized for Katherine getting hurt because of his inconsideration, and gently told her that he would be more mindful of putting down the toilet seat in the future.

As I watched Katherine and Karl's demonstration, it reminded me of the first Thriving Families lesson on active listening I observed in another class taught by Joseph, a Latino in his thirties. Addressing the four couples in the small classroom, he said: "Let's talk about your last argument and how you might have applied the active listening techniques we've just discussed to prevent those fights." One of the fathers, Cody, there with his girlfriend Mindy, reluctantly offered to share with the group. Both eighteen years old and white, Cody and Mindy were living together, raising their eight-month-old daughter, and struggling to make ends meet on the money Cody earned from intermittent construction work. They had recently had an argument over how to spend the last

$5 they had between them before Cody's next payday. Mindy needed the money to buy formula for the baby, while Cody needed the money for bus fare to get to work. Cody explained:

> Mindy never tells me things straight! Why can't women just say what they mean? . . . It was just last week. We were having a fight about completely running out of money by Wednesday. Then, when it was time for me to take the bus to work on Thursday, I didn't even have enough money for bus fare. Why was she going on and on about this day, that day? Why didn't she just tell me that we were broke? I would have understood that.

To Cody, what instigated this argument was neither that they were about to run out of money nor that they were facing a difficult choice between food for their daughter or getting Cody to work. Rather, from his perspective, the real problem was Mindy's inability to communicate clearly. As Mindy stared at the wall, visibly annoyed at Cody for blaming her for running out of money, Joseph thanked Cody for sharing and concluded, "There you go, that's a good example of why it's so important to communicate clearly and lovingly with your partner and be an active listener."

The Thriving Families curriculum and instructors acknowledged couples' economic constraints. Nevertheless, they proposed generic behavioral strategies, such as active listening and budgeting, to manage what was for most Thriving Families couples their most significant perpetual problem: poverty. Instructors taught that learning to be skilled communicators was important whether a couple was a fighting about the toilet seat or how they should spend their last few dollars. This was one of the main misconceptions of healthy marriage policy and programs like Thriving Families that it funded: They narrowly focused on the idea that it matters less what couples fight about than how they fight. Neither the curricula nor instructors meaningfully acknowledged how poverty is a unique perpetual problem that constrains couples' abilities to develop and practice the skills taught in healthy marriage programs. Consequently, the most valuable lesson many of the parents told me they learned in Thriving Families had little to do with active listening or budgeting.

Parents found the program useful because classes offered them a rare opportunity to communicate free of the financial constraints that overwhelmingly characterized their daily lives. It gave them the necessary time and space to focus on their partners. Classes also provided a unique collective forum for discussion about the particular challenges of parenting and partnering in poverty. Ultimately, it allowed them to interpret much of their emotional stress and, in many cases, their unfulfilled hopes for marriage, as the result of trying to sustain romantic relationships amid severe economic disadvantage.

Parenting, Partnering, and the Price of Poverty

The Thriving Families curriculum rarely discussed poverty explicitly. Though many lessons focused on money, few addressed how most of the couples were living well below the poverty line. This is why Rochelle's favorite class exercise was the baby essentials "Price Is Right" game. African American and in her forties, she taught the classes with her husband, John, an African American in his fifties. Rochelle told me that the game allowed her to talk about money and couples' "circumstances" without talking about the scarcity she knew most of the couples were facing. Before class, she went to a discount department store and bought several baby items—tiny pastel nail clippers, baby lotion, diaper rash cream, baby powder, a rattle, and a bodysuit. She arranged all the items in a row on a desk in front of the classroom. One by one, parents guessed the total cost of the items, and the person whose guess was closest to the actual amount got to take everything home as part of a new baby care package. After Rochelle announced the game's winner, she asked the group why they thought the items cost more or less than the actual price. As she had anticipated, most of the parents underestimated the cost. "Having a kid is a lot more expensive than I thought," one of the mothers exclaimed. As part of the follow-up lesson on "What a Child Needs," Rochelle asked the parents to write down an exhaustive list of baby necessities and how they planned to provide for those needs. Pointing to a chart in the curriculum outlining expenses associated with raising a child—food, clothes, housing, child care—she told the parents that it costs the typical family $194,838 to raise one child from birth to eighteen. In other words, she concluded, "Kids are very expensive."

Next, Rochelle walked to the classroom whiteboard and drew a triangle with equidistant horizontal lines across it. As she drew, she described Maslow's classic psychological theory of the hierarchy of human needs.[3]

"Needs can be ranked in order of importance," she noted. If we cannot fulfill our lowest-level needs for food, shelter, physical safety, and financial security, she explained, we will not be able to focus on our higher-level needs for love, belonging, self-actualization, and achievement. Rochelle later told me during our interview that talking about Maslow's hierarchy of needs was her favorite topic because it best captured how parents "have all these different layers they have to take care of that make it difficult to accept the information from class and apply it. . . . You lose a lot of people because of their life circumstances." It was often hard for couples to focus on their relationships and learn new skills, she elaborated, because so much of their mental and physical energy is consumed with just getting by. That is, they must focus on meeting their and their children's lower-level needs.

Economist Sendhil Mullainathan and psychologist Eldar Shafir have similarly argued that living in poverty depletes individuals' psychological resources and emotional energy.[4] Those living in economic poverty are poor in more than one way, they claimed; like a muscle, our cognitive abilities to learn new information and exercise self-control are limited resources. Scarcity of any kind—too little money, time, or human connection—taxes what they called *bandwidth*, or mental capacity. Poverty especially reduces bandwidth. People who are constantly worried about money have less time and mental energy to focus on other important aspects of their lives. Time and energy spent budgeting down to the last penny, being on the constant lookout for jobs, and coping with the emotional toll of deprivation are time and energy spent not doing something else—such as engaging in the complex and steadfast behaviors associated with being an attentive partner and engaged parent. It is easy to look at a stressed, detached parent and assume that they simply lack skills; what we often overlook, Mullainathan and Shafir argued, is that even learning new skills imposes a bandwidth tax. Skills programs can come with hidden costs: "When the person actually focuses on the training or the incentives, what is he *not* focusing on? Is that added class really worth what little quality time he managed to spend reading or with his children?"[5] Might this explain why research on healthy marriage programs for lower-income couples has not found positive results overall?

As I discussed in chapter 1, research has found that middle-class, engaged and married couples seem to benefit more from relationship skills programs than lower-income couples whose finances and commitments are more tenuous. The large government-sponsored evaluations of the Building Strong Families and Supporting Healthy Marriage programs for low-income unmarried and married couples, respectively, found that, overall, classes like Thriving Families did not help couples stay together.[6] This suggests that perhaps couples most overwhelmed by scarcity and meeting basic needs do not have the "bandwidth" to learn and implement the skills taught in healthy marriage programs. Do skills programs further tax low-income couples' bandwidths to the point of being counterproductive?

One evaluation of a skills program found the opposite. In an analysis of the Building Strong Families data, sociologist Paul Amato found that couples who were most disadvantaged in terms of education, unemployment, earnings, and welfare receipt benefited the most from relationship skills training—as long as they stayed together.[7] The most disadvantaged couples were still more likely to break up and less likely to marry. But if they stayed together after fifteen months, couples tended to experience greater increases in relationship quality. What might explain why relationship skills programs potentially have more benefits in terms of relationship quality for couples experiencing greater scarcity?

The hundreds of hours I spent attending Thriving Families classes and talking with parents point to answers to these important questions that are central to understanding the value of skills-focused marriage policies. Couples found the classes useful, but not because they learned how to better manage their money or why they should get married. And it was not because the classes taught couples how to love more skillfully, develop a middle-class marital habitus, or see marriage as a template of middle-class marital masculinity. Neither did the classes persuade couples to adopt the basic logic of healthy marriage policy that marriage—or even committed co-parenting—helps couples achieve greater financial stability and improve their children's life chances. Parents found the classes useful because of the incentives offered by the program and the constructive group format that allowed them to concentrate exclusively on their romantic relationships in ways they rarely did otherwise. Though it provoked discomfort for some, the classes' focus on relationships encouraged parents to positively confront those issues they could more readily ignore amid the busyness, distractions, and economic and emotional strains of daily life.

Meeting in groups with other couples who shared similar socioeconomic and family circumstances enabled parents to understand that many of the challenges they faced were not the result of personal shortcomings or interpersonal conflicts, but the inherent difficulties of trying to keep a family together while poor. Rather than encouraging couples to commit to one another as a route to upward economic mobility, classes helped couples better understand why living in poverty makes commitment more difficult. In Gottman's terminology, the program influenced the emotional affect around which couples coped with their mutual perpetual problems, including poverty.

Because the classes helped parents understand how their seemingly unique relationship challenges were shared by other low-income couples, they learned how those challenges were shaped by scarcity. Though parents could not often recall specific budgeting or communication techniques weeks after leaving the classes, most eloquently articulated without my prompting in the interviews how the classes helped reduce loneliness and blame. By validating one another—and, in many cases, serving as a relationship quality barometer for other couples—parents learned that their relationships challenges were neither unique nor an indication of individual failings or couple incompatibility. According to parents, this was the program's most valuable message about love, family, and inequality. By normalizing and contextualizing their relationship challenges, classes allowed parents to understand how scarcity engenders conflict, resentment, and relational ambiguity. The end result was more empathy between couples and a greater desire to confront their economic and relational challenges together.

Managing Money in Survival Mode

Like most healthy marriage programs, Thriving Families classes included several lessons about how to manage household money more effectively. Instructors often used the acronym OTP—which stood for On The Path—to help parents remember the program's three primary financial strategies: (O)rganize important financial papers, (T)rack how much you spend and earn, and (P)ay your bills in a timely manner and work out a payment plan with creditors if necessary. Instructors distributed plastic shoeboxes and calculators parents were supposed to use to organize receipts, file important financial papers, and keep track of expenses. They also gave parents advice about how they could save money, even on a limited budget. These lessons were important, instructors emphasized, for improving parents' "financial IQs." Families were like businesses that would be stronger, they claimed, if couples were smarter about money.

Rochelle and John once began a class by asking us to take all the change out of our pockets and lay it on the table. Rochelle described how she had a habit of putting all her loose change in a jar each night and encouraged parents to do the same. "It's change you won't even miss, and you'll be surprised how much you can save after a month. You must make saving a daily habit." Another way of doing this, she told us, was to save all our receipts, think carefully about what we did not really need, and find unnecessary expenses we could cut. She used the example of her favorite frivolous expense—a daily $4 cup of coffee—to illustrate how developing this cost-cutting habit could add up quickly and convert into savings. "If I don't buy that one cup of coffee each day on the way to work, how much would I save?" she asked the group. "Five days a week, times four weeks, equals $80 I would save in just one month if I would make coffee at home instead. That's an electric bill." She then asked the parents to write down a list of all the expenses they had during a typical week and circle two they could do without. Rochelle and John also promoted the concept of "paying yourself first." This involved putting a little money away, even as little as $10, from each paycheck in a savings account as a way to, as John explained, "invest in your family and value yourself." Paying yourself first, Rochelle and John stressed above all else, is a way to develop self-respect and show love for your children. John concluded: "This is about investing in your future and your children's future. When it comes to money, what could be more important than that?"

Janice and Carl, another set of married co-instructors, African American and in their fifties, especially liked teaching the lesson on "Needs versus Wants." Janice would begin by listing the following items on the board: college degree, bus pass, car, high school diploma, four-bedroom house, housing, cigarettes, milk, beer, vitamins, fresh fruit, clothing, cellular phone, leather jacket, food, steak, jeans, brand-name jeans, shampoo, soap, toothpaste, toys, and video game equipment. As a class, we went down the list one item at a time and discussed if it was a need or just a want. Everyone in the class agreed that some things were definitely luxuries—a four-bedroom house, a leather jacket, and brand-name jeans—but other items were harder for parents to categorize. "You don't *have* to have fresh fruit and a cell phone to make it," said one mom, "but I know the fruit is better for my kids, and I need a cell phone when I'm trying to get a job if a boss needs to call me." "That's a good point," admitted Janice, "and think about what you could do without if you had other things. For example, you might not really need vitamins if you have a lot of fresh fruit in your diet." One of the fathers added that, though he knew beer and cigarettes were expensive and not absolutely necessary, his nightly beer and pack a day really helped him relax after work. Carl said he empathized and that people need rewards after working hard all day: "You can't deny yourself of all pleasure in life. Pleasure's a need." Paraphrasing from the curriculum, Janice ended the lesson by emphasizing that needs and wants differ for everyone and that some of our wants may come to seem like needs when our family or economic situation changes.

Some parents told me these strategies for how to better manage money were hypothetically useful. Others found them condescending and judgmental. How instructors chose to personalize the material significantly influenced how parents interpreted it. Amber, twenty-four and white, took classes taught by Rochelle and John with her fiancé Saul, Latino and thirty-five. She told me that Rochelle and John's strategies for saving money took for granted that parents had any money to save and that couples were financially struggling because they did not prioritize the right expenses:

> They talked about how they put money away in a savings jar because they have lots of money to do that. I'm sorry, but I live check to check, and I can't afford to put money away like that. I have rent, children, bills, and they're like, "If you have money, you'll find a way to put it away." No we can't! We need our money to save for our bills and our children. . . . Then, the last day of class, [Rochelle] said that job means "just over broke." That's what they were telling us. J.O.B. means "just over broke." . . . So my [fiancé's] job is nothing? How did I feel? I felt like they were putting me down all the time. . . . How can you say that to people? We're in this class. We're not rich people. I just couldn't believe I was sitting in this class, and they were telling me what I don't have and why I'm this way and you're that way.

To Amber, these recommended strategies for saving signaled that instructors had little understanding of just how much the couples in the classes were struggling financially. Some couples' budgets were so tight that even the pocket change at the end of the day was a meaningful amount of money they could not afford to let sit in a jar until the end of the month.

Parents tended to respond differently to Katherine and Karl, who used another approach to teach about financial literacy. They asked parents to collectively create a monthly budget based on an income of $1,500 a month, including typical expenses for a couple with young children, such as housing, food, and transportation. They relied on the parents to suggest the amounts and encouraged them to include a rainy-day fund for unanticipated expenses, like car repairs. But there was always a lot of disagreement among the parents about how much certain things actually cost. Once during the budgeting exercise, one of the mothers said that she could grocery shop for a family of four for the entire month for just $100. "I don't know where you shop," another mother interrupted, "but I've never been to that store!" This lesson, too, revealed that most of the couples lived in very precarious financial situations. Even accounting for government-subsidized housing, food stamps, and free health care through Medicaid, we were never able as a class to get our total monthly expenses under the $1,500 amount for a family of four as Katherine instructed. We got close once with a budget of $1,600, but when Katherine threw in the hypothetical crisis of having our one family car break down and need $500 in repairs, we were in the red again. She stressed that this is why we needed a rainy-day fund, but she never explained how we were supposed to save for that when our monthly budget did not even cover the basic essentials of food, rent, and gas. The exercise seemed even less practical considering that more than half of parents in the classes lived in households that collectively made less than $1,000 per month.

Nevertheless, several parents who took Katherine and Karl's classes told me that even though the budgeting exercise overestimated how much money was coming in, knowing exactly how much they spent was useful. As Abigail, twenty-one and Latina, told me:

> They started teaching me how to manage money, what you want to spend your money on, all the things you don't need, that you should save money for the baby, for your bills. That helped me out a lot. It reminded me that now we got a baby to think about, and it's not about us no more. It's about her, what she needs, what she wants.

However, others described that because their money problems were not the result of bad budgeting or frivolous spending, as the curriculum and instructors seemed to assume, they were useless. Josh, eighteen and white, also took Katherine and Karl's classes and explained: "The stuff on money would have been much more helpful if we had any. If we had money, I could walk into a store, go down the aisles, put everything in the cart I need, and calculate right there." Josh boasted that he had always been good at math and had been doing his mother's taxes since he was eleven. He also offered me money-saving tips during our interview, including a story of how he was able to save his family $200 one month by buying everything they needed in bulk at a warehouse discount store. He also kept track of which foods could stay frozen the longest and prevented overspending by always paying fixed expenses, like rent and utilities, first. The problem with the money management lessons in the classes, he told me, was not that he and his pregnant fiancée, Sarah, seventeen and white, did not know how to stretch their money as far as possible. The problem was that the little money they did have could only be stretched so far.

Susan and José used another tactic that parents especially liked to teach about finances. Instead of talking directly about money, they asked participants to list all their most important values. Family, love, and honesty always topped the list. José then asked parents to brainstorm about how their spending and saving habits aligned with those values. Though parents found Rochelle and John's budgeting tips judgmental, and Katherine and Karl's strategies impractical, Susan and José's approach was useful to parents because it initiated conversations about how and why money was a common source of conflict. Disagreements over money were particularly salient for Thriving Families couples because choosing what to spend money on—and by implication what they would have to do without—usually meant choosing which basic necessity seemed most important in the moment.

The healthy marriage curricula I studied often taught about competing financial values as a matter of choosing between middle-class wants like vacations and new carpeting. Yet, Thriving Families couples tended to fight over more basic needs like gas money for work or baby formula. Couples much preferred discussing how values get expressed through spending over moralistic distinctions between needs and wants and unrealistic budgeting strategies. This helped them understand that, though they frequently fought over money, their disagreements often came down to shared values for family and pleasure. Victor, twenty-four and African American, told me about the money and values exercise: "The best parts to me were the activities that showed you what your differences were and where you're the same." Other parents especially appreciated how this lesson encouraged them to discuss deeply held principles about life and money that they likely would not have talked about otherwise. It also revealed that, like Josh, they were not deficient in budgeting skills but were already skillfully stretching what they did have. Discussing values was a good reminder of this without the insinuation that parents simply needed to learn better ways of managing money. Lewis, a fifty-seven-year-old African American father who took classes with Susan and José, reflected on how this lesson changed his plans for the graduation stipend he and his girlfriend got for completing the program:

> I told her I'm going to do something with my part and she said, "No, you're not. We're going to take the $100 and go get some baby clothes." And I said, "No, I'm going to take $10 and do something for myself." And then after that class about money and values, I was listening to her and I knew she was right when she first said it.

Deborah and Mark also briefly talked about carefully calculating and keeping track of expenses. But they used most of their time allotted for lessons on money to encourage parents to spend time together as a family for free. They urged couples to rethink the common assumption that quality family time has to be about consumption and spending a lot of money. In one class, we brainstormed at length about all the many low- or no-cost activities available in the community, such as going to the zoo or taking a homemade lunch to the park for a picnic. Deborah and Mark asked us to write down as many free family activities we could think of on a piece of paper. We then decorated family boxes—the plastic ones other instructors advised parents to use as receipt organizers—with magazine photos of kids and families. When we were done, we cut up our list of activities, folded the pieces of paper, and took them home with the instruction to pick out one activity to do as a family per week. Mark concluded the lesson with: "The time you spend with family matters most. In the end, time is free and ultimately more valuable anyway."

Chelsea, thirty-two and white, loved this part of the class because she got a year's worth of ideas about "things we can do as a family . . . that are healthy and cheap and just together."

Though some of the lessons on money appealed more to parents than others, ultimately none were helpful for directly improving couples' financial situations. Diane, twenty-nine and Latina, was bringing in $180 a month through unemployment when she took the classes. She perhaps best articulated the problem with the financial literacy lessons when she told me in resignation, "The financial tips might have been helpful, but . . . what was $90 every two weeks going to do? Even the best bargain shopper in the store, even in the cheapest grocery store, couldn't make that work." One simply cannot manage poverty-level income that is already being stretched to its limits month after month.

This is why, most parents told me, the incentives offered by the program were the most important financial benefit they received from attending the classes. Staff recognized that bus fare, gas, and babysitting expenses would be prohibitively expensive for very low-income couples. Therefore, the program provided several incentives—$10 per class for transportation, free child care, and free hot meals—to defray any costs associated with getting and being there. These incentives not only allowed parents to focus exclusively on their relationships during class, they enabled them to be in the class at all.

Even with these inducements, classes were initially small, some with only one couple. Staff were constantly troubled about low attendance and retention because it was common for couples to show up to one or two classes, never to return, or to only attend sporadically throughout the seven-week class series. Program coordinators experimented with several modifications to the program to increase attendance, including offering longer classes on Saturdays for fewer weeks and expanding outreach efforts in the community. Yet nothing substantially increased attendance and retention until the program implemented a graduation stipend, whereby if both partners attended fourteen hours of class time, they received a $100 stipend in cash or gift certificates for local businesses, such as those for grocery or children's stores. Before the graduation stipend, the largest Thriving Families classes had only three or four couples, with many attending only occasionally. Once the program began to offer graduation stipends, instructors, staff, and I often had to rearrange chairs and tables before the beginning of class just to have room for the ten to twenty couples who would show up.

Though the graduation stipend totaled less than $4.00 per person, per hour, this was a lot more than most of the parents—many of whom were unemployed and making nothing at all—were earning through work or collecting in government assistance. Diane emphasized that because she was only bringing in $180 per month and her fiancé, Pedro, thirty-five and Latino, was out of work and making nothing, the money they got for going to the classes doubled their income that month. Not incidentally, Diane learned about the state's TANF welfare program through another mother taking the classes and was receiving cash assistance by the time of our interview. For those couples who were neither employed nor on government assistance, the gas money and graduation stipend were their only income for those weeks.

When instructors asked at the beginning of a new class series why couples decided to attend the classes, many parents candidly responded that they were there, in large part, because of the money. The interviews confirmed this. Only unmarried couples who were pregnant or had infants qualified for the program's incentives per federal funding guidelines. If the program staff found out that a couple was already married, they were still welcome to stay for class, use the child care, and eat with the rest of the group, but they did not receive any money or gift cards. During the two occasions I saw staff discover that a couple was already married, the couples left once they realized they would not get any money for gas or graduation.

Money was also a particularly powerful incentive when one of the partners in a couple was not very engaged. In one case, Maria, a program coordinator, realized that a father who had signed up was sitting in his car in the parking lot for most of the class, but the mother was actively participating and seemed like she really wanted to be there. Maria told the mother that they would not get the stipend if her boyfriend was not physically present for the entire class. The mother went out to the car to get him. The father said nothing and appeared annoyed the entire class, but stayed just for the stipend. As with this couple, money was especially important to the men, while women were more likely to say in interviews that money was a good incentive in addition to the other benefits, especially learning communication skills that they hoped would improve their relationships. Peter, thirty-five and white, told me that he feared a communication class would blame men for relationship problems:

I feel like a lot of times those classes are biased in one way or another. . . . I thought those classes were out to get the men. . . . Just like, "The woman is always right and you're always wrong and you have to check yourself." . . . But after I took the class I realized it wasn't like that, but before then that was a big reason why I was so reluctant.

The money motivated Peter to overcome his reluctance to "get my foot in the door" for the first class. Jennifer, his twenty-four-year-old, white girlfriend, agreed: "The money was a good incentive for me and Lila [a friend who also took the classes with her boyfriend], but we wanted to have the other benefits, you know. [The money] was good to get the guys in there, and the girls were helping pull them in."

That the money was so important for getting couples to come and stay revealed just how much they were struggling financially—and how futile the budgeting lessons really were. I asked parents during interviews how they spent the graduation stipend. Most used it within a day or two of receiving it. Some spent it to take their family out for a nice dinner or to buy baby toys or clothes they otherwise would not have been able to afford. For most though, the $10 transportation stipend they received after each class was the only way they could afford food or diapers for the very next day, while the $100 graduation stipend was necessary to cover that month's electric bill or rent. Thomas, a twenty-one-year-old African American, explained, "We got the $100 probably about two weeks before I got paid. . . . We needed gas in the car and diapers for the baby. We also needed the car smogged. Then we had money left to get something to eat, so we really needed the money at the time."

As Sonia, the program coordinator, told me, most of the couples were simply trying to survive on a day-to-day basis, both relationally and economically:

I call them to confirm they're coming to class. If we have a list of twenty couples who have enrolled in the class, five of those phone numbers are now disconnected because they can no longer pay the bill. Four of the couples have broken up in the last five days, but half of those couples will probably be back together next week in the class, and they love each other. Some people can't come because of the health care situation. There are a lot of sick babies, and people have problems with their pregnancies. . . . We've had people in the classroom who are homeless. They're just going from place to place, and one of the reasons they come to our class is because it's safe. It's a good place for their kids to play because there's nothing dangerous going on, and they're able to get a warm meal. . . . It's just a lot of people in survival mode.

Some parents showed up because, for two or more hours, they and their children were off the streets and could depend on a hot meal or two if there were leftovers, which the instructors and staff always encouraged them to take. Their kids got to eat and, for at least a little while, could play or watch videos in the company of other children in a heated room if it was cold outside or in air-conditioning if it was hot. I observed on several occasions parents using the bathrooms to clean kids, brush their teeth, and wash clothes. Thus, for many of the couples, classes offered something much more immediately important for their families' futures than budgeting or communication skills—help to make it to the next day.

The Healthy Marriage Initiative mission statement and other promotional materials officially stated that participation in healthy marriage programs was voluntary. However, for many couples, because the program paid them to attend, their dire economic circumstances induced them to participate. For some couples, attending the classes also fulfilled a Child Protective Services court-mandated requirement to keep custody of their children. Tim and Louisa, both Latino and in their early twenties, were at one of the first classes I attended. Their demeanor signaled they were not happy to be there. He did not speak once. She was constantly disruptive, reluctant to answer instructors' questions, and frequently rolled her eyes.

Later, during a focus group, I discovered they were there because, as Louisa bluntly told me, "I want to keep my son." Tim was incarcerated during much of Louisa's pregnancy, and she had recently been arrested for assault. The judge told her that she had to take an anger management class, or the court was going to place their son with a foster family. Because the program included lessons on conflict resolution, the court approved Thriving Families to fulfill Louisa's course requirement. She told me that most of the activities were "stupid and gay," but she stayed because "anger management classes cost $100 an hour, and at least here they give you money and food and take care of your kids." Plus, she said, in one of the activities on being honest and affectionate with your partner, Tim told her he loved her. Holding back tears, Louisa confessed: "I can't remember the last time he said that. It really meant a lot to me." She likely would not have heard that in a $100-per-hour anger management session.

Most parents, however, were not in class to fulfill a court order. They learned about Thriving Families through their obstetricians or the Women, Infants, and Children (WIC) government nutrition program. Staff and instructors knew that many couples were primarily there for the money, but they were confident that once the money got them to the classes, the information they received would keep them there. Instructors even acknowledged this at the beginning of a new series of classes. José once asked a new group why they came. Two of the fathers quickly responded in unison, "For the money!" José replied, "The money is good, but hopefully we'll learn something here, too." My interviews revealed they did.

Communicating the Challenges of Partnering and Parenting in Poverty

Once there, parents appreciated how the incentives enabled them to focus on talking with their partners and other couples experiencing similar challenges with money, relationships, and kids. With few exceptions, parents were more interested in learning communication skills than financial management strategies. This preference was not in spite of their financial constraints, but because of them. Long accustomed to stretching the meager resources they did have through skillful budgeting, minimizing their lifestyles, and simply doing without, most parents did not believe that significantly improving their financial situation was amenable to techniques they could learn in a class. This contrasted with how they viewed communication. Most parents told me they could learn a lot about how to be better communicators.

Unlike the lessons on managing money, parents rarely found the communication techniques patronizing or impractical. Some strategies, however, seemed to be more useful than others. One of the communication lessons focused on teaching parents to use "I" and "me" rather than "you" statements. The reasoning behind this strategy was that if one partner spoke from her or his own point of view instead of attacking the other, the couple could talk about the problem with empathy, honesty, and compassion rather than defensiveness, anger, and blame. For example, instead of saying, "He never looks for a job," or "She's always spending money we don't have," couples were supposed to rephrase these statements to give primacy to the feelings underlying them—as in "*I* feel insecure about our financial future because neither of us has a job," or "It worries *me* that we spend more money than we're bringing in." Parents often expressed skepticism in classes and in interviews about how realistic these strategies were, especially in the heat of an argument. How, parents asked instructors, were they really supposed to remember to calmly use their "I" and "me" statements when they were most upset? Would this absolve the other person of wrongdoing related to the conflict? To many parents, this way of communicating seemed nice in theory, but unrealistic in practice. To others, it seemed like a silly semantic tactic that would have no effect on the real meaning of their conversations. When asked by an instructor to convert her claim that "My boyfriend is an asshole sometimes," into an "I" or "me" statement, one mother quipped, "Ok, *I* feel like my boyfriend is an asshole sometimes, and that pisses *me* off."

Couples found other communication strategies more useful. Many thought the lessons on active listening helped them talk more lovingly with both partners and children; they seemed so sensible that several parents referred to them as "common sense." As one father said in class, "This is the way we should all communicate with everyone anyway. It's just a good reminder." In addition to the money, most parents were in the classes to get help with reducing conflict and connecting more with their partners. They generally agreed that the communication skills were effective for these purposes. Learning about open and honest communication was particularly important for couples who were experiencing the transition to first-time parenthood and had not talked about the stress and self-doubt associated with it. Gwen, twenty-four and African American, explained through tears during our interview:

> I'm glad we did it because we actually had time to talk with so many appointments during the end of my pregnancy, . . . and [Isaiah] used the class as an opportunity to talk about his father and about how his childhood had been hard. I was surprised by these things he didn't open up and tell me before.

For experienced parents, the classes encouraged them to refocus on their couple relationships, as their attention had previously been directed toward the kids. Veronica, thirty and African American, told me, "It reverted our focus back to us because for so long it was the kids, and we were learning to balance the kids versus us. So it was him focusing on him, me on me, and then the kids. . . . We've been doing a lot more family time lately." Similarly, Gina, thirty-six and African American, described how:

> The classes helped open our eyes to a lot of things we were taking for granted. We didn't know how to deal with the baby, coming in and still having the same love, you know our respect for each other. . . . I wasn't focused on him no more. I just cared about my baby, and I was pushing him away because of the prior relationships that I had. Because I have older children I was kind of pushing him away from being a father because I was a single mother before he came along.

The classes also taught parents a shared language for how to identify when they or their partners were not communicating effectively or empathically. This led to some parents policing their partners' behavior, such as when Lisa, twenty-four and Latina, described how her boyfriend "repeated everything from class" and would tell her, "Oh, didn't they say not to do that in class." In other cases, without pointedly criticizing their partners, parents acknowledged negative communication dynamics by referring directly or indirectly to specific communication skills they had learned. Isaiah, twenty-four and African American, described fights he had with his girlfriend, Gwen: "If she and I aren't on the same page and the argument starts to escalate, I always tell her to explain exactly what she's trying to say. 'If I don't get it, tell me what I'm missing.' I do that now instead of just shutting down." He could not recall from class the exact term for this technique—active listening—but he remembered that the instructors discussed it and that it helped them communicate better. Other parents, including Gwen, recalled specific concepts and how their partners genuinely tried to use them. Gwen explained:

> When there was any altercation or argument or anything with communication, we had something to refer back to. I am really trying hard to communicate better, and I went to that class, and

[Isaiah] would mention one of the phrases or topics we had talked about, and I thought, "Oh, you were really listening." "Yeah," he'll say, "you know what you're doing right now is not being able to communicate feelings and that's called . . . oh goodness, what's that called . . . defensive listening." He'll refer back to things.

The classes also provided the space and structured time couples needed to focus on one another without distraction. As Victor, twenty-four and African American, noted, "It made time and pushed away other time we didn't need, like for arguments and all that." Even though Lisa found some of the class exercises "silly," she valued how they encouraged couples to simply appreciate one another. "They say 'Tell her you love her,' you know simple things like that. I think it's good when they teach you how to do that because [my boyfriend] never says it. I got teary eyed when he did." Larisa, twenty-one and white, told me: "Before the class, I had never sat down, held his hand, looked him in the face, and told him something personal." Veronica also described how the classes encouraged her and her boyfriend to talk about important issues they did not discuss at home where they were likely to be distracted by their three young children or watching television: "While the pregnancy drew us closer, what drew us even closer was sitting there talking about it because we didn't really talk about it before. We were always in the moment in the classes. I was always in pain, and that helped me open up more to him about it." Many parents commented on how the classes demanded their partners' attention in ways other situations did not. Even for those couples who did have ample time and physical space to communicate frequently, they still appreciated the classes' emphasis on empathy and strong families and how it motivated them to be kinder to one another. As Victor further explained:

> We might have argued all the way until we got to the door, and then we might try to sit away from each other a little bit. But then because I didn't know anyone in there, I couldn't feel the same way. You can't be mad forever, or you don't want to hold a grudge. Going into the class erased all that.

Several parents also used the word *safe* to describe the classes, meaning that they felt secure about opening up and addressing relationship issues without judgment. Peter recounted, "I really felt like it was safe, neutral ground. . . . When I first went in there, I thought I was going to be attacked, but it wasn't like that." Likewise, Chelsea, thirty-two and white, told me that, "You could tell the truth, and I felt like you wouldn't be judged because we're not angels. I believe in going to get help if you need it. They didn't judge us at all, and that made you feel safe."

Couples also described learning how to communicate as co-parents, even when they were no longer together. Though Ramona, thirty and Latina, had broken up with her son's father by the time of our interview, she enthusiastically described how:

> As far as parenting, I did learn a lot, that a lot of your parenting when you have a partner has to do with how good you and your partner get along. You know, it all involves the same circle. If you and your partner practice love and being at peace, and peace within each other, it's like a circle your child falls into. And if you fall into a circle that's negative, your whole relationship also has a big influence on your children. That's what I learned.

Similarly, Malia, twenty-one and African American, had separated from her unborn daughter's father immediately after finishing the classes. Yet, she still felt that she had gained valuable insight about how to create and maintain a cooperative co-parenting relationship despite no longer being together romantically. She said:

> It was good because the class gave us tools to use that are best and healthy for the baby whether we're together or not. It's not about us, it's about her. . . . For them to tell us to treat that person as a business partner if you're not together, that makes a lot of sense. It's strictly business now. Now it's the baby—is she okay—not fighting.

Nevertheless, parents often found it difficult to use their newly learned skills outside the classroom when they did not have the instructors and other couples there to support their efforts. As Chelsea noted during our interview several weeks after she and her partner, Simon, finished the classes, "We don't use them and we forget. That's our fault, not the classes' fault." Like many other parents, Josephine, thirty-three and African American, wanted the classes to be longer because they were too brief and "squeezed too tight. It was easier to communicate in the classes than at home because they asked us to participate. They asked us to say how we felt." At home, she and her boyfriend did not have the motivation or support they felt they needed to keep practicing. Implementing the skills long-term proved to be prohibitively difficult after parents finished the program. Some reasons for this—talking in ways that felt unnatural, not having the group's support, and the tendency over time to forget the techniques—had little to do with finances.

However, other reasons parents gave for not following through with what they had learned pointed to how poverty can undermine the ability to practice relationship skills. Parents found that deliberately making time for and devoting exclusive attention to one another while actively listening was particularly difficult when faced with economic challenges. Constraints such as not having a safe, private space to talk and managing constant financial deprivation and anxiety kept many parents from putting the skills to greater use.

Communication strategies taught in healthy marriage programs, such as active listening, assumed that couples had control over time and space. During another class with Cody and Mindy, Joseph, the instructor, gave the group a homework exercise to do before the next class meeting. He asked the parents to spend fifteen minutes actively listening and talking to one another about their feelings before going to sleep each night. The point, he told us, was to set aside a little time each day just for one's partner to keep the relationship strong. The following week, Joseph asked if everyone had done the homework exercise. Cody answered that they had wanted to, but because they lived in a small studio apartment with his father, their infant daughter, and occasionally a friend who slept at their place because he was homeless, they did not have the chance to talk intimately. Cody told us that their apartment was smaller than the classroom, which meant it could not have been larger than a few hundred square feet. Unless he and Mindy wanted to go into the closet or the bathroom, they had no privacy. Their neighborhood had too much crime for them to feel safe going outside, especially at night. Finally, Cody explained, though he really wanted to know more about Mindy's day at home with the baby, he was simply too tired to keep his eyes open after working two full shifts during the day. Joseph empathically nodded that he understood their predicament and responded, "Okay, but just try for those few minutes a day when you can. They really matter." Cody and Mindy promised they would try.

Other couples faced similar constraints. The majority lived with parents, friends, and other couples. Many parents were therefore hard-pressed to find a quiet, private space to talk without interruption by the many other household members living in the same one- or two-bedroom apartments and houses. This was especially true for couples who already had children because the unemployment of one or both partners made it likely that parents were caring for their children, and often others', around the clock. Unless they were school-age, very few Thriving Families children spent a significant amount of time away from home given that day care was unaffordable for most. Because many parents neither owned a car nor could afford to go out together for entertainment as a couple, finding quality alone time was rare. Most were also adjusting to the fatigue and sleep deprivation associated with having a new baby.

I interviewed most of the parents where they lived, so I experienced firsthand how the frequent traffic of children and other family members would make it difficult to find a quiet space to talk uninterrupted and undistracted. Diane and Pedro lived with her uncle in a one-bedroom apartment. I interviewed them in a vacant lot across the street. Understandably, Diane felt unsafe going there after dark when their most intimate conversations were likely to happen. Elise and Matthew lived with her ex-boyfriend and two children in a 500-square-foot apartment. The ex and eldest child slept in the living room adjacent to where Elise and Matthew slept with the baby in the bedroom. Elise did not feel comfortable discussing private issues with Matthew when her ex was only a few feet away behind a thin wall. Sarah and Josh lived with her two parents and three siblings. To speak privately during our interview, we had to sit outside on the lawn when it was 112 degrees. Sweltering heat made it hard to actively listen. Simon and Chelsea's baby had a bad case of colic. I struggled to hear most of their words during our interviews. I held Nevaeh, Jessica and Mitch's three-day-old daughter, throughout our entire interview because Jessica had not been able to put Nevaeh down without the baby crying since her birth. Jessica relished the opportunity to finally eat a postpartum meal with two hands. I interviewed Sabrina and Jared at a friend's house because that was the only space they considered neutral ground. I interviewed Marcy and Thomas separately in my car because they lived in theirs. These were not circumstances conducive to the methodical, relaxed, and heartfelt conservations parents learned to have in class.

The relationship skills taught in healthy marriage programs took a lot for granted about the material conditions of couples' daily lives. Eating at nice restaurants, purchasing gifts of affection, and hiring babysitters cost money. Beyond that, the low-income couples I interviewed struggled to find adequate energy, space, and time to practice using the skills. While time and energy are resources in short supply for parents of all class backgrounds, couples in poverty confront unique obstacles to concentrating on their romantic relationships. Healthy marriage education presumed that couples have enough psychological distance from deprivation to focus on the emotional aspects of their relationships. It was, therefore, ironic that Rochelle focused on Maslow's hierarchy of needs, a theory about how people must first meet their physical and security needs before they can pursue those for love and belonging.

As the parents I observed and interviewed poignantly exemplified, couples can experience deeply satisfying emotional intimacy as they simultaneously worry about how they will feed and house their children. But it was disingenuous for healthy marriage policy to target low-income families by focusing on techniques—such as "I" statements and active listening—that did not meaningfully acknowledge the larger problems in parents' lives. Effective communication is equally important for low-income and more affluent couples. Yet, relationship programs should not obscure that how well couples get along is shaped by both communication styles *and* structural pressures. That is, they should account for how, when it comes to romantic relationships, poverty is a unique perpetual problem.

"In the Same Boat": Learning to Face Shared Challenges Together

One of the most valuable lesson parents learned was that many of their most difficult relationship struggles were common among other families living in poverty. They experienced the classes as a nonjudgmental forum where they could—perhaps for the first time—discuss shared romantic and parenting challenges with other couples going through similar struggles with love and money. This allowed parents to understand that many of their struggles were not theirs alone, nor the result of personal shortcomings, as they had previously believed. Emilio, the staff recruiter, explained, "Many of the parents come for the money, but they start realizing this is different. . . . They share the same issues. You don't talk about all this in your neighborhood. You don't get together with all your friends from the street and talk about what you're going through in your relationship with your kids at a barbeque." That is exactly what parents talked about in class.

In their classic study of groups focusing on the transition to first-time parenthood, psychologists Carolyn Pape Cowan and Philip Cowan found that one of the main benefits of couples groups was how they normalized the stress that inevitably ensued when partners became parents.[8] Watching and listening as other couples struggled with similar issues— more conflict, less sleep, new identities and responsibilities—allowed parents to reinterpret their challenges as part of the normal and shared experience of new parenthood. The same thing happened in Thriving Families classes, but not just about parenting. By sharing and comparing how their financial problems strained their ability to parent, influenced their intimate dynamics, and prevented them from marrying, couples came to understand many of their common conflicts over jobs, money, and marriage as endemic to poverty rather than as the result of individual inadequacies. By having their own experiences reflected back to them in others' relationship stories, couples felt less alone in their struggles with partners, parenting, and especially poverty.

This was more the result of how the classes brought together similarly situated couples and encouraged them to openly discuss their problems than any explicit lessons in the curriculum about how being poor strains romantic relationships. Though created in the wake of welfare reform that promoted individual responsibility in matters of family and work, the social nature of the classes allowed parents to understand how larger social and economic circumstances shaped many of the relationship and financial challenges they faced as low-income parents. What parents found most useful was how the classes taught them not to take stress related to unemployment or work, kids, in-laws, and exes—and especially with never having enough money—out on one another. It was this message, rather than budgeting tips or communication strategies, that most resonated with parents and helped them reduce conflict.

Parents wanted to hear about the relationship challenges of other couples and the techniques others used for resolving these challenges, especially disagreements over kids, money, and trust. As Saul told me, "I wanted to hear how other couples go through their relationships, how they solve their problems. I wanted feedback from other people and to

be able to relate to the stuff they had been through." Many parents simply wanted to be around and talk with other adults. Elsa, a white focus
group participant in her twenties, told the group, "With three kids, we
don't see other adults very often. We've learned a lot about each other in
a healthier way because we're able to point out things we've learned
from others along the way."

The classes engendered mutual understanding and helped reduce
defensiveness between partners because couples quickly learned that
they shared the same relationship and financial difficulties with others.
When I asked parents which relationship challenges they believed were
most common, they said communication first, followed closely by
money. Marcy, twenty-one and white, told me: "We all had the same
problems. We were trying not to mess up the best thing we had going
on. All of us agreed to why we had come to class, the whole communication thing and how it affects the kids. We all want our kids to be like, 'I
love my mom and dad because they can get along.'" Others described
shared financial difficulties. When I asked him what couples seemed to
struggle with the most, David, a twenty-eight-year-old, African American father, emphatically answered:

> Money! Almost everyone in the class had the exact same prob-
> lems . . . money issues. I would say that was about 50 to 75 percent
> of every relationship. If you have no finances, you're struggling.
> You constantly snap at each other. It's always a headache, a frus-
> tration. Probably 75 percent of people's relationship problems are
> money. If their finances were good, they'd be more open and
> happy, but it's not like that. . . . We didn't argue when we didn't
> have to worry about money.

Parents' realization that their most significant and unrelenting relationship struggles were shared with so many other couples created a
sense of empathic mutual understanding that affected how they interacted with their own partners. As I discovered in the trainings for the
healthy marriage curricula, teaching empathy—especially learning to
see things from a partner's perspective—was a central goal of marriage
education. Thriving Families parents tended to learn more about empathy from other couples not because their perspectives and problems were
particular, but precisely because they were not. As parents came to understand their conflicts as common and shaped by shared economic

constraints, they were less likely to blame their partners and see these conflicts as justifiable reasons to break up. They told me that the empathy they gained by going to the classes reduced their tendency to view each other as adversaries in a me-against-you mindset. This led to a more collaborative outlook that supported couples' efforts to cooperatively confront their shared challenges. As David explained about his girlfriend, Mikalea:

> We're not the only ones going through these problems. . . . The classes made her feel better because . . . if we have a problem, [she thinks] she's the only one going through it. She doesn't think that I'm going through it with her or that other people in this world have the same problems or worse. . . . It doesn't matter where you're from, what race, what religion. Every house has it. It's how you stand up to it. Are you going to overcome it, or are you going to let it take you down?

Mikalea, twenty-seven and white, agreed. She found the classes so powerful that she was planning to become an instructor: "I would recommend the class to others because . . . it really helps out. It shares everybody's lives. It shows people they're not on their own."

Hearing about other couples' relationships, especially those that involved severe financial and interpersonal distress, was often inspirational for those who interpreted their struggles as milder in comparison. Jennifer, twenty-six and white, described how she wanted to attend the classes so that she and Peter, her boyfriend, could lessen the resentment each had for the other:

> I thought if we could be in an environment where it's not just him against me, that maybe he would be able to open up more and maybe we could work on it. That really helped. It was good because so many other couples were going through the same things we were, and others were even worse. To be able to see how some people are in the same boat as us, and some are worse off than us, so it's not as bad as it seems.

Reflecting on others' experiences prompted many couples to reevaluate their own relationship quality. Many parents described how they thought of other couples who took the classes as a relationship barometer, a comparison point to gauge the severity of their own challenges. Even if their relationships did not necessarily improve by taking the classes, they felt much better about them after watching other, more distressed couples communicate about their problems, which often seemed worse in comparison. As Gina described, "I'm the kind of person that feels like you're the only person in the world who is going through something, and the classes opened my eyes to that, that I'm lucky with what I'm dealing with. It's not so bad as I always proclaim. I saw couples that argued and separated over silly stuff that could be resolved." Marcy similarly described what she most appreciated about the classes:

> I met a couple that had been together for twelve years, and they had a couple of kids. They had been in [Child Protective Services], but they were finally allowed to keep them, like the newborn they just had. They were telling me their relationship has hit rock bottom to the point where they had to stay on the street with their kids. They were in class trying to keep things together for the family. That was one of the best things about the class. It kind of hurt me, but it was the best thing. I thought, "Okay, your kids got taken away, but you guys are still trying to make things work," which is pretty awesome.

Hearing about other couples' relationship stories, especially those that involved severe deprivation and interpersonal strife, was often an inspiration for those who interpreted their struggles as easier in contrast.

Parents also relied on the group to help them talk about difficult issues without being defensive, or as Jennifer put it, to discuss things "where it's not just him against me." Other couples and instructors, most of whom were willing to share personal details about their arguments and ongoing relationship challenges, provided a third-party perspective that was less emotionally charged. Josephine told me that it was easier for her to communicate in the classes than at home because:

> It's good to know you have someone who has been in the same position, so you're not so scared to talk to your partner about everything. Because you know other people understand where you're coming from. Because sometimes when you're just with your partner, and you're just trying to explain to him, he doesn't know what you're talking about. But if there's another person who's been

there, either a woman or a man, maybe they can explain to him better or allow him to understand a little better. You feel like you're not so crazy because other people are going through this too. I'm not just crazy.

Jamie, a twenty-year-old white mother, similarly explained how she was more receptive when instructors and other parents identified how she needed to change the way she spoke to her son's father: "It helped us to communicate better because I'm selfish and a stubborn person, but if someone else points out my flaws besides him telling me, well, he's selfish and angry, too. If we're angry and yelling at each other, neither of us wants to listen. But when they sat down and explained it to me, I realized when I'm wrong." Like Jamie, most of the parents were more willing to listen, if not agree, with instructors and other parents who had personally experienced similar challenges, but did not have a subjective stake in couples' personal disagreements. To use Jennifer's words, other couples were "in the same boat," but not emotionally invested in the combative "him-against-me" mentality that might persuade them to side with one partner over the other. When conflicts would occasionally erupt in class, there was a gendered tendency for the fathers in the room to immediately side with other men and for women to do the same with other mothers. But, for the most part, parents were neutral when it came to dispensing relationship advice to fellow participants, and they refused to take sides.

Because they empathized with others who were in the same boat relationally and economically, parents responded most favorably to instructors who had overcome family and financial problems. They did not want to hear from social scientific "experts" about relationship trends and child development theories. They wanted to know how real couples fought, worked things out, interacted with their kids, blended families with children from previous relationships, and made ends meet when money was tight. In describing what they liked about Katherine and Karl's teaching style, one couple, Giovana and Mason, both twenty-four and white, talked at length about how important it was for instructors to have empathy for parents based on shared experiences. Giovana told me:

They were good because they could actually relate to how couples were. . . . They would also say that they would always fight, and she said she needed to work on her problems with herself and her issues before they could work on them. You've got to know what your problems are before you can address them together. . . . Even with the people in the classes, it was like you're not the only one going through it. Everyone has the same problems. It's not just that they've already been through it. It's easier to relate to what they're teaching in class as opposed to someone who just reads a book and starts saying, "You need to do this," like it's scripted. It's easier and better when someone has gone through the same thing, learns from it, and then teaches it.

Mason, Giovana's partner, added:

They were people who actually lived through some of the stuff they're talking about in that class. . . . It was helpful to see that you're not the only couple that fights, . . . even the ones that looked like goodie two shoes. It puts your own relationship in perspective, that it's not just your relationship that's messed up or has problems. Everybody goes through it.

Another couple, Jessica, twenty-two, and Mitch, twenty-six, both white, found out about the program through her Child Protective Services (CPS) caseworker. They, too, especially appreciated the real-life perspective of the instructors. Jessica was eight months pregnant when they took the classes. She also had a four-year-old son who no longer lived with her due to a series of arrests for drug use and possession and writing fraudulent checks. The judge overseeing her case ruled that she had to take a parenting class to retain custody of the new baby and to regain custody of her son, who was now living with relatives several hundred miles away. She told me:

Mitch wasn't required to go, but I couldn't go unless he went. I would have had to go to one of those boring parenting classes sponsored by CPS. So our CPS worker said if both of us went to that, it would count. I told him, "Look we get paid." I didn't tell him we have to go, but I did tell him, "If you don't go, I have to go to a really boring class." I've been to one of the really boring lecture type classes where there's an old, bald guy talking to you for six hours who doesn't even have children. He just has a master's degree in raising kids, but no kids. He says, "Do this, and don't do that, and this is proven." Oh my god! If you don't even know what you're doing, then why are you up there talking? [Thriving Families] was different.

From parents' perspectives, the most valuable knowledge instructors had to share was not what they had read about couples counseling or financial literacy, but what they had learned through real-life experiences of emotional heartbreak and financial adversity. Many of the instructors had struggled with both, and parents responded most favorably to those who shared the intimate details of how they had come back from the brink of relationship strife and economic hardship. This encouraged parents to share stories of their struggles as well, creating a sense of empathy and hope that they, too, could stick it out in the long run.

Despite difficulty implementing them outside the classroom, parents still found the communication skills helpful. They found them particularly useful during group discussions, when everyone talked honestly about their shared struggles with relationship issues more common among low-income couples, including unemployment, alcohol and drug use, incarceration, and depression. Parents understood the communication techniques as tools that would allow them to deal with these issues as a unified team, rather than as adversarial individuals. As sociologist Melanie Heath also found in her study of healthy marriage programs, low-income parents found relationship skills more useful when instructors presented them as generally applicable to their lives—as parents, friends, and coworkers—rather than just for marriages they might never have.[9] This positive view of the lessons on communication contrasted with parents' less enthusiastic appraisal of the tips on managing money that implied couples could fix their financial problems simply by changing their spending habits.

Parents had difficulty recalling details about specific lessons weeks after finishing the classes. They also struggled with using the skills outside the classroom. Nevertheless, during our interviews, they easily described why the program meant so much to them. It was not because they learned skills that allowed them to solve their relationship and money problems. It was because they learned just how common those problems were. By revealing how economic forces shape experiences of love and parenting in strikingly similar ways across different families, the classes reduced parents' tendencies to individualize these challenges. They discovered that it was normal for couples struggling with scarcity to have the same persistent conflicts over money, kids, and where their relationship was headed. It was this lesson—that they were not alone in their experiences of parenting and partnering in poverty—that helped the most.

Loving in Poverty

Relationship and budgeting skills assume a certain level of privilege. Poverty inhibited couples' abilities to practice the communication and financial management techniques taught in healthy marriage classes. Parents' experiences with Thriving Families classes did not suggest that living in poverty reduced their mental capacity to learn new skills or that time and energy spent learning these skills depleted "bandwidth." What they did reveal was that people can only manage the money they have, and they can only practice communication skills with adequate energy, time, and space. Given the challenges of balancing work, care, and romance, mustering the wherewithal to consistently be empathic parents and partners can be difficult for couples of any economic background. Low-income parents faced additional daily constraints—such as inadequate housing and the emotional stresses of poverty—that exacerbated these challenges.

As Cody and Mindy's predicament illustrated, it can be very difficult for low-income couples to find just fifteen minutes a day for active listening when their lives are characterized by multiple, overlapping disadvantages. The strains and stresses of poverty—working multiple low-paying jobs or not working at all, being constantly stressed about money, sharing housing with many people or being homeless, and not feeling safe in a crime-ridden neighborhood—were not conducive to practicing the skills taught in healthy marriage programs. Marriage education classes temporarily suspended these constraints. They did not provide the means to escape them. Couples cannot simply learn to love or budget their way out of poverty, regardless of how actively they listen or how well they manage their money.

Parents valued Thriving Families because the classes allowed them to focus on their relationships, thoughtfully consider their long-term marriage prospects, and enact their commitments to their partners and children. Most importantly, shared relationship experiences revealed the economic underpinnings of couples' common conflicts. Parents came to better understand how poverty—rather than ill-fated pairings or inherently flawed partners—shaped these persistent struggles. This allowed them to understand that many of their problems would only get worse if they took their money-related anxieties out on one another and that they likely would not be resolved by breaking up. Parents realized they were in the same boat with similarly disadvantaged couples—and with their partners. By pointing to how stress and conflict in romantic relationships are intimately connected to larger structures of inequality, parents learned to interpret their shared conflicts over money, kids, and commitment as normal perpetual problems among low-income, unmarried families. This realization did not put any more money into their pockets or ensure that they would stay together. It did, however, lessen parents' tendency to individualize their relationship problems, and that made coping with them together a little easier.

8 Conclusion

Family Inequality and the Limits of Skills

My goal in writing this book was to provide an on-the-ground ethnographic analysis of the dominant strategies used in government-supported healthy marriage classes. At the extremes of the political debate over healthy marriage policy are portrayals of marriage as a panacea for families in poverty on one end and a misguided push to the altar for poor couples on the other. Neither captures what was actually taught in healthy marriage classes. The government has funded hundreds of relationship skills programs using numerous curricula taught by thousands of instructors and taken by hundreds of thousands of participants. My findings necessarily reflected only a portion of these experiences. Nevertheless, they clearly revealed that healthy marriage education was neither a poverty panacea nor simply marriage promotion. It was, however, a profoundly political and moral statement about how American families should live—and specifically how they should love.

Healthy marriage education institutionalized a particular understanding of the causes of inequality. At the heart of the controversy over healthy marriage policy—and that over all policy interventions that seek to address poverty—is how much policy should target individual behavior and how much it should focus on changing the social and economic context of that behavior. Research on relationships, marriage, and parenthood suggests that they cannot be disentangled. Teaching couples that learning communication and money management skills will allow them to reap the benefits of marriage and avoid poverty presumes that economic disadvantage results primarily from a combination of ill-informed relationships and irresponsible spending habits. Healthy marriage classes took for granted that couples' relationship and financial problems are behavioral—that is, a result of bad choices and negative interpersonal dynamics. To be sure, individuals' behaviors and choices contribute to family and economic instability. But behaviors and choices do not happen in a social vacuum where all individuals have equal opportunity to make the same choices and face the same consequences for those choices. Privilege often protects more affluent individuals and families from the negative ramifications of bad romantic and financial choices.

Throughout this book, I have summarized and synthesized family research as it relates to the marriage promotion strategies used in healthy marriage programs. This research points to a variety of mechanisms that explain the oft-noted "benefits of marriage," none of which were described fully and accurately in the healthy marriage classroom. I focused on why married people are, on average, less likely to live in poverty, including selection effects, how marriage can shape behavior, and discrimination against the unmarried. Though marriage can be part of the path to middle-class stability for some, marriage does not benefit everyone equally, and marriage would not improve most poor families' day-to-day economic circumstances. "Evidence-based" healthy marriage classes have an obligation to acknowledge the complexity of this research. Otherwise, simplistically teaching couples that marriage always and directly produces emotional and financial benefits is disingenuous and does a disservice to couples and their children.

Over the past two centuries, cultural views of marriage have transitioned from the idea that marriage is a social and economic relationship necessary to serve the larger communal needs of society, to the idea that marriage is an intimate relationship intended to serve the emotional needs of two individuals.[1] Still, marriage continues to be an important institution for pooling assets. Before romantic love became the focus of marriage, this was assumed to be one of its primary purposes.[2] It helped families in poverty get by through increasing kin networks that combined meager resources. For more affluent families, marriage merged fortunes and further increased family wealth. Marriage has, therefore, always been both a way to cope with social inequality and a way to perpetuate it. Then and now, those with less access to resources and opportunities to create normative married families have profited less from this resource-pooling benefit of marriage.

Debates over the causes of the marriage gap between poor and non-poor Americans often focus on whether the growing class divide in marriage is an economic or cultural phenomenon. It is both. Widening economic disparities combined with an ascendant middle-class marriage culture since the 1960s have had serious repercussions for American families. Social and economic privileges—namely, those related to education, employment, income, wealth, and race—have become some of the strongest predictors of who gets married, stays married, and stays happily married. Though companionship and emotional fulfillment are central to modern marriage, economic factors still significantly shape ideas about whether one is ready for marriage. Growing economic inequality has converged with shifting cultural norms of marriageability to create a retreat from marriage among those who cannot easily achieve middle-class markers of success.

Healthy marriage classes attempted to intervene at this juncture by reshaping American marriage culture, but without addressing the economic underpinnings of these changes. On the surface, healthy marriage policy promoted a pro-marriage culture in which two-parent, married families are considered the most valuable family form. Beyond this, healthy marriage classes challenged the dominant norms of middle-class marriage culture by promoting the idea that marriage can be a socio-economic survival mechanism for low-income families and an unqualified engine of upward mobility. Classes focused less explicitly on endorsing marriage as a preferred relationship status and more on teaching couples to develop a specific state of mind about love and marriage and their connection to economic prosperity. Healthy marriage policy has been critiqued as an unnecessary attempt to get parents in poverty to aspire to marriage. Yet, my research did not reveal this as one of the major goals of healthy marriage programs. Instead of assuming that low-income parents neither valued nor aspired to marriage, educators assumed that fear of marriage combined with deficient relational knowledge and skills has caused the retreat from marriage in low-income communities.

What people really needed to learn, many of the programs presumed, was how to follow a prosperous life script—that is, to make their lives unfold along a middle-class life course by finishing school; getting a well-paying job; finding a highly educated spouse; and then, and only then, having children. This was a tall order given that only three in ten Americans earn a four-year college degree, and fewer than one in ten go on to earn the graduate and professional degrees that are increasingly necessary to qualify for secure, well-paying, middle-class jobs.[3] For unmarried, low-income couples who already shared children, educators assumed that developing relationship and financial skills would help parents overcome their fear of marriage; allow couples to save more money; and, especially for men, work and earn more. By teaching them to think of committed co-parenting as a resource that enhances their children's life chances, classes tried to overcome couples' reluctance associated with the economic bar to marriage.

For the low-income couples who took healthy marriage classes, talk of marriage conjured up anxieties about financial risk and insecurity more than fear about not doing marriage well. In a middle-class marriage culture, couples in emotionally and economically tenuous romantic relationships often see marriage as something they simply cannot afford. These curtailed commitments are both a cultural and economic problem. Lower-income couples do not devalue marriage as a relationship status; they value it highly as an economic benchmark they are not financially equipped to realize. Economic disadvantage often undermines couples' abilities to act on their pro-marriage cultural values. As growing social inequality has converged with growing cultural acceptance of diverse family forms, it is likely that more couples will indefinitely delay marriage the more it becomes a cultural and economic marker of middle-class achievement. Relationship skills programs that seek to reinvigorate a marriage-only culture are insufficient to reverse these trends.

Marital stability now depends more on couples' assessments of the emotional qualities of their relationships and less on external constraints like social norms and laws, as was the case during the marriage-only era. Class differences significantly shape whether couples are able to generate and sustain the emotional qualities typically associated with happy marriages. When couples have little education, cannot find work or work in low-status jobs, and make little money, they tend to have more interpersonal problems in their relationships and are less likely to stay together.[4] By focusing on communication and conflict resolution, healthy marriage programs reflected how modern marriage requires ongoing emotional investments. But notably absent from relationship skills education in the programs I studied was a meaningful discussion of how social and economic conditions affect individuals' abilities to make these investments with partners deemed economically worthy of marriage.

The Costs of Skills

There are three main interrelated problems with how relationship skills were taught in the healthy marriage classroom. First, the focus on individual skills obscured the insidious effects of institutionalized inequalities—classism, sexism, racism, and heterosexism—on romantic and economic opportunity. "Skills" were often an ideological cover for normative understandings of intimate life that privilege the two-parent, heterosexually married family. Educators distinguished between "healthy" and "unhealthy" relationship behaviors to emphasize that the goal of marriage education was to only encourage healthy marriage, not just marriage in general. Healthy relationship behaviors included showing empathy, active listening, and avoiding violence and abuse. But they also included moral directives about sex, marriage, and family—such as abstaining from premarital sex and ensuring that children have both mothers and fathers—which educators also promoted as matters of making "smart" research-based romantic choices that lead to prosperity.

Using the language of *strengthening relationships* in lieu of *promoting marriage*, as did those who ran Thriving Families, does not depoliticize the strategies and messages of healthy marriage programs. Even without explicitly encouraging marriage, any government-supported program claiming that a particular family type, relationship dynamic, or parenting practice can significantly mitigate the impacts of economic inequality is making a strong political and moral statement. As historian Alice O'Connor has shown, American welfare policy throughout the twentieth century has reflected the idea that government can address poverty by amassing social scientific knowledge about the presumably distinct personal characteristics, behaviors, and choices of the poor.[5] Healthy marriage policy is another case of how American anti-poverty policies have scrutinized the work and family behaviors of those in poverty, while the larger social institutions that structure inequality—including the labor market and the privatized family—are assumed to be the natural order of things and beyond reproach. The supposedly ill-informed sexual behaviors and romantic choices of the poor are offered as evidentiary proof for why some prosper while others do not. This renders invisible how inequitable access to educational and employment opportunities stratifies the chances of living in poverty.

In a highly unequal country like the United States that has few redistributive policies, a minimal social safety net, and meager public funding for education, resources are mostly mediated privately through the family. Access to opportunity is, therefore, fundamentally shaped by what individual parents can afford to provide for their own children. Healthy marriage policy reinforced this privatized logic of individual parental responsibility by focusing on parents' relationship status without paying adequate attention to the structural causes of family inequality. Children benefit when they have access to the time, care, and economic resources that two (or more) adults can provide; parents' romantic and sexual choices can indeed influence their ability to provide these resources. But a policy premised on the assumption that we need "healthy" families to be a private safety net because we do not have the political will to create a stronger social one will only perpetuate and politically legitimate the intergenerational transmission of poverty from parents to children.

The second major problem with healthy marriage education was how it took for granted middle-class life chances—namely, access to quality education; well-paying jobs; and highly educated, high-earning spouses. It privileged a therapeutic understanding of love, romance, and relationship work more closely associated with a middle-class worldview not consumed by immediate need and deprivation. Sociologist Eva Illouz has argued that by emphasizing self-awareness and communicative expression, therapeutic models of romantic love and emotional competence—such as that promoted in healthy marriage programs—assume access to linguistic, cultural, and economic capital that is typically associated with being college educated and middle class.[6] That is, the kind of romantic love now understood to be the glue of modern marriage necessitates resources that allow couples to focus on the emotional aspects of their relationships. Yet, healthy marriage education presented marriage as an emotional and economic partnership through which communication, conflict resolution, and financial management skills can buffer families, especially those in poverty, against the structural inequalities that reduce relationship satisfaction and stability. These messages did more than disparage those who do not conform to the two-parent, married family type; without regard for social circumstance, they promoted the mistaken idea that relationship and economic success depend on individual ability.

Third, there is no evidence that differences in relationship abilities or skills, however defined, influence social and economic trends that are the focus of family and welfare policies. Marriage, single parenthood, divorce, and poverty rates do not track differences in communication and budgeting skills. Yet, this was a fundamental premise of healthy marriage programs. Though many skills programs have helped couples improve how happy they are with their relationships—including the Thriving Families program highlighted in this book—this has not translated into measurable impacts on family and economic stability. The Healthy Marriage Initiative required that federal grantees use evidence-based curricula in their programs. However, most studies of relationship education programs have only evaluated a narrow set of individual-level outcomes, such as couples' subjective assessments of changes in communication and conflict-resolution abilities. These are important outcomes. Couples and their children benefit when partners get along and have supportive, low-conflict relationships. The problem is the leap of logic that outcomes related to communication translate into population-level changes in rates of family stability and poverty that justify public expenditures for and government endorsement of relationship skills programs.

Family scholars Ted Huston and Heidi Melz argued that there is "no convincing evidence that a lack of skills or a loss of skills is driving the presumed retreat from marriage in America."[7] There is, however, a large and ever-growing literature that I have cited throughout this book detailing how a rising middle-class marriage culture, combined with the increasing difficulty of accomplishing middle-class economic stability, is driving this retreat. Huston and Melz also noted that couples are more likely to work through their differences and cooperatively cope with stressors, including economic ones, if their relationships are characterized by goodwill, admiration, warmth, and mutual respect.[8] Problem-solving skills focused on communication and conflict resolution, they claimed, cannot compensate for deficiencies in these areas. To their credit, all the healthy marriage education programs I studied encouraged goodwill, admiration, and mutual respect based on the well-researched claim that relationships thrive most within a warm emotional climate, not just in the absence of conflict. Nevertheless, healthy marriage classes mostly ignored how emotions within intimate relationships are also shaped by the larger economic climate of marriage.

The most significant way the curricula and classes addressed couples' economic circumstances was by teaching financial literacy focused on budgeting, identifying needless expenses, and negotiating money-related conflict. This presumed that couples, especially low-income couples, lacked the skills and knowledge to effectively manage money. Ironically, the one financial topic that likely would have most helped families in poverty—if they qualify for and how to access government and social services—was rarely and (if at all) only briefly covered in the curricula and classes. At the time of my research, healthy marriage grantees were *required* to teach lessons on "commitment to a healthy marriage," communication, conflict resolution, and the benefits of marriage and *advised* to include lessons on financial literacy and responsibility; topics such as locating safe and stable housing and referrals for mental health services and TANF cash assistance were *optional* content areas, and the latter focused in part on "preparing to discontinue TANF supports."[9] Though some of the curricula did provide brief information about TANF eligibility and other services, not one of the trainers and instructors I observed spent more than a minute discussing these issues with parents or educators in training. Tellingly, most did not talk about it at all.

Though many assumed that federal support for healthy marriage programs would disappear with the end of the George W. Bush administration, President Obama advocated for continued funding with a greater emphasis on fatherhood involvement and employment. As of 2016, Congress and President Obama included $150 million annually for healthy marriage and responsible fatherhood programs in the federal budget. Avoiding welfare reform's explicit emphasis on promoting marriage to prevent poverty, these more recent grantees have been referred to as "relationship strengthening programs" with the goal of "strengthening families to improve the lives of children and parents to promote economic stability."[10] Grantees were required to provide "comprehensive healthy relationship and marriage education services, responsible parenting [education], and job and career advancement activities," including vocational training, financial literacy training, and job-related services, such as résumé workshops.[11] Though there was a greater focus on employment opportunities for parents, communication and money management skills were still central to more recently funded healthy marriage and responsible fatherhood programs.

Despite the government's official move away from the language of "marriage promotion" as a means to "poverty prevention," many of those who have recently received public funding for marriage education programming continue to frame their activities in these terms. The National Association for Relationship and Marriage Education (NARME)—the country's premiere professional association for marriage educators—consistently lobbies Congress to reauthorize funding for healthy marriage programs. When continuation funding was announced in 2010, NARME issued a press release advocating for relationship and marriage education as "cost-effective programs that help families stay together[,] which reduces the poverty that can result from divorce and family breakdown. Taxpayers benefit from lowering the drain on [welfare] funding."[12] The organization has actively lobbied for funding for relationship and marriage education to become a permanent provision of welfare policy as a preventive, low-cost alternative to expensive social services.[13]

Whether relationship education services are low-cost is a matter of debate.[14] The $150 million in annual federal funding for healthy marriage and responsible fatherhood programs is less than 1 percent of federal expenditures on TANF, which have totaled more than $16.5 billion each year since the passage of the 1996 welfare reform law.[15] States have also used a portion of their federal block grants to provide additional funding for state-based relationship and marriage initiatives. The cost for the Building Strong Families program and evaluation ranged from $9,000 to $14,000 per couple and averaged $11,000 per couple.[16] The per-couple cost for Supporting Healthy Marriage was $7,400 to $11,500, with an average of $9,100.[17] According to what a recruiter once told a group of parents, the Thriving Families program cost $4,000 per couple. As of 2011 when I completed my research with Thriving Families, the monthly TANF cash benefit for a single-parent family of three ranged from a low of $170 in Mississippi to a high of $923 in Alaska. In California, where Thriving Families was located, the monthly cash benefit was $638.[18] Fourteen hours of healthy marriage education—including meals, child care, and cash stipends—cost more than six months of cash-assistance benefits the families would have received if they were on TANF. Moreover, not all healthy marriage funding has supported programs for poor and low-income couples that qualify for means-tested benefits. As sociologist Melanie Heath has argued, diverting public funding to relationship education could ultimately widen the class-based marriage gap because much of the money spent on healthy marriage programs has paid for free marriage classes for middle-class couples who could afford other relationship support services.[19]

Given that federal and state governments incur public costs through a wide variety of programs, services, and tax breaks, supporting poor families is not just a matter of spending on either relationship education or cash assistance. Still, public funding for any program is money not spent elsewhere and, therefore, requires political justification. The Administration for Children and Families has claimed that marriage increases the economic self-sufficiency of American families by reducing poverty for women and children and increasing employment and wages for men. However, there is no evidence that healthy marriage programs improve families' economic situations other than to provide small, short-term financial incentives for participation. Though healthy marriage funding may be small compared to the total TANF budget, it emerged as part of a welfare policy overhaul that significantly curtailed public support for families in poverty. More than just a choice about where to allocate limited funding for social welfare programs, it reflected and reinforced political ideology regarding the causes and consequences of poverty. Two decades later, there is still no evidence that more than $1 billion in federal funding for healthy marriage programs has had any measureable positive economic impacts on poor families.

The cost–benefit argument often used to justify continued funding for healthy marriage programs relies on the premise that investments in preventive relationship interventions save taxpayers money by reducing unmarried childbearing, divorce, and absentee fatherhood. Some scholars have even tried to quantify the public costs of these trends as a way to advocate for healthy marriage programs. One example frequently cited by supporters is economist Benjamin Scafidi's analysis that concluded: "Family fragmentation costs U.S. taxpayers at least $112 billion each year, or over $1 trillion per decade" on public expenditures, including welfare programs, the criminal justice system, food stamps, and lower taxes paid by those who grow up in poverty and earn less.[20] Yet, existing research does not support the claim that relationship education directly leads to more stable marriages that in turn help families escape poverty.

What is supported by research is that better job opportunities promote marriage. Unmarried parents are more likely to marry when they are employed and experience increases in income.[21] However, since welfare reform in the 1990s, low-income mothers have been less likely to marry men who make enough to lift their families out of poverty.[22] Work and more generous family benefits, such as public subsidies for child care, have reduced childhood poverty in families headed by single mothers significantly more than marriage has.[23] This suggests that labor market interventions, such as a higher minimum wage and tax credits for working parents, would be more effective than relationship skills for directly preventing poverty and indirectly encouraging marriage. Assistance policies and skills programs are not necessarily an either/or proposition, and defunding the latter would not automatically create more support for the former. But in a tenuous fiscal environment where funding for social services for the poor is already low, any money spent on relationship programs should be supported by evidence that they actually help accomplish policy goals. To date, there is no evidence that healthy marriage funding has contributed to either relationship or economic stability among American families.

Moreover, many policies intended to help low-income families—including the Earned Income Tax Credit and many states' TANF programs—still financially penalize parents, especially working mothers, when they get married. Even spouses' low wages can be enough to reduce benefits or disqualify them from eligibility. Though the Healthy Marriage Initiative included provisions that states could, in conjunction with marriage education, use funds to experiment with policies that reduce marriage penalties, few states have pursued this option. Cynthia, the Thriving Families director, acknowledged this dilemma:

> Let's say if you and I were a couple. You have a job, but it doesn't have any health insurance, and if I marry you we lose [Medicaid], and now we have no health insurance for us or our kid. What am I going to do? Am I going to put our child at risk because we got married? Not hardly. I think that's a wise choice. And until those barriers get eliminated, we can't expect our couples to get married because they're not stupid.

The marriage penalty in means-tested benefits is yet another reason that marriage can be unaffordable and expensive for low-income families.

These various costs have significant implications for how to create a relationship policy that can best support families. Rather than programs that presume differences in relationship and financial skills contribute to inequality, we need a policy that better reflects how inequities in opportunities and resources influence romantic experiences, marital decisions, and family stability.

A Smarter Relationship Policy

Family scholars and policymakers all along the political spectrum agree that antipoverty policy should promote secure, loving families. Individuals' and couples' abilities to make their own well-informed choices about commitment, marriage, and parenting are an important part of that agenda. In many ways, the curricula and classes I studied supported this goal. Because skills training did not carry the same stigma as therapy for couples, the focus on education allayed parents' concerns that seeking counseling meant their relationships were in jeopardy. Couples also learned that their struggles with parenting, communication, and money were shared among similarly disadvantaged couples. This encouraged cooperative problem solving and reduced couples' tendencies to see one another as adversaries.

These were primary goals of many of the marriage education curricula I studied. For example, in the workshop for *Smart Steps for Stepfamilies*, Francesca Adler-Baeder, the curriculum's lead author, told our audience that: "A lot of what you do in working with stepfamily couples is just normalize their experience, . . . to raise awareness of stepfamily dynamics and teach that mutual agreement is the goal, rather than a prescribed level of love between stepparent and stepchild." John Gottman's *Bringing Baby Home* for new parents likewise focused on normalizing the challenges that almost all couples experience after having a baby. And not all federally funded relationship programs have taken a skills-based approach or focused on promoting marriage using the strategies described throughout this book. A notable example is the Supporting Father Involvement program, led by psychologists Philip Cowan and Carolyn Pape Cowan, which has had positive results.[24] Rather than using minimally trained instructors, they used clinically trained leaders to oversee couples groups that helped unmarried couples normalize and address common relationship and parenting challenges.

Most parents I interviewed believed that taking Thriving Families classes improved their relationships. The program did not, however, fundamentally change their views or decisions about marriage. Two parents told me the classes reinforced their prior decisions to marry. Three others decided to break up with their children's other parents after learning about the characteristics of a viable relationship. The classes led these participants to conclude that their own relationship problems were irreparable and that staying together would be detrimental for them and their children. They also learned how to better negotiate the challenges of co-parenting without being together as couples. Most of the healthy marriage educators I observed and interviewed would consider both choices—marrying in warm, supportive relationships and breaking up in high-conflict, deeply troubled relationships—successful outcomes of relationship skills training. An important part of healthy marriage education is learning when getting married would *not* be a smart decision for the adults and kids involved. As Cynthia noted, there are two kinds of success in relationship skills programs: "Couples get married, or they make an informed decision to stay or get out. The goal isn't to save every couple. The goal is to save those marriages that can be saved by learning skills."

While it is important to recognize that not every couple should marry, a smarter relationship policy would reflect that promoting marriage and teaching skills are not actually one and the same. Rather than marriage, most of the healthy marriage programs I studied promoted the dubious message that there are ways of loving, parenting, and budgeting that directly create middle-class opportunities. Effective family policies are those that help create a socioeconomic and political context in which people can act in accordance with their own freely chosen family values. For the parents I interviewed, their values almost always included a desire to get married or have a loving, committed partnership while raising their children. Policy does not need to promote marital aspirations. It needs to promote the social and economic conditions in which people can fulfill them.

Relationship programs can be a valuable social service—especially for low-income couples who have less access to costly counseling—but only if they meaningfully address the socioeconomic context of romantic relationships, rather than simply valorizing marriage as a preferred family form. Parents told me that the classes helped them better understand how many of the barriers to having good relationships are social, not just personal. This suggests that relationship programs could better support disadvantaged families if they taught about how poverty affects relationship quality and commitment decisions. Teaching people about the findings of relationship and marital research is a valid policy goal. But a selective interpretation of that research describing the social and economic benefits of marriage as a unidirectional causal relationship does not realistically support couples in making the best relationship choices for them and their children. It is deceptively simplistic to ignore how selection and discrimination also play a role in shaping the connection between marriage and economic well-being. It is also insufficient to say that people should avoid "unhealthy" relationships; brief caveats about relationships deemed "unhealthy," such as those involving abuse, are not enough.

A broader sociologically informed relationship education program would teach about the benefits *and* costs of marriage and under what specific conditions marriage is beneficial and when it could be harmful. Instead of simply using the challenges more commonly experienced by low-income couples as material for hypothetical case studies, the program would also need to address how economic disadvantage shapes these challenges. It would teach about the history of marriage, the rise of middle-class marriage culture, how the unmarried experience discrimination, and how inequality shapes intimate life. It would also require instruction in how resources and public support play an important role in creating cooperative and satisfying romantic and family relationships. Most importantly, it would not teach that economic inequalities are the result of deficient relationship and budgeting skills. These are all evidence-based findings that reflect a more balanced and fairer interpretation of research on marriage and families.

Teaching couples about the complexity of the correlation between marital and economic status—especially how poverty tends to undermine relationship stability—would likely not discourage them from marrying. If anything, taking a more nuanced approach to teaching about family-formation trends would validate couples' experiences with interpersonal difficulties that are exacerbated by economic distress. This would help them recognize that many of their relationships problems are socially patterned and, therefore, less likely to solved by faulting their partners, breaking up, or moving on to another person with whom they are likely to experience similar challenges.

Programs that focus more on the relationship effects of couples' economic constraints would not solve their relationship problems. Nor would expanding the social safety net by increasing welfare cash assistance and other support programs. Money alone does not make or break a relationship. As parents described to me, numerous and overlapping personal, psychological, financial, and social issues shaped their relationship challenges. Nevertheless, a smarter relationship policy would reflect that couples need a lot more than love—no matter how rational or skilled—to create happy, stable families. Encouraging a love-is-all-you-need mentality, as the Thriving Families program often did, does families in poverty a disservice by individualizing and romanticizing economic disadvantage. Romantic commitment via skills will not allow couples to transcend scarcity. Relationship programs that teach couples to understand their challenges in relation to the external stressors in their lives—rather than relational or personal deficiencies—would help them more. Instead of assuming that parents' communication and spending habits are deficient, relationship programs should also recognize and validate the skills many of those in poverty already possess, such as the abilities to stretch limited resources, navigate social service bureaucracies, and juggle care and work responsibilities.

Ultimately, any policy that proposes to promote family stability must contend with the intimate inequalities that lead to curtailed commitments, especially those related to gender. Programs that link economic prosperity with marriage will likely only reinforce couples' tendencies to make marital decisions based on the middle-class marriage bar and the male breadwinner ethic. Classist gender norms, such as those embedded in marital masculinity, make it harder for couples, especially men, to seem worthy of marriage. It is counterproductive to teach couples to communicate and budget more effectively without also addressing the outdated gender ideologies and growing economic disparities that influence their romantic relationships.[25] The most effective policy approach to proposing prosperity will not be grounded in notions of self-sufficiency, middle-class marriage culture, and paternal provision, which all tend to undermine, rather than promote, stable relationships among low-income couples. It will reflect the fundamental sociological premise that love and commitment thrive most within the context of social and economic opportunity.

Notes

1. Introduction

1. I use pseudonyms for the individuals I studied in nonpublic settings. In the spirit of fair use copyright standards, I name and/or cite my sources when I draw from data obtained in public settings and published materials.

2. Carlson, McLanahan, and England, "Union Formation in Fragile Families."

3. McLanahan and Beck, "Parental Relationships in Fragile Families."

4. The HMI has been alternatively referred to as the "Healthy Families Initiative" and the "Healthy Marriage and Relationships Initiative." This varied terminology reflects controversy over how much policy should focus explicitly on marriage. Though I have chosen to use *healthy marriage policy* to reflect legislators' and administrators' semantic choice, I critically analyze the meaning of both "healthy" and "marriage/relationships" throughout the book when discussing how the policy was implemented.

5. See van Acker, *Governments and Marriage Education Policy*, for a comparative analysis of how marriage education policies have been implemented in the United States, the United Kingdom, and Australia.

6. Hawkins, *The Forever Initiative*; Manning et al., "Healthy Marriage Initiative Spending."

7. Personal Responsibility and Work Opportunity Reconciliation Act of 1996, Public Law 104-193. 104th Congress.

8. The Healthy Marriage Initiative home page is archived at http://archive.acf .hhs.gov/healthymarriage/. Retrieved April 22, 2016.

9. Archive.acf.hhs.gov/healthymarriage/about/mission.html#goals. Retrieved April 22, 2016.

10. See http://www.acf.hhs.gov/programs/ofa/programs/healthy-marriage /about. Retrieved April 22, 2016.

11. "HHS Grants Forecast," United States Department of Health and Human Services. https://extranet.acf.hhs. gov/hhsgrantsforecast/index.cfm?switch=grant. Retrieved February 10, 2015.

12. Cott, *Public Vows.*

13. Abramovitz, *Regulating the Lives of Women*; Cott, *Public Vows*; Hays, *Flat Broke with Children*; Mink, "The Lady and the Tramp"; Skocpol, *Protecting Soldiers and Mothers.*

14. Fineman, *The Neutered Mother.*

15. Hays, *Flat Broke with Children.*

16. Healthy marriage funding could be used for ten activities, including: "1) public advertising campaigns on the value of healthy marriages and the skills needed to increase marital stability and the health of the marriage; 2) education in high schools on the value of healthy marriages, healthy relationship skills, and budgeting; 3) marriage education, marriage skills, and relationship skills programs, that may include parenting skills, financial management, conflict resolution, and job and career advancement, for non-married pregnant women and non-married expectant fathers; 4) pre-marital education and marriage skills training for engaged couples and for couples or individuals interested in marriage; 5) marriage enhancement and marriage skills training programs for married couples; 6) divorce reduction programs that teach healthy relationship skills; 7) marriage mentoring programs which use married couples as role models and mentors in at-risk communities; 8) programs to reduce the disincentives to marriage in means-tested aid programs, if offered in conjunction with any activity described above; 9) research on the benefits of healthy marriages and healthy marriage education; and 10) technical assistance to grantees who are implementing any of the above activities to help them succeed." http://archive.acf.hhs.gov /healthymarriage/about/mission.html#activities. Retrieved April 22, 2016.

17. "Premarital and Marriage Education" Fact Sheet, U.S. Department of Health and Human Services. http://www.healthymarriageinfo.org/resource -detail/index.aspx?rid=3274. Retrieved July 16, 2012.

18. Halford, *Marriage and Relationship Education.*

19. Andrews et al., "A Guide to Low-Cost Curricula and Resources."

20. Avishai, Heath, and Randles, "Marriage Goes to School" and "The Marriage Movement."

21. Dion, "Healthy Marriage Programs."

22. Fletcher, *The New Science of Intimate Relationships.*

23. Regan, *Close Relationships.*

24. Edin and Reed, "Why Don't They Just Get Married?"; Carbone and Cahn, *Marriage Markets.*

25. Gibson-Davis, "Expectations and the Economic Bar to Marriage among Low-Income Couples"; McLanahan and Percheski, "Family Structure and the

Reproduction of Inequality"; Silva, *Coming Up Short*; Watson and McLanahan, "Marriage Meets the Joneses."

26. Edin and Kefalas, *Promises I Can Keep*; Edin, Kefalas, and Reed, "A Peak Inside the Black Box."

27. Edin and Kefalas, *Promises I Can Keep*; Edin and Nelson, *Doing the Best I Can*; Gibson-Davis, "Money, Marriage, and Children"; Gibson-Davis, Edin, and McLanahan, "High Hopes but Even Higher Expectations"; Smock, Manning, and Porter, "Everything's There Except the Money."

28. Conger, Conger, and Martin, "Socioeconomic Status, Family Processes, and Individual Development"; Fry, "New Census Data Show More Americans Are Tying the Knot"; Fry and Cohn, "Women, Men, and the New Economics of Marriage"; Zagorsky, "Marriage and Divorce's Impact on Wealth."

29. Amato, "Strengthening Marriage is an Appropriate Social Policy Goal"; Fagan, Patterson, and Rector, "Marriage and Welfare Reform"; Haskins and Sawhill, *Creating an Opportunity Society*; Horn, "Wedding Bell Blues"; Howell, "Marriage Education"; Hymowitz, *Marriage and Caste in America*; Marquardt et al., "The President's Marriage Agenda for the Forgotten Sixty Percent"; Waite and Gallagher, *The Case for Marriage*.

30. Nock, *Marriage in Men's Lives*; Popenoe, *Families without Fathers*; Waite and Gallagher, *The Case for Marriage*.

31. Cahill, "Welfare Moms and Two Grooms"; Coontz and Folbre, "Briefing Paper: Marriage, Poverty, and Public Policy"; Furstenberg, "Should Government Promote Marriage"; Hardisty, *Pushed to the Altar*; Heath, *One Marriage under God*; Smith, "The Politicization of Marriage in Contemporary American Public Policy"; Solot and Miller, *Let Them Eat Wedding Rings*.

32. Hardie and Lucas, "Economic Factors and Relationship Quality Among Young Couples."

33. Smock, Gupta, and Manning, "The Effect of Marriage and Divorce on Women's Economic Well-Being."

34. Brown, "Marriage and Child Well-Being."

35. Ahituv and Lerman, "How do Marital Status, Work Effort, and Wage Rates Interact?"

36. Cherlin, *The Marriage-Go-Round*.

37. Manning, Fettro, and Lamidi, "Child Well-Being in Same-Sex Parent Families."

38. Autor and Wasserman, *Wayward Sons*; Carlson and McLanahan, "Strengthening Unmarried Families"; Hofferth, "Residential Father Family Type and Child Well-Being."

39. Thomas and Sawhill, "For Richer or for Poorer."

40. Sigle-Rushton and McLanahan, "For Richer or Poorer?"

41. Lichter, Graefe, and Brown, "Is Marriage a Panacea?"

42. Lichter and Graefe, "Men and Marriage Promotion"; Williams, Sassler, and Nicholson, "For Better or For Worse?"

43. Lichter, Graefe, and Brown, "Is Marriage a Panacea?"

44. DeNavas-Walt and Proctor, "Income and Poverty in the United States: 2014."

45. Brown, Manning, and Stykes, "Family Structure and Child Well-Being."

46. Amato, "The Consequences of Divorce for Adults and Children."

47. Acs, "Can We Promote Child Well-Being by Promoting Marriage?"

48. Gerstel and Sarkisian, "Marriage: The Good, the Bad, and the Greedy."

49. DePaulo, *Singled Out*.

50. Musick and Bumpass, "Reexamining the Case for Marriage."

51. Soons and Kalmijn, "Is Marriage More than Cohabitation?"

52. Though Hawkins, Amato, and Kinghorn, "Are Government-Supported Healthy Marriage Initiatives Affecting Family Demographics?" found that states with higher levels of healthy marriage funding had higher rates of marriage and lower rates of single parenthood and childhood poverty, this association disappeared when one extreme outlier, Washington, D.C., was removed from the analysis. See also Manning et al., "Healthy Marriage Initiative Spending and U.S. Marriage & Divorce Rates."

53. Blanchard et al., "Investigating the Effects of Marriage and Relationship Education on Couples' Communication Skills"; Carrol and Doherty, "Evaluating the Effectiveness of Premarital Prevention Programs"; Cowan, Cowan, and Knox, "Marriage and Fatherhood Programs"; Dion, "Healthy Marriage Programs"; Fagan, Paterson, and Rector, "Marriage and Welfare Reform"; Hawkins et al., "Does Marriage and Relationship Education Work?"; Markman and Rhoades, "Relationship Education Research"; Reardon-Anderson et al., "Systematic Review of the Impact of Marriage and Relationship Programs."

54. Cowan, Cowan, and Knox, "Marriage and Fatherhood Programs"; Dion, "Healthy Marriage Programs"; Johnson, "Healthy Marriage Initiatives"; Ooms, "Adapting Healthy Marriage Programs for Disadvantaged and Culturally Diverse Populations."

55. Hawkins and Fackrell, "Does Relationship and Marriage Education for Lower-Income Couples Work?"

56. Kirkland et al., "Effects of Relationship/Marriage Education on Co-Parenting and Children's Social Skills."

57. Einhorn et al., "PREP Inside and Out."

58. Lundquist et al., *A Family-Strengthening Program for Low-Income Families*.

59. Wood et al., "The Long-Term Effects of Building Strong Families."

60. Sparks, "Implementation of 'Within my Reach'."

61. Heath, *One Marriage under God*.

62. Cherlin, "Should the Government Promote Marriage?"

63. Heath, *One Marriage under God*; Heath, "Making Marriage Promotion into Public Policy."

64. Heath, "State of Our Unions."

65. This list was available on the HMI website at http://www.acf.hhs.gov/healthymarriage/pdf/june18_list_ marriageedprograms.PDF. Retrieved January 31, 2008.

66. There was no curriculum listed among the comprehensive list of grantees specifically for Latinos or Native Americans. For Spanish-speaking participants,

educators used a Spanish version of one of the common general relationship skills curricula because most were available in Spanish translations.

67. In many cases, the same developer or company offered numerous curricula for different target audiences. I specify when relevant which curricula I studied.

68. See Hauer et al., "Marriage Education Curriculum Assessment Guide," 7.

69. For example, see Ponzetti, *Evidence-Based Approaches to Relationship and Marriage Education*.

70. Department of Health and Human Services, 2008 Poverty Guidelines. *Federal Register*, Vol. 73, No. 15, January 23, 2008, pp. 3971–3972.

71. Latino participants were underrepresented in my interview sample because many exclusively spoke Spanish and took the Spanish Thriving Families classes. I do not speak Spanish, so I did not observe the Spanish classes or interview any of the parents who took them.

2. Rationalizing Romance

1. Coontz, *Marriage, a History*.

2. Ibid.

3. Davis, *More Perfect Unions*.

4. Coontz, *Marriage, a History*.

5. Cherlin, "The Deinstitutionalization of Marriage."

6. Bellah et al., *Habits of the Heart*, 85, 93.

7. Furstenberg and Cherlin, *Divided Families*.

8. Beck-Gernsheim, "On the Way to a Post-Familial Family."

9. Beck and Beck-Gernsheim, *The Normal Chaos of Love*, 48.

10. Hackstaff, *Marriage in a Culture of Divorce*.

11. Celello, *Making Marriage Work*.

12. Hochschild, "Emotion Work, Feeling Rules, and Social Structure"; Hochschild, *The Second Shift*.

13. Sprecher and Metts, "Romantic Beliefs."

14. Ingraham, *White Weddings*.

15. Swidler, *Talk of Love*.

16. van Acker, "Administering Romance."

17. Illouz, *Consuming the Romantic Utopia*.

18. Apple, *Perfect Motherhood*; Ehrenreich and English, *For Her Own Good*; Gillis, *A World of Their Own Making*.

19. Groves, *The Marriage Crisis*.

20. Bailey, "Scientific Truth . . . and Love."

21. Weber, "Science as a Vocation." See also Schaff, *Fleeing the Iron Cage*.

22. Illouz, *Why Love Hurts*.

23. Van Epp, *How to Avoid Marrying a Jerk (or Jerkette)*.

24. Van Epp, *How to Avoid Falling in Love with a Jerk*, 27.

25. Ibid., 308.

26. Ennis, *The Third Option*, 78.

27. Pearson, Stanley, and Kline, *Within My Reach*, 28.

28. Pearson, *Love U2*, 62.

29. Gordon, *Passage to Intimacy*, 26.

30. Simpson, *Active Relationships*.

31. Markman, Stanley, and Blumberg, *Fighting for Your Marriage*, 6.

32. Van Epp, *How to Avoid Falling in Love with a Jerk*, 10.

33. Mackenzie, *Wait Training*, 19.

34. Ibid.

35. Goleman, *Emotional Intelligence*.

36. Gordon, *PAIRS Professional Training*, 8.

37. Simpson, *Active Relationships*, 104.

38. Ibid., 101.

39. Guerney and Ortwein, *Mastering the Mysteries of Love*, 30–31.

40. Arp and Arp, *10 Great Dates to Energize Your Marriage*, 120.

41. Ibid.

42. Gottman et al., *Bringing Baby Home*, 64.

43. Pearson, *Love U2*, xiii-xiv.

44. Mackenzie, *Wait Training*.

45. Ennis, *The Third Option*, 175.

46. Van Epp, *How to Avoid Falling in Love with a Jerk*, 17, 19.

47. Gottman et al., *Bringing Baby Home*, 56.

48. Simpson, *Active Relationships*, 65.

49. Ibid., 42.

50. Hochschild, *The Commercialization of Intimate Life*, 123.

51. Waite and Gallagher, *The Case for Marriage*.

52. Coontz, *The Way We Never Were*; Stacey, *In the Name of the Family*.

3. Teaching Upward Mobility

1. Karney and Bradbury, "The Longitudinal Course of Marital Quality and Stability."

2. Karney and Bradbury, "Contextual Influences on Marriage."

3. Amato et al., *Alone Together*; Conger, Conger, and Martin, "Socioeconomic Status, Family Processes, and Individual Development"; Cutrona et al., "Neighborhood Context and Financial Strain as Predictors of Marital Interaction"; Dakin and Wampler, "Money Doesn't Buy Happiness, But It Helps"; Duncan, Huston, and Weisner, *Higher Ground*; Martin, "Trends in Marital Dissolution by Women's Education in the United States"; Orbuch et al., "Who Will Divorce"; Rauer et al., "Relationship Risks in Context."

4. Conger and Elder, *Families in Troubled Times*; Rubin, *Worlds of Pain*.

5. Hardie and Lucas, "Economic Factors and Relationship Quality among Young Couples."

6. Cutrona et al., "Neighborhood Context and Financial Strain as Predictors of Marital Interaction."

7. Kitson, *Portrait of Divorce*.

8. Amato and Previti, "People's Reasons for Divorcing."

9. Reed, "Anatomy of a Breakup."

10. England and Fitzgibbons, "Everyday Gender Conflicts in Low-Income Couples."

11. Avellar and Smock, "The Economic Consequences of the Dissolution of Cohabiting Unions"; Dush, "Marital and Cohabitation Dissolution and Parental Depressive Symptoms in Fragile Families."

12. Brock and Lawrence, "A Longitudinal Investigation of Stress Spillover in Marriage."

13. Karney and Bradbury, "Contextual Influences on Marriage."

14. Carlson and Furstenberg, "The Prevalence and Correlates of Multipartnered Fertility among Urban U.S. Parents"; Carlson, McLanahan, and England, "Union Formation in Fragile Families"; Reed, "Anatomy of a Breakup."

15. Edin and Kefalas, *Promises I Can Keep*.

16. Sherman, *Those Who Work, Those Who Don't*.

17. Levine, *Ain't No Trust*.

18. Edin and Nelson, *Doing the Best I Can*; Roy, "You Can't Eat Love."

19. Western, *Punishment and Inequality in America*.

20. Anderson, *Code of the Street*.

21. Alexander, *The New Jim Crow*; Western, *Punishment and Inequality in America*.

22. Frye and Karney, "The Context of Aggressive Behavior in Marriage."

23. Duggan, *The Twilight of Equality*; Rose, *Governing the Soul*; Soss, Fording, and Schram, *Disciplining the Poor*.

24. Lewis, *La Vida*.

25. Wilson, *The Marriage Problem*.

26. Fineman, *The Neutered Mother, the Sexual Family, and Other Twentieth Century Tragedies*; Gilens, *Why Americans Hate Welfare*; Hays, *Flat Broke with Children*; Reese, *Backlash Against Welfare Mothers*.

27. Murray, *Losing Ground*.

28. Mead, *Beyond Entitlement*.

29. Somers and Block, "From Poverty to Perversity."

30. Haskins and Sawhill, *Creating an Opportunity Society*.

31. Ortwein and Guerney, *Love's Cradle Leader's Guide*, 194.

32. Stanley et al., *PREP Leader Manual*, 74.

33. Edin and Kefalas, *Promises I Can Keep*.

34. Ortwein and Guerney, *Love's Cradle Leader's Guide*, 124.

35. For a discussion of the political implications of asset building as an antipoverty strategy, see Schram, *Welfare Discipline*. Also see: Miller-Adams, *Owning Up*; Shapiro and Wolff, *Assets for the Poor*; and Sherraden, *Assets and the Poor*.

36. Hauer et al., "Marriage Education Curriculum Assessment Guide."

37. Zhan, Anderson, and Scott, "Financial Knowledge of the Low-Income Population."

38. Papp, Cummings, and Goeke-Morey, "For Richer, For Poorer"; Stanley, Markman, and Whitton, "Communication, Conflict, and Commitment."

39. Markey, Micheletto, and Becker, *FOCCUS Facilitator Manual*, 57.

40. Arp and Arp, *10 Great Dates to Energize Your Marriage*, 96.

41. Olson, *PREPARE/ENRICH*, 19.

42. Buettner et al., *Marriage Savers Mentor's Guide*, 100.

43. Ibid., 68, 71.

44. Pearson, *Love U2*, 321.

45. Ibid.

46. Kamper, *Connections*, 13.

47. Ibid., 77.

48. Ortwein and Guerney, *Love's Cradle Leader's Guide*, 145.

49. Dixon, *African American Relationships, Marriages, and Families*, 1.

50. Ibid., 6.

51. Pearson, Stanley, and Kline, *Within My Reach*, 27.

52. O'Connor, *Poverty Knowledge*.

53. Sawhill, "The Behavioral Aspects of Poverty."

54. Sawhill, *Generation Unbound*.

55. Barnes, "Debunking Deficiency Theories"; Barnes, "Achievement or Ascription Ideology?"

56. Edin and Kefalas, *Promises I Can Keep*; Hays, *Flat Broke with Children*.

57. Newman, *Chutes and Ladders*; Shipler, *The Working Poor*.

58. Carter, *Keepin' It Real*; Dohan, *The Price of Poverty*; Edin and Kefalas, *Promises I Can Keep*; Edin and Nelson, *Doing the Best I Can*; Hays, *Flat Broke with Children*; Levine, *Ain't No Trust*; Newman, *No Shame in My Game*; Waller, *My Baby's Father*; Young, *The Minds of Marginalized Black Men*.

4. Intimate Inequalities and Curtailed Commitments

1. Some of the material in this chapter originally appeared in Randles, "Marriage Promotion Policy and Family Inequality."

2. Cherlin, "The Deinstitutionalization of Marriage"; Cherlin, *The Marriage-Go-Round*.

3. Burgess and Wallin, *Courtship, Engagement, and Marriage*; Burgess, Locke, and Thomes, *The Family*; Cherlin, "The Deinstitutionalization of Marriage"; Cherlin, *The Marriage-Go-Round*.

4. Cherlin, *Love's Labor Lost*.

5. Coontz, *Marriage, a History*.

6. Cherlin, "American Marriage in the Early Twenty-First Century."

7. McLanahan, Donahue, and Haskins, "Introducing the Issue."

8. Lichter, McLaughlin, and Ribar, "Economic Structuring and the Retreat from Marriage."

9. Cherlin, "The Deinstitutionalization of Marriage."

10. Ibid.

11. Edin and Reed, "Why Don't They Just Get Married?"; Isen and Stevenson, "Women's Education and Family Behavior."

12. McLaughlin and Lichter, "Poverty and the Marital Behavior of Young Women."

13. Carbone and Cahn, *Marriage Markets*.

14. Edin and Reed, "Why Don't They Just Get Married?"

15. England and Edin, *Unmarried Couples with Children*; Gibson-Davis and Rackin, "Marriage or Carriage?"

16. Martin et al., "Births: Final Data for 2010"; McLanahan and Sandefur, *Growing Up with a Single Parent*; U.S. Census Bureau, "Selected Characteristics in the United States: 2008–2012."

17. Carlson, McLanahan, and England, "Union Formation in Fragile Families."

18. Massey, *Categorically Unequal*; McLanahan and Percheski, "Family Structure and the Reproduction of Inequality"; Western, *Punishment and Inequality in America*.

19. See Goode, "Why Men Resist," and Hackstaff, *Marriage in a Culture of Divorce*, for a discussion of this perspective.

20. Collins, "Shifting the Center"; Mintz, *Huck's Raft*.

21. Fry and Cohn, "Women, Men, and the New Economics of Marriage."

22. U.S. Department of Education, *The Condition of Education*.

23. Hegewisch, Williams, and Edwards, "The Gender Wage Gap: 2012."

24. U.S. Bureau of Labor Statistics, "Labor Force Statistics from the Current Population Survey: Earnings."

25. Rosenfeld, "Racial, Educational, and Religious Endogamy in Comparative Historical Perspective."

26. Stone, *Opting Out?*

27. Isen and Stevenson, "Women's Education and Family Behavior."

28. Lichter, Graefe, and Brown, "Is Marriage a Panacea?"

29. Glei, Garfinkel, and McLanahan, "Assortative Mating among Unmarried Parents."

30. Fry and Cohn, "Women, Men, and the New Economics of Marriage."

31. Cherlin, "Between Poor and Prosperous."

32. Isen and Stevenson, "Women's Education and Family Behavior."

33. McLanahan and Percheski, "Family Structure and the Reproduction of Inequality"; Gibson-Davis, "Expectations and the Economic Bar to Marriage among Low-Income Couples."

34. Marsiglio and Roy, *Nurturing Dads*; Sweeney, "Two Decades of Family Change"; Wilson, *The Truly Disadvantaged*; Wilson, *When Work Disappears*.

35. Edin and Kefalas, *Promises I Can Keep*.

36. Watson and McLanahan, "Marriage Meets the Joneses."

37. Gibson-Davis, Edin, and McLanahan, "High Hopes but Even Higher Expectations."

38. Clarkberg, "The Price of Partnering"; Edin and Kefalas, *Promises I Can Keep*; Smock, Manning, and Porter, "Everything's There Except the Money."

39. Smock, Manning, and Porter, "Everything's There Except the Money"; see also Gibson-Davis, "Money, Marriage, and Children."

40. Trail and Karney, "What's (Not) Wrong with Low-Income Marriages."

41. Oppenheimer, "A Theory of Marriage Timing"; also see Dew and Price, "Beyond Employment and Income," for a discussion of how assets shape marital timing independently of income and employment.

42. Wilson, *The Truly Disadvantaged*; Wilson, *When Work Disappears*.

43. Bridges and Boyd, "On the Marriageability of Men."

44. Gould and Paserman, "Waiting for Mr. Right"; Loughran, "The Effect of Rising Male Wage Inequality on Female Age at First Marriage"; Watson and McLanahan, "Marriage Meets the Joneses."

45. McLanahan and Percheski, "Family Structure and the Reproduction of Inequality."

46. Osborne, Manning, and Smock, "Married and Cohabiting Parents' Relationship Stability."

47. Edin and Kefalas, *Promises I Can Keep*.

48. Carlson, McLanahan, and England, "Union Formation in Fragile Families"; Edin and Kefalas, *Promises I Can Keep*; Hill, "Steppin' Out"; Levine, *Ain't No Trust*.

49. Edin and Nelson, *Doing the Best I Can*.

50. Carlson and Furstenberg, "The Prevalence and Correlates of Multipartnered Fertility among Urban U.S. Parents."

51. Monte, "Blended but Not the Bradys."

52. This is the one instance where I do not use a pseudonym. "Jessica" and "Mitch's" daughter was actually named Nevaeh. I chose not to change the baby's name given how indicative it was of the hope and solace she symbolized for her parents. Three of the newborns of couples I interviewed were named Nevaeh.

53. This finding aligns with those of Edin and Kefalas, *Promises I Can Keep*; Edin and Nelson, *Doing the Best I Can*; and Gibson-Davis, "Money, Marriage, and Children."

54. Lewis and Gossett, *Disarming the Past*.

5. The Missing "M Word"

1. The U.S. Court of Appeals for the Ninth Circuit later ruled that Proposition 8 was unconstitutional in 2012, a decision the U.S. Supreme Court remanded in 2013 in *Hollingsworth v. Perry*. See Ball, *Same-Sex Marriage and Children*.

2. Lipsky, *Street-Level Bureaucracy*.

3. Maynard-Moody and Musheno, *Cops, Teachers, Counselors*.

4. Brodkin, "Street-Level Research."

5. Watkins-Hayes, "Race-ing the Bootstrap Climb," 1.

6. Musick and Mare, "Recent Trends in the Inheritance of Poverty and Family Structure."

7. D'Addio, "Intergenerational Transmission of Disadvantage."

8. Bourdieu, *Distinction*; *The Logic of Practice*.

9. Gibson-Davis, "Money, Marriage, and Children."

10. Edin and Kefalas, *Promises I Can Keep*.

11. Anderson, *Streetwise*; "Sex Codes and Family Life among Poor Inner-City Youth."

12. Furstenberg, "Fathering in the Inner City"; Nelson, "Low-Income Fathers"; Sullivan, "Young Fathers and Parenting in Two Inner-City Neighborhoods"; Waller, *My Baby's Father*.

13. Edin and Nelson, *Doing the Best I Can*; Nurse, *Fatherhood Arrested*.

14. Edin, Nelson, and Reed, "Daddy Baby, Momma Maybe."

15. Edin and Nelson, *Doing the Best I Can*.

16. Ibid.

17. Ibid., 17.

18. McLanahan and Beck, "Parental Relationships in Fragile Families."

19. Ibid.

20. Graefe and Lichter, "Marriage Patterns among Unwed Mothers."

21. Cabrera, Fagan, and Farrie, "Explaining the Long Reach of Fathers' Influence on Prenatal Involvement"; Shannon et al., "Who Stays and Who Leaves?"

22. Tach, Mincy, and Edin, "Parenting as a 'Package Deal'"; Hohmann-Marriott, "Coparenting and Father Involvement in Married and Unmarried Co-resident Couples."

23. Roy, Buckmiller, and McDowell, "Together but Not 'Together'."

24. Moore, Kinghorn, and Bandy, "Parental Relationship Quality and Child Outcomes across Subgroups."

25. "Healthy Marriage: Why Love Is Good for You." Mayo Clinic.com Health Library. www.riversideonline.com/health_reference/Senior-Health/MH00108 .cfm. Retrieved June 25, 2014. Because the Mayo report does not cite the studies reviewed for the report, it is unclear if these studies reflect outcomes specifically from low-income samples or if the findings are from longitudinal studies that measure changes in relationship stress or the economic effects of low-income couples getting married.

26. Shirer et al., *Together We Can: Creating a Healthy Future for Our Family*, 225.

27. Maynard-Moody and Musheno, *Cops, Teachers, Counselors*.

28. Moore, Kinghorn, and Bandy, "Parental Relationship Quality and Child Outcomes across Subgroups."

29. Mintz, *Huck's Raft*; Sealander, *The Failed Century of the Child*.

30. Ludwig and Mayer, "Culture and the Intergenerational Transmission of Poverty."

31. Folbre, *Valuing Children*.

6. Men, Money, and Marriageability

1. Barack Obama, "We Need Fathers to Step Up," *Parade*, June 19, 2009. http://parade.condenast.com/104895/presidentbarackobama/barack-obama-we -need-fathers-to-step-up/. Retrieved July 11, 2014.

2. Some of the material in this chapter originally appeared in Randles, "Repackaging the 'Package Deal'."

3. Gottman et al., *Bringing Baby Home*.

4. Coltrane, "Marketing the Marriage 'Solution'."

5. These grants received continuation funding through 2016. See the Office of Family Assistance Responsible Fatherhood page at www.acf.hhs.gov/programs/ofa /programs/healthy-marriage/responsible-fatherhood. Retrieved May 10, 2016.

6. Cott, *Public Vows*; Curran and Abrams, "Making Men into Dads"; Haney and March, "Married Fathers and Caring Daddies."

7. Killewald, "A Reconsideration of the Fatherhood Premium"; Killewald and Gough, "Does Specialization Explain Marriage Penalties and Premiums"; Lincoln, "Gender, Productivity, and the Marital Wage Premium"; Nock, *Marriage in Men's Lives*.

8. Becker, *A Treatise on the Family*.

9. Nock, *Marriage in Men's Lives*.

10. Ashwin and Isupova, " 'Behind Every Great Man . . .'."

11. Glauber, "Race and Gender in Families and at Work"; Hodges and Budig, "Who Gets the Daddy Bonus?"; Killewald, "A Reconsideration of the Fatherhood Premium."

12. Glauber, "Race and Gender in Families and at Work"; Killewald, "A Reconsideration of the Fatherhood Premium."

13. Correll, Bernard, and Paik, "Getting a Job"; Glauber, "Race and Gender in Families and at Work"; Lundberg and Rose, "Parenthood and the Earnings of Married Men and Women."

14. Hodges and Budig, "Who Gets the Daddy Bonus?"

15. Cohen, "Cohabitation and the Declining Marriage Premium for Men."

16. Ahituv and Lerman, "How do Marital Status, Work Effort, and Wage Rates Interact?"; Nock, *Marriage in Men's Lives*.

17. Petersen, Penner, and Høgsnes, "The Male Marital Wage Premium."

18. Cohen, "Cohabitation and the Declining Marriage Premium for Men"; Killewald and Gough, "Does Specialization Explain Marriage Penalties and Premiums"; Lincoln, "Gender, Productivity, and the Marital Wage Premium."

19. Cooke, "Doing Gender in Context."

20. Randles, "Redefining the Marital Power Struggle through Relationship Skills."

21. Marsiglio and Pleck, "Fatherhood and Masculinities."

22. Townsend, *The Package Deal*.

23. Furstenberg and Cherlin, *Divided Families*.

24. Nock, *Marriage in Men's Lives*.

25. Cabrera, Shannon, and Tamis-LeMonda, "Fathers' Influence on Their Children's Cognitive and Emotional Development"; Carlson, "Family Structure, Father Involvement, and Adolescent Behavior Outcomes"; Carlson and Magnuson, "Low-Income Fathers' Influence on Children"; Choi and Pyun, "Nonresident Fathers' Financial Support"; King and Sobolewski, "Nonresident Fathers' Contribution to Adolescent Well-Being"; Lamb, "How Do Fathers Influence Children's

Development?"; McLanahan, Tach, and Schneider, "The Causal Effects of Father Absence"; Menning, "Nonresident Fathering and School Failure."

26. Cowan et al., "Promoting Fathers' Engagement with Children."

27. Blankenhorn, *Fatherless America*; Popenoe, *Life without Father*.

28. Coley and Chase-Lansdale, "Stability and Change in Paternal Involvement among Urban African American Fathers"; King, Harris, and Heard, "Racial and Ethnic Diversity in Nonresident Father Involvement."

29. Carlson et al., "Couples as Partners and Parents over Children's Early Years"; Cowan et al., "Supporting Fathers' Engagement with Their Kids"; Gibson-Davis, "Family Structure Effects on Maternal and Paternal Parenting in Low-Income Families."

30. Adamsons and Pasley, "Parents' Fathering Identity Standards and Later Father Involvement"; Goldberg, "Identity and Involvement among Resident and Nonresident Fathers"; Henley and Pasley, "Conditions Affecting the Association between Father Identity and Father Involvement."

31. Danziger and Ratner, "Labor Market Outcomes and the Transition to Adulthood"; Smeeding, Garfinkel, and Mincy, "Young Disadvantaged Men"; Sum et al., "No Country for Young Men."

32. Harris and Marmer, "Poverty, Paternal Involvement, and Adolescent Well-Being."

33. Magnuson and Gibson-Davis, "Child Support among Low-Income Non-custodial Fathers."

34. Sinkewicz and Garfinkel, "Unwed Fathers' Ability to Pay Child Support."

35. Edin and Nelson, *Doing the Best I Can*; Tach and Edin, "The Relationship Contexts of Young Disadvantaged Men"; Tach, Mincy, and Edin, "Parenting as a 'Package Deal'."

36. Monte, "Blended but Not the Bradys."

37. Marsiglio and Roy, *Nurturing Dads*; Orloff and Monson, "Citizens, Workers, or Fathers"; Smeeding, Garfinkel, and Mincy, "Young Disadvantaged Men."

38. Gring-Pemble, "Legislating a 'Normal, Classic Family'"; Haney and March, "Married Fathers and Caring Daddies."

39. Quoted in Gring-Pemble, "Legislating a 'Normal, Classic Family'," 14.

40. Doherty, Kouneski, and Erickson, "Responsible Fathering."

41. Popenoe, *Life without Father*.

42. Nock, *Marriage in Men's Lives*.

43. Gibson-Davis, "Expectations and the Economic Bar to Marriage among Low-Income Couples"; Gibson-Davis, "Money, Marriage, and Children."

44. Marsiglio and Roy, *Nurturing Dads*.

45. Linnenberg, "#1 Father or Fathering 101?"

46. Shirer et al., *Together We Can: Creating a Healthy Future for Our Family*, 74.

47. Gavanas, *Fatherhood Politics in the United States*.

48. Shirer et al., *Together We Can: Creating a Healthy Future for Our Family*, 74.

49. See Gavanas, *Fatherhood Politics in the United States* and "Domesticating Masculinity and Masculinizing Domesticity" for an analysis of this as a common strategy in the pro-marriage wing of the fatherhood responsibility movement.

50. Biblarz and Stacey, "How Does the Gender of Parents Matter?"; Pleck, "Fatherhood and Masculinity."

51. Biblarz and Stacey, "How Does the Gender of Parents Matter?"

52. Coltrane, *Family Man*; Doucet, *Do Men Mother?*; Hamer, *What It Means to Be Daddy*; Marsiglio and Hutchinson, *Sex, Men, and Babies*; Miller, "It's a Triangle that's Difficult to Square"; Waller, *My Baby's Father*.

53. Sherman, *Those Who Work, Those Who Don't*.

54. Linnenberg, "#1 Father or Fathering 101?"; Waller, *My Baby's Father*.

55. See Cowan et al., "Promoting Fathers' Engagement with Children," for a full discussion of the implementation and effects of the federally funded Supporting Fatherhood Involvement program.

56. Marsiglio and Roy, *Nurturing Dads*.

7. "It's Not Just Us"

1. Some of the material in this chapter originally appeared in Randles, "Partnering and Parenting in Poverty."

2. Gottman, *The Marriage Clinic*, 96.

3. Maslow, "A Theory of Human Motivation."

4. Mullainathan and Shafir, *Scarcity*.

5. Ibid., 174.

6. Wood et al., "The Long-Term Effects of Building Strong Families"; Lundquist et al., *A Family-Strengthening Program for Low-Income Families*.

7. Amato, "Does Social and Economic Disadvantage Moderate the Effects of Relationship Education on Unwed Couples?"

8. Cowan and Cowan, *When Partners Become Parents*.

9. Heath, *One Marriage under God*.

8. Conclusion

1. Coontz, *Marriage, a History*.

2. Ibid.

3. U.S. Department of Education, *The Condition of Education*.

4. Amato et al., *Alone Together*.

5. O'Connor, *Poverty Knowledge*.

6. Illouz, *Consuming the Romantic Utopia*.

7. Huston and Melz, "The Case for (Promoting) Marriage," 255.

8. Ibid.

9. Hauer et al., "Marriage Education Curriculum Assessment Guide," 7–11.

10. "About Healthy Marriage and Responsible Fatherhood," Office of Family Assistance website. www.acf.hhs.gov/programs/ofa/programs/healthy-marriage/about. Retrieved May 18, 2016.

11. Ibid.

12. "Congress Makes Key Vote for Marriage Education," National Association for Relationship and Marriage Education, Press Release. www.narme.org/ =documents/12-2010/NARME-Press%20Release-%20TANF%20Reauth%20 FY2011-Final.doc. Retrieved May 15, 2012.

13. See Howell, *The Case for Relationship Education.*

14. For example, see the exchange between Johnson, "Healthy Marriage Initiatives" and "Optimistic or Quixotic" and Hawkins et al., "A More Optimistic Perspective on Government-Supported Marriage and Relationship Education Programs for Lower Income Couples."

15. Congressional Budget Office, "Temporary Assistance for Needy Families."

16. Wood et al., "The Long-Term Effects of Building Strong Families."

17. Lundquist et al., "A Family-Strengthening Program for Low-Income Families."

18. Finch and Schott, "TANF Benefits Fell Further in 2011 and Are Worth Much Less than in 1996 in Most States."

19. Heath, *One Marriage under God.*

20. Scafidi, *The Taxpayer Costs of Divorce and Unwed Childbearing,* 5.

21. Gibson-Davis, "Money, Marriage, and Children"; Waller and McLanahan, " 'His' and 'Her' Marriage Expectations."

22. Graefe and Lichter, "Marriage Patterns among Unwed Mothers."

23. Lichter and Crowley, "Welfare Reform and Child Poverty"; Lieb and Thistle, "The Changing Impact of Marriage, Motherhood, and Work on Women's Poverty"; Misra, Moller, and Budig, "Work-Family Policies and Poverty for Partnered and Single Women in Europe and North America"; Press, Fagin, and Laughlin, "Taking Pressure Off Families"; Usdansky and Wolf, "When Child Care Breaks Down."

24. Cowan et al., "Promoting Fathers' Engagement with Children."

25. See Randles, "Redefining the Marital Power Struggle through Relationship Skills."

References

Abramovitz, Mimi. 1996. *Regulating the Lives of Women: Social Welfare from Colonial Times to the Present*. Boston: South End Press.

Acs, Gregory. 2007. "Can We Promote Child Well-Being by Promoting Marriage?" *Journal of Marriage and Family* 69(5): 1326–1344.

Adamsons, Kari, and Kay Pasley. 2016. "Parents' Fathering Identity Standards and Later Father Involvement." *Journal of Family Issues* 37(2): 221–244.

Ahituv, Avner, and Robert I. Lerman. 2007. "How do Marital Status, Work Effort, and Wage Rates Interact?" *Demography* 44(3): 623–647.

Alexander, Michelle. 2010. *The New Jim Crow: Mass Incarceration in the Age of Colorblindness*. New York: New Press.

Amato, Paul R. 2004. "The Consequences of Divorce for Adults and Children." *Journal of Marriage and Family* 62(4): 1269–1287.

——. 2007. "Strengthening Marriage is an Appropriate Social Policy Goal." *Journal of Policy Analysis and Management* 26(4): 951–964.

——. 2014. "Does Social and Economic Disadvantage Moderate the Effects of Relationship Education on Unwed Couples? An Analysis of Data from the 15-Month Building Strong Families Evaluation." *Family Relations* 63(3): 343–355.

Amato, Paul, Alan Booth, David Johnson, and Stacy Rogers. 2007. *Alone Together: How Marriage in America Is Changing*. Cambridge, MA: Harvard University Press.

Amato, Paul R., and Denise Previti. 2003. "People's Reasons for Divorcing: Gender, Social Class, the Life Course, and Adjustment." *Journal of Family Issues* 24(5): 602–626.

Anderson, Elijah. 1990. *Streetwise: Race, Class, and Change in an Urban Community.* Chicago: University of Chicago Press.

——. 1993. "Sex Codes and Family Life among Poor Inner-City Youth." Pp. 74–98 in *Young Unwed Fathers: Changing Roles and Emerging Policies,* edited by R. Lerman and T. Ooms. Philadelphia, PA: Temple University Press.

——. 1999. *Code of the Street: Decency, Violence, and the Moral Life of the Inner City.* New York: Norton.

Andrews, Barbara, Bill Coffin, Karen Elliott, Josephine Hauer, Larry McDowell, and Sandy Naatz. 2009. "A Guide to Low-Cost Curricula and Resources: Marriage and Relationship, Fatherhood and Parenting, and Financial Education." Washington, D.C.: United States Department of Health and Human Services. Retrieved January 20, 2014 (http://www. wvdhhr.org/bcf/children _adult/cabuseprev/documents/acfresourceguide.pdf).

Apple, Rima D. 2006. *Perfect Motherhood: Science and Childrearing in America.* New Brunswick, NJ: Rutgers University Press.

Arp, David, and Claudia Arp. 1997. *10 Great Dates to Energize Your Marriage.* Grand Rapids, MI: Zondervan.

Ashwin, Sarah, and Olga Isupova. 2014. "'Behind Every Great Man . . .': The Male Marriage Wage Premium Examined Qualitatively." *Journal of Marriage and Family* 76(1): 37–55.

Autor, David, and Melanie Wasserman. 2013. *Wayward Sons: The Emerging Gender Gap in Labor Markets and Education.* Washington, D.C.: Third Way.

Avellar, Sarah, and Pamela J. Smock. 2005. "The Economic Consequences of the Dissolution of Cohabiting Unions." *Journal of Marriage and Family* 67(2): 315–327.

Avishai, Orit, Melanie Heath, and Jennifer Randles. 2012. "Marriage Goes to School." *Contexts* 11(3): 34–38.

——. 2015. "The Marriage Movement." Pp. 308–320 in *Families as They Really Are,* second edition, edited by B. Risman and V. Rutter. New York: Norton.

Bailey, Beth. 1987. "Scientific Truth . . . and Love: The Marriage Education Movement in the United States." *Journal of Social History* 20(4): 711–732.

Ball, Carlos A. 2014. *Same-Sex Marriage and Children: A Tale of History, Social Science, and Law.* New York: Oxford University Press.

Barnes, Sandra. 2001. "Debunking Deficiency Theories: Evaluating Non-Traditional Attitudes and Behavior among Residents in Poor Urban Neighborhoods." *Journal of Poverty* 5(1): 43–66.

——. 2002. "Achievement or Ascription Ideology? An Analysis of Attitudes about Future Success for Residents in Poor Urban Neighborhoods." *Sociological Focus* 35(2): 207–225.

Beck, Ulrich, and Elisabeth Beck-Gernsheim. 1995. *The Normal Chaos of Love.* Malden, MA: Polity.

Beck-Gernsheim, Elisabeth. 1998. "On the Way to a Post-Familial Family: From a Community of Need to Elective Affinities." *Theory, Culture & Society* 15(3): 53–70.

Becker, Gary S. 1981. *A Treatise on the Family.* Cambridge, MA: Harvard University Press.

Bellah, Robert, Richard Marsden, William M. Sullivan, Ann Swidler, and Steven M. Tipton. 1985. *Habits of the Heart: Individualism and Commitment in America*. Berkeley, CA: University of California Press.

Biblarz, Timothy J., and Judith Stacey. 2010. "How Does the Gender of Parents Matter?" *Journal of Marriage and Family* 72(1): 3–22.

Blanchard, Victoria L., Alan J. Hawkins, Scott A. Baldwin, and Elizabeth B. Fawcett. 2009. "Investigating the Effects of Marriage and Relationship Education on Couples' Communication Skills: A Meta-Analytic Study." *Journal of Family Psychology* 23(2): 203–214.

Blankenhorn, David. 1996. *Fatherless America: Confronting Our Most Urgent Social Problem*. New York: Harper Perennial.

Bourdieu, Pierre. [1979] 1984. *Distinction: A Social Critique of the Judgment of Taste*, translated by Richard Nice. Cambridge, MA: Harvard University Press.

——. 1990. *The Logic of Practice*, translated by Richard Nice. Stanford, CA: Stanford University Press.

Bridges, Tristan, and Melody L. Boyd. 2016. "On the Marriageability of Men." *Sociology Compass* 10(1): 48–64.

Brock, Rebecca L., and Erika Lawrence. 2008. "A Longitudinal Investigation of Stress Spillover in Marriage: Does Spousal Support Adequacy Buffer the Effects?" *Journal of Family Psychology* 22(1): 11–20.

Brodkin, Evelyn A. 2003. "Street-Level Research: Policy at the Front Lines." Pp. 145–163 in *Policy into Action: Implementation Research and Welfare Reform*, edited by M. Clare Lennon and R. Corbett. Washington, D.C.: Urban Institute Press.

Brown, Susan L. 2010. "Marriage and Child Well-Being: Research and Policy Perspectives." *Journal of Marriage and Family* 72(5): 1059–1077.

Brown, Susan L., Wendy D. Manning, and J. Bart Stykes. 2015. "Family Structure and Child Well-Being: Integrating Family Complexity." *Journal of Marriage and Family* 77(1): 177–190.

Buettner, Rudy, Faith Buettner, Mike McManus, and Harriet McManus. 2006. *Marriage Savers Mentor's Guide Using the FOCCUS Premarital Inventory*. Potomac, MD: Marriage Savers, Inc.

Burgess, Ernest, Harvey Locke, and Mary Thomes. 1963. *The Family: From Institution to Companionship*. New York: American Book Company.

Burgess, Ernest, and Paul Wallin. 1954. *Courtship, Engagement, and Marriage*. Philadelphia, PA: J.B. Lippincott.

Cabrera, Natasha, Jay Fagan, and Danielle Farrie. 2008. "Explaining the Long Reach of Fathers' Prenatal Involvement on Later Paternal Engagement with Children." *Journal of Marriage and Family* 70(5): 1094–1107.

Cabrera, Natasha J., Jacqueline D. Shannon, and Catherine Tamis-LeMonda. 2007. "Fathers' Influence on Their Children's Cognitive and Emotional Development: From Toddlers to Pre-K." *Developmental Science* 11(4): 208–213.

Cahill, Sean. 2005. "Welfare Moms and Two Grooms: The Concurrent Promotion and Restriction of Marriage in US Public Policy." *Sexualities* 8(2): 169–187.

Carbone, June, and Naomi Cahn. 2014. *Marriage Markets: How Inequality Is Remaking the American Family*. New York: Oxford University Press.

Carlson, Marcia J. 2006. "Family Structure, Father Involvement, and Adolescent Behavior Outcomes." *Journal of Marriage and Family* 68(1): 137–154.

Carlson, Marcia. J., and Frank F. Furstenberg. 2006. "The Prevalence and Correlates of Multipartnered Fertility among Urban U.S. Parents." *Journal of Marriage and Family* 68(3): 718–732.

Carlson, Marcia J., and Katherine A. Magnuson. 2011. "Low-Income Fathers' Influence on Children." *The ANNALS of the American Academy of Political and Social Science* 635(1): 95–116.

Carlson, Marcia, and Sara McLanahan. 2006. "Strengthening Unmarried Families: Could Enhancing Couple Relationships also Improve Parenting?" *Social Service Review* 80(2): 297–321.

Carlson, Marcia, Sara McLanahan, and Paula England. 2004. "Union Formation in Fragile Families." *Demography* 41(2): 237–261.

Carlson, Marcia J., Natasha V. Pilkauskas, Sara S. McLanahan, and Jeanne Brooks-Gunn. 2011. "Couples as Partners and Parents over Children's Early Years." *Journal of Marriage and Family* 73(2): 317–334.

Carroll, Jason, and William Doherty. 2003. "Evaluating the Effectiveness of Premarital Prevention Programs: A Meta-Analytic Review of Outcome Research." *Family Relations* 52(2): 105–118.

Carter, Prudence. 2005. *Keepin' It Real: School Success Beyond Black and White.* New York: Oxford University Press.

Celello, Kristin. 2009. *Making Marriage Work: A History of Marriage and Divorce in the Twentieth-Century United States.* Chapel Hill, NC: University of North Carolina Press.

Cherlin, Andrew. 2003. "Should the Government Promote Marriage?" *Contexts* 2(4): 22–30.

——. 2004. "The Deinstitutionalization of American Marriage." *Journal of Marriage and Family* 66(4): 848–861.

——. 2005. "American Marriage in the Early Twenty-First Century." *The Future of Children* 15(2): 33–55.

——. 2009. *The Marriage-Go-Round.* New York: Random House.

——. 2011. "Between Poor and Prosperous: Do the Family Patterns of Moderately Educated Americans Deserve a Closer Look?" Pp. 68–84 in *Social Class and Changing Families in an Unequal America*, edited by M. Carlson and P. England. Stanford, CA: Stanford University Press.

——. 2014. *Labor's Love Lost: The Rise and Fall of the Working-Class Family in America.* New York: Russell Sage Foundation.

Choi, Jeong-Kyun, and Ho-Soon Pyun. 2014. "Nonresident Fathers' Financial Support, Informal Instrumental Support, Mothers' Parenting, and Child Development in Single-Mother Families with Low Income." *Journal of Family Issues* 35(4): 526–546.

Clarkberg, Marin. 1999. "The Price of Partnering: The Role of Economic Well-Being in Young Adults' First Union Experiences." *Social Forces* 77(3): 945–968.

Cohen, Philip N. 2002. "Cohabitation and the Declining Marriage Premium for Men." *Work and Occupations* 29(3): 346–363.

Coley, Rebekah Levine, and Lindsay P. Chase-Lansdale. 1999. "Stability and Change in Paternal Involvement among Urban African American Fathers." *Journal of Family Psychology* 21(3): 416–435.

Collins, Patricia Hill. 2008. "Shifting the Center: Race, Class, and Feminist Theorizing about Motherhood." Pp. 173–187 in *American Families: A Multicultural Reader*, edited by S. Coontz. New York: Routledge.

Coltrane, Scott. 1996. *Family Man: Fatherhood, Housework, and Gender Equity.* New York: Oxford University Press.

——. 2001. "Marketing the Marriage 'Solution': Misplaced Simplicity in the Politics of Fatherhood." *Sociological Perspectives* 44(4): 387–418.

Conger, Rand D., Katherine J. Conger, and Monica J. Martin. 2010. "Socioeconomic Status, Family Processes, and Individual Development." *Journal of Marriage and Family* 72(3): 685–704.

Conger, Rand D., and Glen H. Elder Jr. 1994. *Families in Troubled Times: Adapting to Change in Rural America.* Hawthorne, NY: Aldine de Gruyter.

Congressional Budget Office. 2015. "Temporary Assistance for Needy Families: Spending and Policy Options." *Congressional Budget Office Report.* Retrieved December 14, 2015 (https://www.cbo.gov/publication/49887#section0).

Cooke, Lynn Prince. 2006. " 'Doing' Gender in Context: Household Bargaining and Risk of Divorce in Germany and the United States." *American Journal of Sociology* 112(2): 442–472.

Coontz, Stephanie. 1992. *The Way We Never Were: American Families and the Nostalgia Trap.* New York: Basic Books.

——. 2005. *Marriage, a History: From Obedience to Intimacy, or How Love Conquered Marriage.* New York: Viking Press.

Coontz, Stephanie, and Nancy Folbre. 2010. "Briefing Paper: Marriage, Poverty, and Public Policy." Pp. 185–193 in *Families as They Really Are*, edited by B. J. Risman. New York: Norton.

Correll, Shelley, Stephen Bernard, and In Paik. 2007. "Getting a Job: Is There a Motherhood Penalty?" *American Journal of Sociology* 112(5): 1297–1338.

Cott, Nancy. 2002. *Public Vows: A History of Marriage and the Nation.* Cambridge, MA: Harvard University Press.

Cowan, Carolyn Pape, and Philip A. Cowan. 1992. *When Partners Become Parents: The Big Life Change for Couples.* New York: Routledge.

Cowan, Philip A., Carolyn Pape Cowan, and Virginia Knox. 2010. "Marriage and Fatherhood Programs." *The Future of Children* 20(2): 205–230.

Cowan, Philip, Carolyn Pape Cowan, Nancy Cohen, Marsha Klein Pruett, and Kyle Pruett. 2008. "Supporting Fathers' Engagement with Their Kids." Pp. 44–80 in *Raising Children: Emerging Needs, Modern Risks, and Social Responses*, edited by J. Duerr Berrick and N. Gilbert. New York: Oxford University Press.

Cowan, Philip A., Carolyn Pape Cowan, Marsha Kline Pruett, Kyle Pruett, and Jessie J. Wong. 2009. "Promoting Fathers' Engagement with Children: Preventative Interventions for Low-Income Families." *Journal of Marriage and Family* 71(3): 663–679.

Curran, Laura, and Laura S. Abrams. 2000. "Making Men into Dads: Fatherhood, the State, and Welfare Reform." *Gender & Society* 14(5): 662–678.

Cutrona, Carolyn E., Daniel W. Russell, W. Todd Abraham, Kelli A. Gardner, Janet N. Melby, Chalandra Bryant, and Rand D. Conger. 2003. "Neighborhood Context and Financial Strain as Predictors of Marital Interaction and Marital Quality in African American Couples." *Personal Relationships* 10(3): 389–409.

D'Addio, Anna Cristina. 2007. "Intergenerational Transmission of Disadvantage: Mobility or Immobility across Generations? A Review of the Evidence of OECD Countries." OECD Social, Employment and Migration Working Papers, No. 52. Retrieved June 23, 2014 (http://www.oecd.org/social/family/38335410.pdf).

Dakin, John, and Richard Wampler. 2008. "Money Doesn't Buy Happiness, But It Helps: Marital Satisfaction, Psychological Distress, and Demographic Differences between Low- and Middle-Income Clinical Couples." *American Journal of Family Therapy* 36(4): 300–311.

Danziger, Sheldon, and David Ratner. 2010. "Labor Market Outcomes and the Transition to Adulthood." *The Future of Children* 20(1): 133–158.

Davis, Rebecca. 2010. *More Perfect Unions: The American Search for Marital Bliss*. Cambridge, MA: Harvard University Press.

DeNavas-Walt, Carmen, and Bernadette D. Proctor. 2015. "Income and Poverty in the United States: 2014 Current Population Reports." P60-252. U.S. Department of Commerce, Economics and Statistics Administration, United States Census Bureau. Retrieved April 21, 2016 (https://www.census.gov/content/dam/Census/library/publications/2015/demo/p60-252.pdf).

DePaulo, Bella. 2006. *Singled Out: How Singles Are Stereotyped, Stigmatized, and Ignored, and Still Live Happily Ever After*. New York: St. Martin's Press.

Dew, Jeffrey, and Joseph Price. 2011. "Beyond Employment and Income: The Association between Young Adults' Finances and Marital Timing." *Journal of Family and Economic Issues* 32(3): 424–436.

Dion, M. Robin. 2005. "Healthy Marriage Programs: Learning What Works." *The Future of Children* 15(2): 139–156.

Dixon, Patricia. 2007. *African American Relationships, Marriages, and Families: An Introduction*. New York: Routledge.

Dohan, Daniel. 2003. *The Price of Poverty: Money, Work, and Culture in the Mexican American Barrio*. Berkeley, CA: University of California Press.

Doherty, William, Edward F. Kouneski, and Martha Farrell Erickson. 1996. "Responsible Fathering: An Overview and Conceptual Framework." Report prepared for the Administration for Children and Families, U.S. Department of Health & Human Services. Contract HHS-100-93-0012, The Lewin Group. Retrieved July 10, 2014 (http:// fatherhood.hhs.gov/concept.htm).

Doucet, Andrea. 2006. *Do Men Mother?: Fathering, Care, and Domestic Responsibility*. Toronto, Canada: University of Toronto Press.

Duggan, Lisa. 2003. *The Twilight of Equality: Neoliberalism, Cultural Politics, and the Attack on Democracy*. Boston: Beacon Press.

Duncan, Greg J., Aletha C. Huston, and Thomas Weisner. 2007. *Higher Ground: New Hope for the Working Poor and Their Children*. New York: Russell Sage.

Dush, Claire M. Kamp. 2013. "Marital and Cohabitation Dissolution and Parental Depressive Symptoms in Fragile Families." *Journal of Marriage and Family* 75(1): 91–109.

Edin, Kathryn, and Maria Kefalas. 2005. *Promises I Can Keep: Why Poor Women Put Motherhood before Marriage.* Berkeley, CA: University of California Press.

Edin, Kathryn, Maria Kefalas, and Joanna Reed. 2004. "A Peek Inside the Black Box: What Marriage Means to Low-Income Unmarried Parents." *Journal of Marriage and Family* 66(4): 1007–1014.

Edin, Kathryn, and Timothy J. Nelson. 2013. *Doing the Best I Can: Fatherhood in the Inner City.* Berkeley, CA: University of California Press.

Edin, Kathryn, Timothy J. Nelson, and Joanna Miranda Reed. 2011. "Daddy Baby, Momma Maybe: Low-Income Urban Fathers and the 'Package Deal' of Family Life." Pp. 85–107 in *Social Class and Changing Families in an Unequal America,* edited by M. Carlson and P. England. Stanford, CA: Stanford University Press.

Edin, Kathryn, and Joanna Reed. 2005. "Why Don't They Just Get Married? Barriers to Marriage among the Disadvantaged." *The Future of Children* 15(2): 117–137.

Ehrenreich, Barbara, and Deirdre English. 2005. *For Her Own Good: Two Centuries of the Experts' Advice to Women.* New York: Anchor.

Einhorn, Lindsey, Tamara Williams, Scott Stanley, Nicole Wunderlin, Howard Markman, and Joanne Eason. 2008. "PREP Inside and Out: Marriage Education for Inmates." *Family Process* 47(3): 341–356.

England, Paula, and Kathryn Edin (eds.). 2007. *Unmarried Couples with Children.* New York: Russell Sage Foundation.

England, Paula, and Emily Fitzgibbons Shafer. 2007. "Everyday Gender Conflicts in Low-Income Couples." Pp. 55–83 in *Unmarried Couples with Children,* edited by P. England and K. Edin. New York: Russell Sage Foundation.

Ennis, Patricia Crane. 1989. *The Third Option: Instructor's Manual.* Syracuse, NY: The Third Option and the Roman Catholic Diocese of Syracuse.

Fagan, Patrick F., Robert Patterson, and Robert Rector. 2002. "Marriage and Welfare Reform: The Overwhelming Evidence that Marriage Education Works." Washington, D.C.: Heritage Foundation.

Finch, Ife, and Liz Schott. 2011. "TANF Benefits Fell Further in 2011 and Are Worth Much Less than in 1996 in Most States." Washington, D.C.: Center on Budget and Policy Priorities. Retrieved August 1, 2014 (http://www.cbpp.org/cms/index.cfm?fa=view&id=3625).

Fineman, Martha Albertson. 1995. *The Neutered Mother, the Sexual Family, and Other Twentieth Century Tragedies.* New York: Routledge.

Fletcher, Garth. 2002. *The New Science of Intimate Relationships.* Malden, MA: Blackwell.

Folbre, Nancy. 2008. *Valuing Children: Rethinking the Economics of the Family.* Cambridge, MA: Harvard University Press.

Fry, Richard. 2014. "New Census Data Show More Americans Are Tying the Knot, but Mostly It's the College-Educated." Pew Research Center. Retrieved May 22, 2014 (http://www.pewresearch.org/fact-tank/2014/02/06/new

-census-data-show-more- americans-are-tying-the-knot-but-mostly-its-the-college
-educated/).

Fry, Richard, and D'Vera Cohn. 2010. "Women, Men, and the New Economics of Marriage." Pew Research Center. Retrieved June 12, 2014 (http://pewsocial trends.org/files/2010/11/new-economics-of-marriage.pdf).

Frye, Nancy E., and Benjamin R. Karney. 2006. "The Context of Aggressive Behavior in Marriage: A Longitudinal Study of Newlyweds." *Journal of Family Psychology* 20(1): 572–583.

Furstenberg, Frank. 1995. "Fathering in the Inner City: Paternal Participation and Public Policy." Pp. 119–147 in *Fatherhood: Contemporary Theory, Research, and Social Policy*, edited by W. Marsiglio. Thousand Oaks, CA: Sage.

——. 2007. "Should Government Promote Marriage?" *Journal of Policy Analysis and Management* 26(4): 951–964.

Furstenberg, Frank F., and Andrew J. Cherlin. 1991. *Divided Families: What Happens to Children when Parents Part.* Cambridge, MA: Harvard University Press.

Gavanas, Anna. 2004a. *Fatherhood Politics in the United States: Masculinity, Sexuality, Race, and Marriage.* Urbana, IL: Illinois University Press.

——. 2004b. "Domesticating Masculinity and Masculinizing Domesticity in Contemporary U.S. Fatherhood Politics." *Social Politics* 11(2): 247–266.

Gerstel, Naomi, and Natalia Sarkisian. 2006. "Marriage: The Good, the Bad, and the Greedy." *Contexts* 5: 16–21.

Gibson-Davis, Christina. 2007. "Expectations and the Economic Bar to Marriage among Low-Income Couples." Pp. 84–103 in *Unmarried Couples with Children*, edited by P. England and K. Edin. New York: Russell Sage Foundation.

——. 2008. "Family Structure Effects on Maternal and Paternal Parenting in Low-Income Families." *Journal of Marriage and Family* 70(2): 452–465.

——. 2009. "Money, Marriage, and Children: Testing the Financial Expectations and Family Formation Theory." *Journal of Marriage and Family* 71(1): 146–160.

Gibson-Davis, Christina, Kathryn Edin, and Sara McLanahan. 2005. "High Hopes but Even Higher Expectations: The Retreat from Marriage among Low-Income Couples." *Journal of Marriage and Family* 67(5): 1301–1312.

Gibson-Davis, Christina, and Heather Rackin. 2014. "Marriage or Carriage?: Trends in Union Context and Birth Type by Education." *Journal of Marriage and Family* 76(3): 506–519.

Gilens, Martin. 1999. *Why Americans Hate Welfare: Race, Media, and the Politics of Antipoverty Policy.* Chicago: University of Chicago Press.

Gillis, John. 1997. *A World of Their Own Making: Myth, Ritual, and the Quest for Family Values.* Cambridge, MA: Harvard University Press.

Glauber, Rebecca. 2008. "Race and Gender in Families and at Work: The Fatherhood Premium." *Gender & Society* 22(1): 8–30.

Glei, Dana, Irwin Garfinkel, and Sara McLanahan. 2002. "Assortative Mating among Unmarried Parents: Implications for Child Support Enforcement." *Journal of Population Economics* 15(3): 417–432.

Goldberg, Julia S. 2015. "Identity and Involvement among Resident and Nonresident Fathers." *Journal of Family Issues* 36(7): 852–879.

Goleman, Daniel. 1995. *Emotional Intelligence: Why It Can Matter More Than IQ.* New York: Bantam.

Goode, William J. 1992. "Why Men Resist." Pp. 287–310 in *Rethinking the Family: Some Feminist Questions,* edited by B. Thorne and M. Yalom. Boston: Northeastern University Press.

Gordon, Lori H. 1993. *Passage to Intimacy.* Wichita, KS: Fireside.

——. 2004. *PAIRS Professional Training.* Weston, FL: PAIRS Foundation.

Gottman, John. 1999. *The Marriage Clinic: A Scientifically Based Marital Therapy.* New York: Norton.

Gottman, John M., Julie Schwartz Gottman, Carolyn Pirak, and Joni Parthemer. 2007. *Bringing Baby Home: A Program for New Parents Experiencing the Transition to Parenthood, Instructor's Manual.* Seattle, WA: Relationship Research Institute.

Gould, Eric D., and M. Daniele Paserman. 2003. "Waiting for Mr. Right: Rising Inequality and Declining Marriage Rates." *Journal of Urban Economics* 53(2): 257–281.

Graefe, Deborah Roempke, and Daniel T. Lichter. 2008. "Marriage Patterns among Unwed Mothers: Before and After PRWORA." *Journal of Policy Analysis and Management* 27(3): 479–497.

Gring-Pemble, Lisa. 2003. "Legislating a 'Normal, Classic Family': The Rhetorical Construction of Families in American Welfare Policy." *Political Communication* 20(4): 473–498.

Groves, Ernest R. 1928. *The Marriage Crisis.* New York: Longmans, Green, and Co.

Guerney, Bernard G., and Mary Ortwein. 2008. *Mastering the Mysteries of Love: Relationship Enhancement Program for Couples, Leader's Guide.* Frankfort, KY: Relationship Press.

Hackstaff, Karla. 1999. *Marriage in a Culture of Divorce.* Philadelphia: Temple University Press.

Halford, W. Kim. 2011. *Marriage and Relationship Education: What Works and How to Provide It.* New York: Guilford Press.

Hamer, Jennifer. 2001. *What It Means to Be Daddy: Fatherhood for Black Men Living Away from Their Children.* New York: Columbia University Press.

Haney, Lynne, and Miranda March. 2003. "Married Fathers and Caring Daddies: Welfare Reform and the Discursive Politics of Paternity." *Social Problems* 50(4): 461–481.

Hardie, Jessica Halliday, and Amy Lucas. 2010. "Economic Factors and Relationship Quality among Young Couples: Comparing Cohabitation and Marriage." *Journal of Marriage and Family* 72(5): 1141–1154.

Hardisty, Jean. 2008. *Pushed to the Altar: The Right Wing Roots of Marriage Promotion.* Somerville, MA: Political Research Associates/Women of Color Resource Center.

Harris, Kathleen Mullan, and Jeremy K. Marmer. 1996. "Poverty, Paternal Involvement, and Adolescent Well-Being." *Journal of Family Issues* 17(5): 614–640.

Haskins, Ron, and Isabel V. Sawhill. 2009. *Creating an Opportunity Society.* Washington, D.C.: Brookings Institution Press.

Hauer, Josephine, Larry McDowell, Barbara Andrews, Lewissa Swanson, Pam Marr, Bridget Minor, and Bill Coffin. 2008. "Marriage Education Curriculum Assessment Guide." Washington, D.C.: Administration for Children and Families. Retrieved April 25, 2014 (http://www.healthymarriageinfo.org/resource-detail/index.aspx?rid=2046).

Hawkins, Alan J. 2013. *The Forever Initiative: A Feasible Public Policy Agenda to Help Couples Form and Sustain Healthy Marriages and Relationships*. North Charleston, SC: CreateSpace.

Hawkins, Alan J., Paul R. Amato, and Andrea Kinghorn. 2013. "Are Government-Supported Healthy Marriage Initiatives Affecting Family Demographics? A State-Level Analysis." *Family Relations* 62(3): 501–513.

Hawkins, Alan, Victoria Blanchard, Scott Baldwin, and Elizabeth Fawcett. 2008. "Does Marriage and Relationship Education Work? A Meta-Analytic Study." *Journal of Consulting and Clinical Psychology* 76(5): 723–734.

Hawkins, Alan, and Tamara Fackrell. 2010. "Does Relationship and Marriage Education for Lower-Income Couples Work? A Meta-Analytic Study of Emerging Research." *Journal of Couple & Relationship Therapy* 9(2): 181–191.

Hawkins, Alan J., Scott M. Stanley, Philip A. Cowan, Frank D. Fincham, Steven R. H. Beach, Carolyn Pape Cowan, Galena Kline Rhoades, Howard J. Markman, and Andrew P. Daire. 2013. "A More Optimistic Perspective on Government-Supported Marriage and Relationship Education Programs for Lower Income Couples." *American Psychologist* 68(2): 110–111.

Hays, Sharon. 2003. *Flat Broke with Children: Women in the Age of Welfare Reform*. New York: Oxford University Press.

Heath, Melanie. 2009. "State of Our Unions: Marriage Promotion and the Contested Power of Heterosexuality." *Gender & Society* 23(1): 27–48.

———. 2012a. *One Marriage under God: The Campaign to Promote Marriage in America*. New York: New York University Press.

———. 2012b. "Making Marriage Promotion into Public Policy: The Epistemtic Culture of a Statewide Initiative." *Qualitative Sociology* 35(4): 385–406.

Hegewisch, Ariane, Claudia Williams, and Angela Edwards. 2013. "The Gender Wage Gap: 2012." Institute for Women's Policy Research Fact Sheet, #C350. Retrieved June 12, 2014 (http://www.iwpr.org/publications/pubs/the-gender-wage-gap-2012/).

Henley, Kari, and Kay Pasley. 2005. "Conditions Affecting the Association between Father Identity and Father Involvement." *Fathering* 3(1): 59–80.

Hill, Heather. 2007. "Steppin' Out: Infidelity and Sexual Jealousy Among Unmarried Parents." Pp. 104–132 in *Unmarried Couples with Children*, edited by P. England and K. Edin. New York: Russell Sage Foundation.

Hochschild, Arlie Russell. 1979. "Emotion Work, Feeling Rules, and Social Structure." *American Journal of Sociology* 85(3): 551–575.

———. 2003. *The Commercialization of Intimate Life: Notes from Home and Work*. Berkeley, CA: University of California Press.

Hochschild, Arlie Russell, with Anne Machung. [1989] 2012. *The Second Shift: Working Families and the Revolution at Home*. New York: Penguin Books.

Hodges, Melissa J., and Michelle J. Budig. 2010. "Who Gets the Daddy Bonus? Organizational Hegemonic Masculinity and the Impact of Fatherhood on Earnings." *Gender & Society* 24(6): 717–745.

Hofferth, Sandra L. 2006. "Residential Father Family Type and Child Well-Being: Investment Versus Selection." *Demography* 43(1): 53–77.

Hohmann-Marriott, Bryndl. 2011. "Coparenting and Father Involvement in Married and Unmarried Coresident Couples." *Journal of Marriage and Family* 73(1): 296–309.

Horn, Wade F. 2001. "Wedding Bell Blues." *Brookings Review* 19: 39–42.

Howell, Patty. 2008. *Marriage Education: An Important Investment in Cultural Change*. California Association of Marriage and Family Therapists (CAMFT). Retrieved June 30, 2014 (http://www.camarriage.com/content/resources/ c76dfc8a-2ed8-4551- aab5- 380b63febcb8.pdf).

———. 2011. *The Case for Relationship Education: Creating Social Benefit through Skills Training*. Leucadia, CA: Healthy Relationships California.

Huston, Ted, and Heidi Melz. 2004. "The Case for (Promoting) Marriage: The Devil Is in the Details." *Journal of Marriage and Family* 66(4): 943–958.

Hymowitz, Kay. 2006. *Marriage and Caste in America: Separate and Unequal Families in a Post-Marital Age*. Chicago: Ivan R. Dee Press.

Illouz, Eva. 1997. *Consuming the Romantic Utopia: Love and the Cultural Contradictions of Capitalism*. Berkeley, CA: University of California Press.

———. 2012. *Why Love Hurts*. Malden, MA: Polity.

Ingraham, Chrys. 1999. *White Weddings: Romancing Heterosexuality in Popular Culture*. New York: Routledge.

Isen, Adam, and Betsey Stevenson. 2010. "Women's Education and Family Behavior: Trends in Marriage, Divorce, and Fertility." Pp. 107–142 in *Demography and the Economy*, edited by J. Shoven. Chicago: University of Chicago Press.

Johnson, Matthew D. 2012. "Healthy Marriage Initiatives: On the Need for Empiricism in Policy Implementation." *American Psychologist* 67(4): 296–308.

———. 2013. "Optimistic or Quixotic?: More Data on Marriage and Relationship Education Programs for Lower Income Couples." *American Psychologist* 68(2): 111–112.

Kamper, Charlene R. 2003. *Connections: Relationships and Marriage, Instructor's Manual*. Berkeley, CA: Dibble Fund.

Karney, Benjamin, and Thomas N. Bradbury. 1995. "The Longitudinal Course of Marital Quality and Stability: A Review of Theory, Method, and Research." *Psychological Bulletin* 118(1): 3–34.

———. 2005. "Contextual Influences on Marriage: Implications for Policy and Intervention." *Current Directions in Psychological Science* 14(4): 171–174.

Killewald, Alexandra. 2013. "A Reconsideration of the Fatherhood Premium: Marriage, Residence, Biology, and the Wages of Fathers." *American Sociological Review* 78(1): 96–116.

Killewald, Alexandra, and Margaret Gough. 2013. "Does Specialization Explain Marriage Penalties and Premiums." *American Sociological Review* 78(3): 477–502.

King, Valarie, Kathleen Mullan Harris, and Holly E. Heard. 2004. "Racial and Ethnic Diversity in Nonresident Father Involvement." *Journal of Marriage and Family* 66(1): 1–21.

King, Valerie, and Juliana M. Sobolewski. 2006. "Nonresident Fathers' Contribution to Adolescent Well-Being." *Journal of Marriage and Family* 68(3): 537–557.

Kirkland, Cassandra L., Emily Moye Skuban, Francesca Adler-Baeder, Scott A. Ketring, Angela Bradford, Thomas Smith, and Mallory Lucier-Greer. 2011. "Effects of Relationship/Marriage Education on Co-Parenting and Children's Social Skills: Examining Rural Minority Parents' Experiences." *Early Childhood Research and Practice* 13. Retrieved June 24, 2015 (http://ecrp.uiuc.edu/v13n2/kirkland.html).

Kitson, Gay. 1992. *Portrait of Divorce: Adjustment to Marital Breakdown.* New York: Guilford Press.

Lamb, Michael E. 2010. "How Do Fathers Influence Children's Development? Let Me Count the Ways." Pp. 1–26 in *The Role of the Father in Child Development,* fifth edition, edited by M. Lamb. Hoboken, NJ: Wiley.

Levine, Judith A. 2013. *Ain't No Trust: How Bosses, Boyfriends, and Bureaucrats Fail Low-Income Mothers and Why It Matters.* Berkeley, CA: University of California Press.

Lewis, Jerry, and John Gossett. 1999. *Disarming the Past: How an Intimate Relationship Can Heal Old Wounds.* Redding, CT: Zeig, Tucker & Theisen.

Lewis, Oscar. 1966. *La Vida: A Puerto Rican Family in the Culture of Poverty—San Juan and New York.* New York: Random House.

Lichter, Daniel, Deborah Roempke Graefe, and J. Brian Brown. 2003. "Is Marriage a Panacea?: Union Formation among Economically Disadvantaged Unwed Mothers." *Social Problems* 50(1): 60–86.

Lichter, Daniel T., and Martha L. Crowley. 2004. "Welfare Reform and Child Poverty: Effects of Maternal Employment, Marriage, and Cohabitation." *Social Science Research* 33(3): 385–408.

Lichter, Daniel T., and Deborah Roempke Graefe. 2007. "Men and Marriage Promotion: Who Marries Unwed Mothers?" *Social Service Review* 81(3): 397–421.

Lichter, Daniel T., Diane K. McLaughlin, and David C. Ribar. 2002. "Economic Structuring and the Retreat from Marriage." *Social Science Research* 31(2): 230–256.

Lieb, Hilarie, and Susan Thistle. 2005. "The Changing Impact of Marriage, Motherhood, and Work on Women's Poverty." *Journal of Women, Politics and Policy* 27(3–4): 5–22.

Lincoln, Anne E. 2008. "Gender, Productivity, and the Marital Wage Premium." *Journal of Marriage and Family* 70(3): 806–814.

Linnenberg, Kathryn. 2007. "#1 Father or Fathering 101?: Couple Relationship Quality and Father Involvement when Fathers Live with Their Children." Pp. 59–182 in *Unmarried Couples with Children,* edited by P. England and K. Edin. New York: Russell Sage Foundation.

Lipsky, Michael. 1983. *Street-Level Bureaucracy: Dilemmas of the Individual in Public Services.* New York: Russell Sage.

Loughran, David. 2002. "The Effect of Rising Male Wage Inequality on Female Age at First Marriage." *Review of Economics and Statistics* 84(2): 276–286.

Ludwig, Jens, and Susan Mayer. 2006. "'Culture' and the Intergenerational Transmission of Poverty: The Prevention Paradox." *The Future of Children* 16(2): 175–196.

Lundberg, Shelly, and Elaina Rose. 2000. "Parenthood and the Earnings of Married Men and Women." *Labour Economics* 7(6): 689–710.

Lundquist, Erika, JoAnn Hsueh, Amy E. Lowenstein, Kristen Faucetta, Daniel Gubits, Charles Michalopoulos, and Virginia Knox. 2014. *A Family-Strengthening Program for Low-Income Families: Final Impacts from the Supporting Healthy Marriage Evaluation.* OPRE Report 2014-09A. Washington, D.C.: Office of Planning, Research and Evaluation, Administration for Children and Families, U.S. Department of Health and Human Services.

Mackenzie, Joneen. 2008. *Wait Training: It's All About M.E. (Marriage Education): Teaching the Skills to Live Well, Love Well and Marry Well in the Future.* Denver, CO: Center for Relationship Education.

Magnuson, Katherine, and Christina Gibson-Davis. 2007. "Child Support among Low-Income Noncustodial Fathers." Pp. 228–251 in *Unmarried Couples with Children,* edited by P. England and K. Edin. New York: Russell Sage Foundation.

Manning, Wendy D., Susan L. Brown, Krista K. Payne, and Hsueh-Sheng Wu. 2014. "Healthy Marriage Initiative Spending and U.S. Marriage & Divorce Rates, A State-Level Analysis." (FP-14-02). National Center for Family & Marriage Research. Retrieved March 1, 2014 (http://www.bgsu.edu/content ./dam/BGSU/college-of-arts-and-sciences/NCFMR/documents/FP/FP-14 -02.pdf).

Manning, Wendy D., Marshal Neal Fettro, and Esther Lamidi. 2014. "Child Well-Being in Same-Sex Parent Families: Review of Research Prepared for American Sociological Association Amicus Brief." *Population Research and Policy Review* 33(4): 485–502.

Markey, Barbara, M. Micheletto, and A. Becker. 2000. *FOCCUS (Facilitating Open Couple Communication, Understanding & Study): Facilitator Manual.* Omaha, NE: FOCCUS, Inc.

Markman, Howard J., and Galena K. Rhoades. 2012. "Relationship Education Research: Current Status and Future Directions." *Journal of Marriage and Family Therapy* 38(1): 169–200.

Markman, Howard J., Scott M. Stanley, and Susan L. Blumberg. 2001. *Fighting for Your Marriage: Positive Steps for Preventing Divorce and Preserving a Lasting Love.* San Francisco, CA: Jossey-Bass.

Marquardt, Elizabeth, David Blankenhorn, Robert I. Lerman, Linda Malone-Colón, and W. Bradford Wilcox. 2012. "The President's Marriage Agenda for the Forgotten Sixty Percent." *The State of Our Unions.* Charlottesville, VA: National Marriage Project and Institute for American Values.

Marsiglio, William, and Sally Hutchinson. 2002. *Sex, Men, and Babies: Stories of Awareness and Responsibility.* New York: New York University Press.

Marsiglio, William, and Joseph H. Pleck. 2004. "Fatherhood and Masculinities." Pp. 249–269 in *The Handbook of Studies on Men and Masculinities*, edited by M. Kimmell, J. Hearn, and R. W. Connell. Thousand Oaks, CA: Sage.

Marsiglio, William, and Kevin Roy. 2012. *Nurturing Dads: Social Initiatives for Contemporary Fatherhood*. New York: Russell Sage Foundation.

Martin, Joyce A., Brady E. Hamilton, Stephanie J. Ventura, Michelle J. K. Osterman, Elizabeth C. Wilson, and T. J. Mathews. 2012. "Births: Final Data for 2010." National Vital Statistics Reports. 60(1). Hyattsville, MD: National Center for Health Statistics. Retrieved June 12, 2014 (http://www.cdc.gov/nchs/data/nvsr/nvsr61/nvsr61_01.pdf).

Martin, Steve P. 2006. "Trends in Marital Dissolution by Women's Education in the United States." *Demographic Research* 15(20): 537–560.

Maslow, Abraham H. 1943. "A Theory of Human Motivation." *Psychological Review* 50(4): 370–396.

Massey, Douglas. 2007. *Categorically Unequal: The American Stratification System*. New York: Russell Sage Foundation.

Maynard-Moody, Steven, and Michael Musheno. 2003. *Cops, Teachers, Counselors: Stories from the Front Lines of Public Service*. Ann Arbor, MI: University of Michigan Press.

McLanahan, Sara, and Audrey N. Beck. 2010. "Parental Relationships in Fragile Families." *The Future of Children* 20(2): 17–38.

McLanahan, Sara, Elisabeth Donahue, and Ron Haskins. 2005. "Introducing the Issue." *The Future of Children*. 15(2): 3–12.

McLanahan, Sara, and Christine Percheski. 2008. "Family Structure and the Reproduction of Inequality." *Annual Review of Sociology* 34: 257–276.

McLanahan, Sara, and Gary Sandefur. 1994. *Growing Up with a Single Parent: What Hurts, What Helps*. Cambridge, MA: Harvard University Press.

McLanahan, Sara, Laura Tach, and Daniel Schneider. 2013. "The Causal Effects of Father Absence." *Annual Review of Sociology* 39: 399–427.

McLaughlin, Diane K., and Daniel T. Lichter. 1997. "Poverty and the Marital Behavior of Young Women." *Journal of Marriage and the Family* 59(3): 582–594.

Mead, Lawrence. 1986. *Beyond Entitlement: The Social Obligations of Citizenship*. New York: Free Press.

Menning, Chadwick L. 2006. "Nonresident Fathering and School Failure." *Journal of Family Issues* 27(10): 1356–1382.

Miller, Tina. 2010. " 'It's a Triangle that's Difficult to Square': Men's Intentions and Practices around Caring, Work, and First-Time Fatherhood." *Fathering* 8(3): 362–378.

Miller-Adams, Michelle. 2002. *Owning Up: Poverty, Assets, and the American Dream*. Washington, D.C.: Brookings Institution Press.

Mink, Gwendolyn. 1990. "The Lady and the Tramp: Gender, Race, and the Origins of the American Welfare State." Pp. 92–122 in *Women, the State, and Welfare*, edited by L. Gordon. Madison, WI: University of Wisconsin Press.

Mintz, Steven. 2004. *Huck's Raft: A History of American Childhood*. Cambridge, MA: Harvard University Press.

Misra, Joya, Stephanie Moller, and Michelle J. Budig. 2007. "Work-Family Policies and Poverty for Partnered and Single Women in Europe and North America." *Gender & Society* 21(6): 804–827.

Monte, Lindsay. 2007. "Blended but Not the Bradys: Navigating Unmarried Multiple Partner Fertility." Pp. 183–203 in *Unmarried Couples with Children*, edited by P. England and K. Edin. New York: Russell Sage Foundation.

Moore, Kristin A., Andrea Kinghorn, and Tawana Bandy. 2011. "Parental Relationship Quality and Child Outcomes across Subgroups." *Child Trends*, April 2011–2013.

Mullainathan, Sendhil, and Eldar Shafir. 2013. *Scarcity: Why Having Too Little Means so Much*. New York: Henry Holt.

Murray, Charles. 1984. *Losing Ground: American Social Welfare Policy, 1950–1980*. New York: Basic Books.

Musick, Kelly, and Larry Bumpass. 2012. "Reexamining the Case for Marriage: Union Formation and Changes in Well-Being." *Journal of Marriage and Family* 74(1): 1–18.

Musick, Kelly, and Robert D. Mare. 2006. "Recent Trends in the Inheritance of Poverty and Family Structure." *Social Science Research* 35(2): 471–499.

Nelson, Timothy J. 2004. "Low-Income Fathers." *Annual Review of Sociology* 30(1): 427–451.

Newman, Katherine. 1999. *No Shame in My Game: The Working Poor in the Inner City*. New York: Vintage Books.

———. 2006. *Chutes and Ladders: Navigating the Low-Wage Labor Market*. New York: Russell Sage Foundation.

Nock, Steven. 1998. *Marriage in Men's Lives*. New York: Oxford University Press.

Nurse, Anne. 2002. *Fatherhood Arrested: Parenting within the Juvenile Justice System*. Nashville, TN: Vanderbilt University Press.

O'Connor, Alice. 2001. *Poverty Knowledge: Social Science, Social Policy, and the Poor in Twentieth-Century U. S. History*. Princeton, NJ: Princeton University Press.

Olson, David H. 2002. *PREPARE/ENRICH: Building a Strong Marriage Workbook*. Minneapolis, MN: Life Innovations.

Ooms, Theodora. 2007. "Adapting Healthy Marriage Programs for Disadvantaged and Culturally Diverse Populations: What Are the Issues?" Center for Law and Social Policy (CLASP) Policy Brief, March 2007, No. 10.

Oppenheimer, Valerie Kincade. 1988. "A Theory of Marriage Timing." *American Journal of Sociology* 94(3): 563–591.

Orbuch, Terri L., Joseph Veroff, Halimah Hassan, and Julie Horrocks. 2002. "Who Will Divorce: A 14-Year Longitudinal Study of Black Couples and White Couples." *Journal of Social and Personal Relationships* 19(2): 179–202.

Orloff, Ann, and Renee Monson. 2002. "Citizens, Workers, or Fathers: Men in the History of U.S. Social Policy." Pp. 61–91 in *Making Men into Fathers: Men, Masculinities, and the Social Politics of Fatherhood*, edited by B. Hobson. New York: Cambridge University Press.

Ortwein, Mary, and Bernard Guerney Jr. 2004. *Love's Cradle Leader's Guide: Building Strong Families through Relationship Enhancement*. Frankfort, KY: Relationship Press.

Osborne, Cynthia, Wendy D. Manning, and Pamela J. Smock. 2007. "Married and Cohabiting Parents' Relationship Stability: A Focus on Race and Ethnicity." *Journal of Marriage and Family* 69(5): 1345–1366.

Papp, Lauren M., E. Mark Cummings, and Marcie C. Goeke-Morey. 2009. "For Richer, for Poorer: Money as a Topic of Marital Conflict in the Home." *Family Relations* 58(1): 91–103.

Pearson, Marline E. 2007. *Love U2: Relationship Smarts Plus: Instructor's Manual*. Berkeley, CA: Dibble Institute.

Pearson, Marline, Scott M. Stanley, and Galena H. Kline. 2005. *Within My Reach: Instructor Manual*. Greenwood Village, CO: PREP for Individuals.

Petersen, Trond, Andrew M. Penner, and Geir Høgsnes. 2011. "The Male Marital Wage Premium: Sorting vs. Differential Pay." *Industrial & Labor Relations Review* 64: 283–304.

Pleck, Joseph H. 2010. "Fatherhood and Masculinity." Pp. 27–57 in *The Role of the Father in Child Development*, fifth edition, edited by M. Lamb. Hoboken, NJ: Wiley.

Ponzetti, James J. Jr., (ed.). 2015. *Evidence-Based Approaches to Relationship and Marriage Education*. New York: Routledge.

Popenoe, David. 1996. *Life without Father: Compelling New Evidence that Fatherhood and Marriage Are Indispensable for the Good of Children and Society*. New York: Free Press.

——. 2009. *Families without Fathers: Fathers, Marriage, and Children in American Society*. Edison, NJ: Transaction.

Press, Julie E., Jay Fagan, and Lynda Laughlin. 2006. "Taking Pressure Off Families: Child-Care Subsidies Lessen Mothers' Work-Hour Problems." *Journal of Marriage and Family* 68(1): 155–171.

Randles, Jennifer. 2012. "Marriage Promotion Policy and Family Inequality." *Sociology Compass* 6(8): 671–683.

——. 2013. "Repackaging the 'Package Deal': Promoting Marriage for Low-Income Families by Targeting Paternal Identity and Reframing Marital Masculinity." *Gender & Society* 27(6): 864–888.

——. 2014. "Partnering and Parenting in Poverty: A Qualitative Analysis of a Relationship Skills Program for Low-Income, Unmarried Families." *Journal of Policy Analysis and Management* 33(2): 385–412.

——. 2016. "Redefining the Marital Power Struggle through Relationship Skills: How United States Marriage Education Programs Challenge and Reinforce Gender Inequality." *Gender & Society* 30(2): 240–264.

Rauer, Amy J., Benjamin R. Karney, Cynthia W. Garvan, and Wei Hou. 2008. "Relationship Risks in Context: A Cumulative Risk Approach to Understanding Relationship Satisfaction." *Journal of Marriage and Family* 70(5): 1122–1135.

Reardon-Anderson, Jane, Matthew Stagner, Jennifer Macomber, and Julie Murray. 2005. "Systematic Review of the Impact of Marriage and Relationship Programs." U.S. Department of Health and Human Services Report. Retrieved January 31, 2014 (http:// www.acf.hhs.gov/programs/opre/strengthen/serv _delivery/reports/systematic_rev/system atic_rev.pdf).

Reed, Joanna. 2007. "Anatomy of a Breakup: How and Why Do Unmarried Couples with Children Break Up?" Pp. 133–155 in *Unmarried Couples with Children*, edited by P. England and K. Edin. New York: Russell Sage Foundation.

Reese, Ellen. 2005. *Backlash against Welfare Mothers: Past and Present*. Berkeley, CA: University of California Press.

Regan, Pamela. 2011. *Close Relationships*. New York: Routledge.

Rose, Nikolas. 1999. *Governing the Soul: The Shaping of the Private Self*. New York: Routledge.

Rosenfeld, Michael. 2008. "Racial, Educational, and Religious Endogamy in Comparative Historical Perspective." *Social Forces* 87(1): 1–32.

Roy, Kevin. 2004. "You Can't Eat Love: Constructing Provider Role Expectations for Low-Income and Working-Class Fathers." *Fathering* 2: 253–276.

Roy, Kevin M., Nicole Buckmiller, and April McDowell. 2008. "Together but Not 'Together': Trajectories of Relationship Suspension for Low-Income Unmarried Parents." *Family Relations* 57(2): 198–210.

Rubin, Lillian Breslow. 1969. *Worlds of Pain: Life in the Working-Class Family*. New York: Basic Books.

Sawhill, Isabel V. 2003. "The Behavioral Aspects of Poverty." *Public Interest* 153: 79–93.

——. 2014. *Generation Unbound: Drifting into Sex and Parenthood without Marriage*. Washington, D.C.: Brookings Institution Press.

Scafidi, Benjamin. 2008. *The Taxpayer Costs of Divorce and Unwed Childbearing: First-Ever Estimates for the Nation and All Fifty States*. New York: Institute for American Values.

Schaff, Lawrence A. 1991. *Fleeing the Iron Cage: Culture, Politics, and Modernity in the Thought of Max Weber*. Berkeley, CA: University of California Press.

Schram, Sanford F. 2006. *Welfare Discipline: Discourse, Governance, and Globalization*. Philadelphia, PA: Temple University Press.

Sealander, Judith. 2003. *The Failed Century of the Child: Governing America's Young in the Twentieth Century*. New York: Cambridge University Press.

Shannon, Jacqueline D., Natasha J. Cabrera, Catherine Tamis-LeMonda, and Michael E. Lamb. 2009. "Who Stays and Who Leaves? Father Accessibility across Children's First Five Years." *Parenting Science and Practice* 9(1–2): 78–100.

Shapiro, Thomas M., and Edward N. Wolff (eds.). 2001. *Assets for the Poor: The Benefits of Spreading Asset Ownership*. New York: Russell Sage Foundation.

Sherman, Jennifer. 2009. *Those Who Work, Those Who Don't: Poverty, Morality, and Family in Rural America*. Minneapolis, MN: University of Minnesota Press.

Sherraden, Michael W. 1991. *Assets and the Poor: A New American Welfare Policy*. Armonk, NY: Sharpe.

Shipler, David. K. 2004. *The Working Poor: Invisible in America*. New York: Vintage Books.

Shirer, Karen, Ching-Ju Chen, Dawn Contreras, Saneya Hamler, Angela Harris, Holly Lacina, Erika London, and José Rubén Parra Cardona. 2007. *Together We Can: Creating a Healthy Future for Our Family: A Curriculum to Improve*

Co-Parenting Relationships of Single Parents. East Lansing, MI: Michigan State University Extension.

Sigle-Rushton, Wendy, and Sara McLanahan. 2003. "For Richer or Poorer? Marriage as an Anti-Poverty Strategy in the United States." *Population* 57(3): 509–526.

Silva, Jennifer. 2013. *Coming Up Short: Working-Class Adulthood in an Age of Uncertainty*. New York: Oxford University Press.

Simpson, Kelly. 2007. *Active Relationships: Active Marriage and Best Practices for Healthy Relationships: Participant's Guide*. Dallas, TX: Active Relationships Center.

Sinkewicz, Marilyn, and Irwin Garfinkel. 2009. "Unwed Fathers' Ability to Pay Child Support: New Estimates Accounting for Multiple-Partner Fertility." *Demography* 46(2): 247–263.

Skocpol, Theda. 1995. *Protecting Soldiers and Mothers: The Political Origins of Social Policy in the United States*. Cambridge, MA: Harvard University Press.

Smeeding, Timothy M., Irwin Garfinkel, and Ronald B. Mincy. 2011. "Young Disadvantaged Men: Fathers, Families, Poverty, and Policy." *The ANNALS of the American Academy of Political and Social Science* 635(1): 6–21.

Smith, Anna Marie. 2001. "The Politicization of Marriage in Contemporary American Public Policy: The Defense of Marriage Act and the Personal Responsibility Act." *Citizenship Studies* 5(3): 303–320.

Smock, Pamela J., Sanjiv Gupta, and Wendy D. Manning. 1999. "The Effect of Marriage and Divorce on Women's Economic Well-Being." *American Sociological Review* 64(6): 794–812.

Smock, Pamela, Wendy Manning, and Meredith Porter. 2005. "'Everything's There Except the Money': How Money Shapes Decisions to Marry Among Cohabitors." *Journal of Marriage and Family* 67(3): 680–697.

Solot, Dorian, and Marshall Miller. 2007. *Let Them Eat Wedding Rings*, second edition. West Hills, CA: Alternatives to Marriage Project

Somers, Margaret R., and Fred Block. 2005. "From Poverty to Perversity: Ideas, Markets, and Institutions over 200 Years of Welfare Debates." *American Sociological Review* 70(2): 260–287.

Soons, Judith P. M., and Matthijs Kalmijn. 2009. "Is Marriage More than Cohabitation?: Well-Being Differences in 30 European Countries." *Journal of Marriage and Family* 71(5): 1141–1157.

Soss, Joe, Richard C. Fording, and Sanford Schram. 2011. *Disciplining the Poor: Neoliberal Paternalism and the Persistent Power of Race*. Chicago: University of Chicago Press.

Sparks, Anne. 2008. "Implementation of 'Within My Reach': Providing a Relationship Awareness and Communications Skills Program to TANF Recipients in Oklahoma." National Poverty Center Working Paper Series, #08-11, July 2008.

Sprecher, Susan, and Sandra Metts. 1999. "Romantic Beliefs: Their Influence on Relationships and Patterns of Change over Time." *Journal of Social and Personal Relationships* 16(6): 834–851.

Stacey, Judith. 1996. *In the Name of the Family: Rethinking Family Values in the Postmodern Age*. Boston: Beacon.

Stanley, Scott M., Howard J. Markman, Natalie H. Jenkins, and Susan L. Blumberg. 2008. *PREP Leader Manual: Version 7.0*. Greenwood Village, CO: PREP Educational Products.

Stanley, Scott M., Howard J. Markman, and Sarah W. Whitton. 2002. "Communication, Conflict, and Commitment: Insights on the Foundations of Relationship Success from a National Survey." *Family Process* 41(4): 659–675.

Stone, Pamela. 2007. *Opting Out?: Why Women Really Quit Careers and Head Home*. Berkeley, CA: University of California Press.

Sullivan, Mercer L. 1993. "Young Fathers and Parenting in Two Inner-City Neighborhoods." Pp. 52–73 in *Young Unwed Fathers: Changing Roles and Emerging Policies*, edited by R. Lerman and T. Ooms. Philadelphia, PA: Temple University Press.

Sum, Andrew, Ishwar Khatiwada, Joseph McLaughlin, and Sheila Palma. 2011. "No Country for Young Men: Deteriorating Labor Market Prospects for Low-Skilled Men in the United States." *The ANNALS of the American Academy of Political and Social Science* 635(1): 24–55.

Sweeney, Megan. 2002. "Two Decades of Family Change: The Shifting Economic Foundations of Marriage." *American Sociological Review* 67(1): 132–147.

Swidler, Ann. 2001. *Talk of Love: How Culture Matters*. Chicago: University of Chicago Press.

Tach, Laura, and Kathryn Edin. 2011. "The Relationship Contexts of Young Disadvantaged Men." *The ANNALS of the American Academy of Political and Social Science* 635(1): 76–94.

Tach, Laura, Ronald Mincy, and Kathryn Edin. 2010. "Parenting as a 'Package Deal': Relationships, Fertility, and Nonresident Father Involvement among Unmarried Parents." *Demography* 47(1): 181–204.

Thomas, Adam, and Isabel Sawhill. 2002. "For Richer or for Poorer: Marriage as an Antipoverty Strategy." *Journal of Policy Analysis and Management* 21(4): 587–599.

Townsend, Nicholas W. 2002. *The Package Deal: Marriage, Work and Fatherhood in Men's Lives*. Philadelphia, PA: Temple University Press.

Trail, Thomas E., and Benjamin R. Karney. 2012. "What's (Not) Wrong with Low-Income Marriages." *Journal of Marriage and Family* 74(3): 413–427.

U.S. Bureau of Labor Statistics. 2014. "Labor Force Statistics from the Current Population Survey: Earnings." Retrieved June 12, 2014 (http://www.bls.gov/cps/ earnings.htm).

U.S. Census Bureau. 2014. "Selected Social Characteristics in the United States: 2008–2012 American Community Survey 5-Year Estimates." Retrieved January 2, 2014 (http://factfinder2.census.gov/faces/tableservices/jsf/pages/product view.xhtml?pid=ACS _12_5YR_DP02).

U.S. Department of Education. 2012. *The Condition of Education* (NCES 2012-045), Indicator 47. National Center for Education Statistics. Retrieved June 12, 2014 (http:// www.edweek.org/media/coe-in-brief-final-33condition.pdf).

Usdansky, Margaret L., and Douglas A. Wolf. 2008. "When Child Care Breaks Down: Mothers' Experience with Child Care Problems and Resulting Missed Work." *Journal of Family Issues* 2(9): 1185–1210.

van Acker, Elizabeth. 2003. "Administering Romance: Government Policies Concerning Pre-Marriage Education Programs." *Australian Journal of Public Administration* 62(1): 15–23.

———. 2008. *Governments and Marriage Education Policy: Perspectives from the UK, Australia, and the US.* New York: Palgrave Macmillian.

Van Epp, John. 2007a. *How to Avoid Marrying a Jerk (or Jerkette): P.I.C.K. (Premarital Interpersonal Choices & Knowledge) a Partner Workbook.* Medina, OH: Lifechangers.

———. 2007b. *How to Avoid Falling in Love with a Jerk: The Foolproof Way to Follow Your Heart without Losing Your Mind.* New York: McGraw-Hill.

Waite, Linda, and Maggie Gallagher. 2000. *The Case for Marriage: Why Married People Are Happier, Healthier, and Better Off Financially.* New York: Doubleday.

Waller, Maureen. 2002. *My Baby's Father: Unmarried Parents and Paternal Responsibility.* Ithaca, NY: Cornell University Press.

Waller, Maureen R., and Sara S. McLanahan. 2005. " 'His' and 'Her' Marriage Expectations: Determinants and Consequences." *Journal of Marriage and Family* 67(1): 53–67.

Watkins-Hayes, Celeste. 2009. "Race-ing the Bootstrap Climb: Black and Latino Bureaucrats in Post-Reform Welfare Offices." *Social Problems* 56(2): 285–310.

Watson, Tara, and Sara McLanahan. 2011. "Marriage Meets the Joneses: Relative Income, Identity, and Marital Status." *Journal of Human Resources* 46(3): 482–517.

Weber, Max. [1946] 1970. "Science as a Vocation." Pp. 129–156 in *From Max Weber: Essays in Sociology,* edited by H. H. Gerth and C. Wright Mills. New York: Oxford University Press.

Western, Bruce. 2006. *Punishment and Inequality in America.* New York: Russell Sage.

Williams, Kristi, Sharon Sassler, and Lisa M. Nicholson. 2008. "For Better or For Worse? The Consequences of Marriage and Cohabitation for Single Mothers." *Social Forces* 86(4): 1481–1511.

Wilson, James Q. 2002. *The Marriage Problem: How Our Culture Has Weakened Families.* New York: Harper Collins.

Wilson, William Julius. 1987. *The Truly Disadvantaged: The Inner City, the Underclass, and Public Policy.* Chicago: University of Chicago Press.

———. 1996. *When Work Disappears: The World of the New Urban Poor.* New York: Vintage Press.

Wood, Robert G., Quinn Moore, Andrew Clarkwest, and Alexandra Killewald. 2014. "The Long-Term Effects of Building Strong Families: A Program for Unmarried Parents." *Journal of Marriage and Family* 76(2): 446–463.

Young, Alford A., Jr. 2004. *The Minds of Marginalized Black Men: Making Sense of Mobility, Opportunity, and Life Chances.* Princeton, NJ: Princeton University Press.

Zagorsky, Jay. 2005. "Marriage and Divorce's Impact on Wealth." *Journal of Sociology* 41(4): 406–424.

Zhan, Min, Steven G. Anderson, and Jeff Scott. 2006. "Financial Knowledge of the Low-Income Population: Effects of a Financial Education Program." *Journal of Sociology and Social Welfare* 33(1): 53.

Index

abstinence education, 42, 46, 206
ACF. *See* Administration for Children and Families
active listening, 8, 37, 39, 52, 170–171, 185–186, 186, 192, 200, 206
Active Relationships (curriculum), 17, 39, 42–43, 48, 75
addiction, 27, 28. *See also* alcohol; drugs
Adler-Baeder, Francesca, 213
Administration for Children and Families, 6, 7, 17, 19, 20, 22, 211
adult status, 87–88, 142
affective awareness, 29
African American Relationships, Marriages, and Families (AARMF) (curriculum), 74–75, 78
African Americans: disadvantaged males and, 56, 93, 161, 163–165; gendered family roles and, 154–155; Healthy Marriage Initiative program for, 17, 78; marriage and, 82, 87, 93–94; normative social stability model and, 16; relationship problems

and, 51–52; relationship skills programs and, 14, 20, 78; single mothers and, 6, 58, 93; structural disadvantages and, 74–75, 93; Thriving Family participants, 20, 22; wage discrimination and, 89; welfare stereotypes and, 58; women's earnings and, 89
alcohol, 55, 75, 94, 95
Amato, Paul, 174
anger, 2, 46, 47, 54, 84; management class, 184–85
antipoverty policies, 90, 206–207, 212, 213. *See also* Healthy Marriage Initiative; welfare reform; welfare system
arguments, 51–56, 83; about money, 52, 55, 56, 74, 179; time-outs from, 35, 39; unresolved, 169
arranged marriage, 28, 39, 40
Asian Americans, 20, 22
asset building, 68–69
assortative mating, 90

attachment, five fundamental dynamics of, 36

Australia, marriage education policy, 31–32

"Baby, Now that I've Found You" (song), 34

bandwidth, 173, 174, 200

behavioral strategies, 5, 6, 39

behavior modification, 7, 78

Bellah, Robert, 29

Beyond Entitlement (Mead), 58

blended families, 45

Blumberg, Susan, 62–64

bonding power, 41–42

Bourdieu, Pierre, 111

brain function, 38–39

breadwinner. *See* male breadwinner

breathing exercises (stress reduction), 48

Bringing Baby Home (curriculum), 17, 44–45, 48, 70–71, 137, 138, 213

Brodkin, Evelyn, 109

budgeting, 67, 70–74, 175–179, 208; needs vs. wants and, 176–177, 209; poverty and, 71–72, 74, 78, 80, 171, 181

budgeting strategies, 4, 67, 70–71, 178–179, 183, 185

Building Strong Families: cost per-couple, 210; evaluations of, 14–15, 174

bureaucracy. *See* street-level bureaucracy theory

Bush, George W., 81, 139, 209

California Healthy Marriages Coalition, 17

California Proposition 8 (same-sex marriage), 108

Caring for My Family: Together We Can (curriculum), 17, 45, 66–67

cash assistance program, 5–6

"Cat's in the Cradle" (song), 152

Celello, Kristin, 30

Chapin, Harry, 152

Cherlin, Andrew, 16, 29, 82, 86, 87, 142

childbearing: decisions about, 45–46, 103, 113–114; teenage, 65, 162;

unmarried, 6, 20, 21, 50, 58, 60, 86, 96–97, 99, 103, 211

child care, 5, 80, 133; by father, 143, 144, 147, 151, 153, 155, 157, 165, 166, 168; public subsidies for, 212

Child Protective Services, 96, 100, 184, 198–199

children: absent fathers and, 161, 162, 211; co-parent commitment to (*see* co-parenting); father's interaction with, 137, 138, 143–144, 150, 152–53, 157, 160, 163, 164, 167; financial costs of raising, 172–173; married parents advantage for, 5, 8, 11–12, 26, 72, 149; parent multiple partners and, 77, 83, 94; poverty and, 212; from previous relationships, 51–52, 55; same-sex parents and, 11, 12, 166; stable environment for, 4; stepfamilies and, 12, 17, 70, 83, 145, 213; upward mobility and, 110, 127–128; welfare reform and, 5

child support, 139, 145

class: differences in, 205, 206; fatherhood bonuses and, 141; gender norms and, 216; inequality factors (*see* inequality); marriage and, 8–15, 56–58, 64, 86, 88, 90–91, 105, 204, 211; success sequence and, 59–64, 79, 89–95, 102, 142. *See also* middle-class marriage culture; socioeconomic status; upward mobility

cohabitation, 9–10, 60, 63, 86–88, 92; historical rarity of, 86–87; social acceptability of, 13, 87, 93; social stigma of, 86; turnover in, 91

college degree, 5, 9, 11, 85, 205, 207; advantages of, 91, 92, 93, 140; women and, 88, 89, 90. *See also* success sequence

commitment, 9, 29, 34, 39, 40, 67; as attachment dynamic, 36; conditional, 146–147; to co-parenting, 23–24, 109, 110–135, 149, 156; as deliberate decision, 61; individual choices and,

213; long-term, 11; love as, 106, 107, 128, 132; marital components, 49–50; poverty effects on, 175; socioeconomic opportunity and, 216. *See also* curtailed commitment

communication skills: African American families and, 75; healthy marriage curricula and, 1, 2, 3, 8, 18, 21, 27, 30, 31, 37, 40, 67, 205, 207, 209; hostility and, 52; improvement strategies for, 13–14, 15, 182–183, 185–190; interpersonal conflict and, 59; managing money and, 68–77; marriage and, 76, 169–170; negative emotions and, 47; painful issues and, 28; parenthood and, 186–188, 189; perpetual problems statistic, 169–170; poverty and, 170–172, 175, 192, 200; relationship problems and, 51–53, 185–186, 194; relationship satisfaction and, 30, 449; 170–171; techniques for, 27–28, 35, 47, 170. *See also* active listening

conflict resolution, 2, 7, 27, 35, 44, 67, 71, 184–185, 205, 207–209

Connections (curriculum), 17, 61, 66, 72–73

Coontz, Stephanie, 28, 50

co-parenting, 14, 15, 23–24, 71, 106, 108, 109, 110–135, 136, 149, 156–160, 189; "breaking the chain" and, 125–132; healthy marriage programs and, 112–135, 214; men's commitment and, 156–157; misguided message of, 132–135. *See also* fathers

cost-benefit analysis, 102–103, 211

Cott, Nancy, 6

couples counseling, 30

couples training, 7, 11, 34–50, 194–195; research citations, 37–38

Cowan, Carolyn Pape, 193, 213

Cowan, Philip, 193, 213

Craigslist, 21

crime, 12, 57, 62, 94, 107, 138, 211; incarceration and, 55, 56, 93, 144, 161; reduction of, 6

cultural values, 3, 57, 76, 112; shift in, 82, 87–88, 105

culture of poverty thesis, 57–58, 78

curricula development, 17, 37–39, 39, 42–45, 48, 68, 75, 77; evidence-based, 208

curtailed commitment, 8–15, 85–105; components of, 85; socioeconomic realties and, 4, 9, 10, 95

cycle of poverty, 111, 128

"daddy bonus," 140–141

Davis, Rebecca, 29

"dead beat" dads, 150

debt, 71, 92

decision-making, 4, 7, 60–61, 65

"deep-dish" policy analysis, 109

delayed gratification, 57

Department of Health and Human Services, 103–105, 145–146

divorce, 6, 12, 28, 30, 38, 40, 44, 46, 208, 211; moderately educated couples and, 91; prevention curricula, 17, 36–37, 45; rates of, 14, 48–49; reasons for, 54; restrictive laws and, 28; romantic love and, 25; social condemnation of, 28, 82, 87

Divorce Busting (curriculum), 17, 45

Dixon, Patricia, 74–75

domestic science, 32

domestic violence, 12, 75

drugs, 57, 75, 94, 95, 96, 97, 103, 107, 162

drug trade, 55, 56

Earned Income Tax Credit, 75, 212

earnings. *See* wages

economic disadvantage. *See* inequality; poverty; socioeconomic status

Edin, Kathryn, 9–10, 55, 94, 114–115; *Promises I Can Keep*, 66–67

education, 5, 6, 9, 11, 12, 13, 78, 137; benefits of, 89–90, 139; economic advantage and, 56–62, 77, 91; marital endogamy and, 88, 90; middle-class advantage and, 77, 85, 92; Thriving

education (*continued*)
Families participants and, 20;
unequal access to, 207. *See also*
college degree; high-school diploma;
marriage education programs
emotional competence, 207; description
of, 42–43
emotional intelligence, definition of,
42, 48
emotional jug exercise, 47
emotional stress. *See* stress
emotions: inappropriate, 46–48;
management techniques, 34, 39, 41,
42, 46–48, 49, 64–65; negative, 27,
47, 54; poverty effects on, 54, 55, 56,
65, 80, 173, 209. *See also* rationality;
specific emotions
empathy, 2, 8, 27, 29, 37, 43, 44, 206;
communication of, 52, 175; healthy
marriage programs and, 194–195,
197–198
employment, 56, 77–81, 94, 165; of both
parents, 156–157; class advantage
and, 9, 57, 77, 81, 86, 90–91, 166,
205; dominant cultural values and,
76; education level and (*see* college
degree; high-school diploma); gender
roles and (*see* male breadwinner);
high-status, high-earning, 64, 77;
interpersonal skills and, 76; lay-offs
and, 83; low-wage, 5, 13, 73, 104;
marital benefits from, 13, 139–141,
147; marital relationship and,
211–212; marriage predicated on,
8–9, 88, 92, 104, 142, 146; success
factors, 139–140; unequal access to,
64, 77, 206, 207; vocational training
and, 209; welfare reform and, 122,
138–139, 209, 212; well- vs. low-
paying, 5, 82; women and, 89, 90,
156–157, 212; work ethic and, 57, 64,
81. *See also* success sequence;
unemployment
evidence-based marriage education
programs, 12–13, 37–38, 80, 203, 208

extended kin, 13, 86, 203–204
extramarital sex, 43

families, 2, 6, 34, 78, 87, 89; African
American, 74–75; antipoverty policies
and, 213; blended, 145; child-rearing
costs and, 172–173; contemporary state
of, 35; diverse forms of, 11–12, 16, 108,
158–160, 166, 205, 206; effective
policies for, 213, 214; extended, 13, 86,
203–204; government benefits and, 211,
212; inequalities and, 4, 143–147, 207;
marriage as basis of, 11, 82, 116; moral
politics and, 16, 58, 64, 206; normative
ideas of, 16, 139, 142, 145, 158–160,
166, 206; stability of, 11–12, 28, 29,
170; strengths of, 106–107; success
definition and, 64. *See also* gender
norms; parenthood; stepfamilies
family research, 202–203
family systems model, 144
family values, 50, 64, 78, 144
family web exercise, 125–132
fathers, 5, 58, 107, 136–168, 213; absent,
6, 161, 162, 211; attitudes of, 114, 142,
155; child care by, 143, 144, 147, 151, 153,
155, 157, 165, 166, 168; child's
relationship with, 137, 143, 157–165;
conditional commitment and,
146–147; daddy differentiated from,
152–153, 155–156; gender norms and,
137, 138, 143, 145, 148–149, 150–168;
government programs and, 6, 139,
167, 209, 210; ideal attributes of, 153;
importance of, 221, 136; involvement
of, 15, 94, 136, 137–138, 144–145,
148–156, 209; marital masculinity
and, 24, 142–143, 147, 155; marriage
"premium" and, 140–41; as
masculinity role model, 157–65;
media portrayals of, 137; non-
biological, 155–156, 163; "package deal"
and, 114, 115, 142, 143–147; play style
of, 137, 138, 143, 150, 157, 163, 164;
positive stereotypes of, 141; problems

of poverty and, 144, 165–168; "real
men" as, 153; responsible, 136, 137,
138–147, 163–165, 210; welfare reform
and, 145–47. *See also* co-parenting;
parenthood
Father's Day, 136
federal funding. *See* Healthy Marriage
Initiative
financial literacy, 68–77, 78, 178,
181, 209
financial management. *See* money
financial security, 10, 23, 57, 84; happy
marriage and, 104; interrelated
factors of, 82; long-term marriages
and, 81–82, 86, 112; marriage
postponement and, 10, 66–67, 82;
relationship choices and, 59–66;
wealth accumulation and, 11
FOCCUS (curriculum), 17, 69–70
food stamps, 20, 100, 178, 211
Furstenberg, Frank, 142

gay couples. *See* same-sex marriage;
same-sex parents
gender norms: class and, 216; equitable
earnings and, 90; ethnicity and race
and, 154–155; financial conflicts and,
55, 56; flexibility in, 166, 167;
government-funded family policies
and, 139; heterosexual family
structure and, 158–160; inequalities
and, 216; marital age and, 88; marital
division of labor and, 28, 86, 89,
140–141, 150, 153; marriage education
programs and, 158–160; marriage
market and, 93–94; masculinity and,
142, 153 (*see also* male breadwinner);
middle-class expectations and, 165;
parenting and, 137, 138, 143, 148–68;
relationship troubles and, 62;
rethinking of, 153–154; sex-based
differences and, 156–159; traditional
marriage and, 86, 89, 90
Gibson-Davis, Christina, 113, 144
goal-setting, 7, 21, 68; teaching of, 4–5

Goleman, Daniel, *Emotional
Intelligence*, 42
Gordon, Lori, 38–39
Gossett, John, 104
Gottman, John, 169, 175; *Bringing Baby
Home* curriculum, 17, 44–45, 48,
70–71, 137, 138, 213; *The Marriage
Clinic*, 169–70
government policy. *See* Healthy
Marriage Initiative; marriage
education programs; welfare reform
Great Depression (1930s), 86–87
group activities, 22
Groves, Ernest, 32
Guerney, Bernard, 51

habitus, concept of, 111
Hackstaff, Karla, 30
Haskins, Ron, 61
Hays, Sharon, 6–7
"healthy" vs. "unhealthy" relationship
behaviors, 206
health care, 20, 73, 133, 178
health insurance, 72, 80, 91
health problems, married vs.
unmarried, 116–117, 118
Healthy Marriage Initiative (2002), 2–4,
18–19, 146–147, 184–185, 205–212;
antipoverty logic of, 90; assessments
of, 173–174, 207–208, 211, 213–216;
assumptions of, 3–4, 204–205, 208;
basic logic of, 174; conclusions about,
15, 202–211, 212; controversial issues
of, 108, 202–203; cost-benefit analysis
and, 211; creation of, 2–3, 6, 103–105;
critiques of, 94–95, 107–108, 134–135,
204; culture of poverty thesis and, 58;
curricula of, 17–18, 34–35, 48, 78, 109,
203, 208, 209; debates over, 10–13;
definition of good relationship by,
52–53; definition of "healthy
marriage" by, 104; dominant
messages of, 18–19, 170; emphasis
of, 23, 26–28, 34–50, 49–50,
53, 64,

Healthy Marriage (*continued*)
94–95, 108; ethnographic in-depth
study of, 10, 202; evaluations of
programs, 13–19, 105, 173–175;
evidence-based claims of, 12–13,
37–38, 80, 203, 208; federal funding
of, 1–2, 5–7, 8, 15, 17, 19–22, 58, 79,
209, 210–211, 213; fundamental
premises of, 208; goals of, 13–16, 120;
grants by, 17–18, 19, 107–108;
legislative intent of, 10–11, 85; main
misconceptions of, 56–57, 171; as
marriage promotion, 25–28, 31, 43,
108, 203, 204, 209; middle-class
assumptions of, 103; moralistic
outlook of, 16, 58, 64; participant
incentives and, 184–185, 209, 210, 211;
political/social implications of, 9, 16;
populations target of, 17–18; primary
goals of, 213–214; recommendations
for, 211–216; socioeconomic realities
and, 10–11; TANF costs vs., 210; total
spending (to 2014) by, 3. *See also*
marriage education programs;
Thriving Families
"Healthy Marriage, Relationship
Education, and Economic Mobility"
grants, 6, 19–22
"Healthy Marriage: Why Love Is Good
for You" Mayo Clinic report, 118
Heath, Melanie, 15, 16, 199, 210–11
heteronormative biases, 13, 16, 108, 206
heterosexual family structure, 11–12, 16,
158–160, 166, 206
hierarchy of human needs, 172–173, 192
higher education. *See* college degree
high-school diploma, 20, 59, 60, 61, 79,
82, 83, 88, 92, 99, 146
HMI. *See* Healthy Marriage Initiative
Hochschild, Arlie Russell, 30, 49
home economics, 32
homelessness, 95–96, 103, 107, 200
homemakers, 86, 89, 90, 140
homeownership, 5, 9, 84, 85, 92, 94,
142, 146, 147

housework, 140, 151, 153, 154, 155, 157, 165
How to Avoid Falling in Love with a Jerk
(Van Epp), 36, 47
human needs, hierarchy of, 172–173, 192
husbands. *See* marriage; men
Huston, Ted, 208

"I" and "me" statements, 185–186, 192
Illouz, Eva, 32, 33, 207
incarceration, 55, 56, 93, 144, 161
income: inequities in, 73, 91, 92, 93, 110;
levels of Thriving Families
participant households, 20; produced
by marriage, 11, 116. *See also* wages
individual choices, 3, 66
individual fulfillment, 49
individual responsibility. *See*
responsibility
inequality, 202–208, 212–216; choices
and, 78; effects on intimate lives of,
4, 24, 54, 59; employment and, 64,
77, 206, 207; erroneous assumptions
about, 9; generational transmission
of, 111; income, 73, 91, 92, 93, 110;
marital effects of, 9–10, 13, 24, 54,
58, 92–94, 95, 102, 104; moral
politics of, 16, 58, 64; neoliberal
ideology and, 57–58; relationship
skills and, 3, 15, 58–59, 65–66,
212–213, 216; root causes of, 64;
structural bases of, 74–75, 93,
206–208; U.S. increase in, 9, 14.
See also class; socioeconomic status;
upward mobility
infatuation, 41, 43; description/warning
signs of, 38, 39
infidelity, 28, 36, 38, 55, 94
interpersonal dynamics, 4, 30, 39, 40,
41, 94; hardships and, 54–55, 59;
rules for, 33. *See also* arguments;
relationship science; relationship
skills programs
intimacy, 27, 30, 54, 59

jobs. *See* employment

Kefalas, Maria, 55, 94, 114; *Promises I Can Keep*, 66–67
Kitson, Gay, 54
Krauss, Alison, 34

labor market. *See* employment
Latino men, 93, 162
lesbian parents, 159–160
Lewis, Jerry, 103–104
Lewis, Oscar, 57–58
Lichter, Daniel, 12
life choices, 60, 62, 65, 146
limbic system, 38
Linnenberg, Kathryn, 154
Lipsky, Michael, 109
listening. *See* active listening
living together. *See* cohabitation
Losing Ground (Murray), 58
love. *See* romantic love; skilled love
Love's Cradle (curriculum), 17, 51–52, 56, 65, 67, 68, 73–74, 76–77
Love U2 (curriculum), 17, 38, 46, 61, 65, 72
low-wage jobs, 5, 13

machismo, 155
Magnuson, Katherine, 144
male breadwinner: assumptions about, 86, 139–155; critique of, 166–168; low-wages as barrier to, 92, 93, 139; middle-class expectations and, 165, 216; "package deal" and, 114, 115, 142, 143–147; welfare policy based on, 6
Manning, Wendy, 92
marital endogamy, 90
marital habitus, 111–112, 125, 143, 174
marital masculinity, 24, 142–143, 147–154, 155, 157–168, 174, 216; critique of, 166–168
marriage, 3, 6–12, 44–45, 48, 81–105; apprehensions and, 66–67; arranged, 28, 39, 40; barriers to, 92–93; benefits of, 26–34, 49–50, 81–82, 116, 208; changing cultural norms and, 28, 82, 87–88, 105, 108, 203–204;

characteristics of "good," 47, 104–105; class-based values and, 9–10, 57–59, 205 (*see also* middle-class marriage culture); collaborative, 146; commitment components of, 49–50; communication skills and, 76, 169–170; contemporary paradox of, 29; as controversial issue, 108; conventional gender roles and, 28, 86, 89, 140–141, 150, 153; cost-benefit analysis of, 102–103; deinstitutionalization of, 29; divorce culture and, 30, 40, 48–49; dominant emotional paradigms and, 30–31; dual demands of, 28, 30; economic factors and, 4, 15, 72, 82–95, 102–111, 114, 115, 116, 129, 204, 209; economic incentives for, 6, 11–12, 16, 68, 84–85, 202, 203, 211, 215, 216; education factor and, 91, 209; emotional sharing and, 28, 29, 30, 31, 86; employment and, 8–9, 13, 88, 92, 104, 139–140, 142, 143–147, 211–212; encouragement of, 24, 69–77, 174, 208, 211–212; family resource-pooling and, 89; fear of, 122–124, 205; gender norms and, 11, 28, 140–141, 146, 216 (*see also* male breadwinner); good decisions about, 45–46; government explicit promotion of (*See* Healthy Marriage Initiative; marriage education programs); historical evolution of, 9–10, 23, 28, 81–82, 86–88, 215; individual choices and, 29, 49, 213; inequalities and, 90–93, 95; infidelity and, 28, 36, 38, 55, 94; as learned aptitude, 112; love-based culture of, 25–28, 50; as luxury, 10, 113, 132, 133; masculine identity and, 24, 139–140, 142–143, 147–149; meanings attached to, 105; modern dilemma of, 29–31, 48–50; monogamy and, 46; morality and, 16, 36, 42, 206; normative values and, 3, 46, 58; perpetual unresolved marriage (*continued*)

problems and, 169–170; personal vs. communal role of, 29; pooled resources and, 89, 203–204; as poverty panacea, 11, 12, 92, 107–108, 109, 202, 203, 206, 209, 211; prosperity and, 23, 58, 81–82, 87, 108–109; rationality and, 39; relationship skills and, 14, 24, 26, 31–34, 55–58 (*see also* relational competence); religious belief and, 44; "retreat" from, 205, 208; role models and, 66, 67, 68, 111; romantic love and, 25–26, 30, 48–49; same-sex, 108; selection effect and, 11, 117; sentimentalization of, 86; skilled love and, 23, 25–26, 48–50; "smart" brain and, 63–64; social legitimacy from, 13; socially accepted alternatives to, 87; social scientific experts on, 32–33; specialization thesis and (*see* gender norms); spousal legal rights and, 119; stability factors and, 116, 82, 205; as status symbol, 82; tax penalties and, 212; two-parent households and, 6, 16, 26, 50, 57–58, 134–135, 138, 139; unaffordability of, 205, 212; upward mobility and, 79, 81–82, 92, 110, 113, 146

Marriage Clinic, The (Gottman), 169–70

marriage education programs, 19–22, 29, 56, 130; characteristics of, 7–8, 21; costs of, 7, 210; cultural context and, 82; curricula of, 17, 35–50, 62, 68, 77; de-emphasis of marriage and, 115–135; emphasis on emotions in, 29–30; empirical basis of, 8; erroneous basis of, 11; evaluations of, 14–15, 173–175; evidence-based claims and, 12–13, 37–38; focus of, 31, 78; goal achievement by, 14, 15; goals of, 139; government funding of, 8, 14; healthy marriage definition and, 104; instructor training for, 7–8, 16–19, 25, 34–35, 121–22, 123, 194–195; interpersonal relations focus of, 8;

marriage gap and, 56–57; nondenominational curriculum, 17; perpetual problems and, 169–170; policy recommendations for, 212–216; poverty sources and, 78; pragmatic skills and, 31–32, 78; premises of, 7–8, 27, 51, 58–59, 104; rationalizing tendencies of, 33; reinforcement of social boundaries by, 16; relationships beliefs and tools of, 31–32; shared problems and, 192–193; as short-term, 7; social scientists and, 32; societal changes in marriage and, 28; success sequence and, 59–64, 79, 89–95; teaching empathy and, 194–195. *See also* relationship skills programs; Thriving Families

marriage gap, 8–10, 56–57, 64, 86, 104; class-based, 210–211; debate over causes of, 204

marriage penalty (tax), 212

marriage premium, 140–142, 147, 166–167

Marriage Savers (curriculum), 71–72

Marsiglio, William, 146–147

Martin, Stephen, 145

masculinity. *See* marital masculinity; men

Maslow, Abraham, hierarchy of needs, 172–173, 192

Mastering the Mysteries of Love (curriculum), 17, 31, 38, 43, 51, 67; training program, 25–28

Maynard-Moody, Steven, 109

Mayo Clinic, 118

McLanahan, Sara, 12

Mead, Lawrence, *Beyond Entitlement*, 58

Medicaid, 178

Melz, Heidi, 208

memory books, 21

men: advantages of marriage for, 11, 139–150, 211; child support and, 139, 145; co-parenting commitment by, 156–157; disadvantaged, 12, 56, 93, 161, 163–166; irresponsible choices and,

62; masculinity and, 24, 142–143, 147, 153, 157–165; trust and, 160; weak labor market and, 56. *See also* fathers; gender norms

mentoring, 68

meritocracy, 64

middle-class marriage culture, 10, 16, 23, 24, 68, 81–82, 85, 102–105, 108, 110, 216; attributes of, 57–58; behaviors diverging from, 79; budgeting strategies and, 74; employment benefits and, 90–91, 205; foundations of, 166; gender norms and, 165; healthy marriage policy assumptions and, 146–147, 207, 214; history of, 215; life course script of, 60, 77, 82, 204–205, 207; markers of, 3, 5, 9, 82; marriageability and, 104–105; marriage as path to middle-class, 203, 204, 215; marriage program assumptions about, 207, 214; masculinity and, 142, 147–168; "package deal" and, 114, 115, 142, 143–147; relationship skills program and, 15, 173–174; "responsibility package" and, 92–93, 141–142, 146; as "retreat from marriage" factor, 208; skills associated with, 57, 78; success sequence and, 59–64, 77, 79, 82, 89–95, 102

minimum wage, 76, 212

modern marriage dilemma, 29–31, 48–50

money, 1–2, 8, 11, 21, 68–77, 78, 89, 172–194; actual costs and, 172–173, 178; committed relationships and, 107; competing values and, 179–180; fights about, 52, 55, 56, 74, 179; financial literacy and, 68–77, 78, 178, 181, 209; frivolous spending and, 176, 179; income inequality and, 73, 91, 92, 93, 110; joint resources and, 77; low-income families and, 9, 55, 69, 73–74, 175–192; management skills and, 68–77, 175–177, 200, 203, 207,

209; marriage postponement and (*see* marriage, delay of); marriage promotion classes and, 14, 15, 23, 51, 81–82, 175–186, 179, 193–194; needs vs. wants and, 176–177; pooling/sharing of, 55–56; savings plan and, 71, 175–76, 177–178; stepfamilies and, 70; symbolic meaning of, 56. *See also* budgeting; financial security; poverty; wages

monogamy, 46

moral judgments, 10, 16, 36, 42, 58, 64, 96, 111, 113, 206; abstinence education and, 42, 46, 206; neutral language and, 78

mothers: father-child relationship and, 137, 153; parenting style of, 158–159; welfare reform requirements for, 138–139; working, 90, 212. *See also* co-parenting; parenthood; single mothers

Mullainathan, Sendhil, 173

Murray, Charles, *Losing Ground,* 58

Musheno, Michael, 109

National Association for Relationship and Marriage Education (NARME), 210

needs: hierarchy of, 172–173, 192; wants vs., 176–177

negative emotions, 27, 54; "big three" of, 47

negotiations, 30, 70, 76, 77

Nelson, Timothy, 114–115

neocortex, 88

neoliberalism, 8, 57–58

neurochemistry, 38–39

Nock, Steven, 143, 146

nonmarital cohabitation. *See* cohabitation

nonmarital pregnancies. *See* unmarried pregnancy

Obama, Barack, 136, 209

O'Connor, Alice, 78, 206

Office of Family Assistance, 20
Oklahoma Marriage Initiative, 15, 16
OTP (On the Path), 175
Ortwein, Mary, 51

"package deal," 114, 115, 142, 143–147
PAIRS (Practical Application of Intimate
    Relationship Skills) (curriculum), 17,
    38–39, 42, 46
Parade magazine, 136
parenthood, 1, 2, 17, 20, 106–135, 212;
    commitment to, 106, 110–135;
    communication skills and, 186–188,
    189; expenses of, 172–173; first-time
    stresses and, 186–187, 192–193;
    gendered style of, 137, 138, 143, 149,
    150, 157, 158–166; individual choices
    and, 213; individual responsibility
    and, 207; men's commitment to,
    147–148; mandatory classes in, 20,
    120, 198; marriage advantages and,
    11–12, 150; poverty effects on, 72, 173;
    responsibility ethos and, 108–112, 114,
    131, 134, 145, 207; same-sex, 11, 12,
    159–160, 166; social science experts
    on, 32; teachable proper practices of,
    3, 127. See also co-parenting; fathers;
    mothers
Pearson, Marline, 59–60
personal responsibility. See
    responsibility
Personal Responsibility and Work
    Opportunity Reconciliation Act of
    1996 (PRWORA): background to
    passage of, 58; four statutory goals
    for, 5–6; grant funds and, 6;
    neoliberal assumptions of, 58;
    parental financial responsibility
    message of, 138–139, 145–146. See also
    welfare reform
Pick a Partner/How to Avoid Marrying
    a Jerk (curriculum), 17
play style, gender and, 137, 138, 143, 150,
    157, 163, 164
policy, "deep dish" analysis of, 109–110

political ideology, 9, 16, 109, 111
Poor Laws, 6
Popenoe, David, 146
pornography, 27
Porter, Meredith, 92
poverty, 4, 13, 15, 59–60, 86–89, 92,
    171–216; preventative behavioral
    strategies for, 5, 6, 39; breaking cycle
    of, 111, 128, 132; budgeting and, 71–72,
    74, 78, 80, 171, 181; cash assistance
    programs and, 75; childbearing and,
    114; children and, 212; committed
    co-parenting effects on, 132–135;
    communication and, 170–172, 175,
    192, 200; couple commitment and,
    107–108; criminal activity and, 56;
    culture of poverty thesis and, 57–58,
    78; daily constraints of, 200; deficient
    relational knowledge and, 78;
    emotional depletion from, 54, 55, 56,
    65, 80, 173, 175; father's level of
    involvement and, 144, 165–168;
    financial literacy and, 68–77, 78, 178,
    181, 209; ideology of causes/
    consequences, 211; individual vs.
    structural causes of, 207;
    intergenerational transmission of, 57,
    110, 115, 134, 207; managing money
    and, 175–177; marital masculinity
    and, 167–168; marriage promotion
    and (see Healthy Marriage Initiative;
    marriage education programs;
    Thriving Families); mental effects of,
    200; neoliberal view of, 57–58, 78;
    official threshold of, 12; "package
    deal" undermining by, 143–47;
    parenting effects of, 72; as perpetual
    problem, 171; presumed causes of,
    203; rates, 14, 208; relationship
    effects of, 53–54, 55, 64, 77, 80,
    132–135, 171–172, 175, 192, 193, 214–216;
    single mothers and, 58, 72; social
    inequality and, 78–79; stereotypical
    beliefs about, 121–122; strains and
    stresses of, 54, 173, 193–194, 200–201;

success sequence and, 60–62, 79, 91; traditional view of, 6. *See also* welfare reform

P.O.W.E.R. technique, 48

pregnancy. *See* childbearing

premarital sex, 103, 206; arguments against, 36, 38, 39, 41, 42, 46, 65

PREP (Prevention and Relationship Enhancement Program), 17, 34–35, 40, 61, 66, 76, 79

PREPARE/ENRICH: Building a Strong Marriage Workbook, 17, 71

PREP Within My Reach (curriculum), 17, 37

problem-solving skills, 45, 65, 67–68, 208; cooperative, 67, 213; perpetual problems and, 169–170

promiscuity, 57, 58

Promises I Can Keep: Why Poor Women Put Motherhood Before Marriage (Edin and Kefalas), 66–67

property ownership, 82, 86

prosperity, 23, 28, 81–82, 87, 108–109, 204–205, 206

PRWORA. *See* Personal Responsibility and Work Opportunity Reconciliation Act

public assistance, 20. *See also* welfare system

public funding, 210–211

purpose, sense of, 4

quality of life, 12

race, 93. *See also* African Americans

racism, 13, 75, 82, 93

RAM. *See* Relationship Attachment Model

rationality, 16, 31, 33–34, 39, 49, 77; skilled love and, 42, 60–61

relational competence, 43, 45–46, 76, 111; challenges to, 58–59, 67, 94, 107, 173; choices and, 60–64, 65; components of, 52–53, 77; money management and, 70–71; success sequence and,

59–61; synonyms for, 42; teaching tools for, 123, 130

relational violence, 47, 54, 55, 56, 75

Relationship Attachment Model (RAM), 36, 37, 40–41

relationship choices, 59–66; bad, 62, 63, 203, 215; educational intervention and, 37; healthy norms for, 34; impulsive emotions and, 38; intentionality and, 65; lessons on, 61–62; moral appraisals of, 35; "smart," 45–46; socioeconomic factors and, 4, 10, 62–64

Relationship Enhancement (curriculum), 17, 18

relationships, 202–203, 209; barometer of, 195–196; basis of conflict in, 56; building of, 67; challenges of, 77, 175, 193–196; definition of good, 52–53; factors affecting, 215–216; inequality and, 3, 15, 58–59, 65–66; poverty effects on, 214–215; shared experience of, 200–201; socioeconomic opportunity and, 12, 65–66, 77, 94, 107; stability of, 53; strengthening of, 206; struggles of, 194–195; unhealthy, 215

relationship science, 8, 32–33; core principles of, 36; universal laws and, 37–38, 40–41

relationship skills programs, 1–3, 9, 11, 19–24, 27, 78, 139, 169–201, 205–208; communication and, 52, 171–172; curricula for, 17, 23, 34–35, 43–44, 45, 47, 51–52; empathy and, 52, 175; evaluations of, 14–15, 24, 173–175; evidence-based assessment of, 212; focus of, 216; goals of, 40–41; healthy marriage policy and, 66–68, 212–216; "healthy" vs. "unhealthy" behaviors and, 206; inequality as focus of, 19–22, 29, 32–33, 34, 49–50, 56, 130, 206–207; instructor training for, 25–28, 34–50; interpersonal dynamics and, 33; marriage apprehensions and,

relationship skills (*continued*)
66–77; marriage benefits and,
26–34, 39, 49–50;
misunderstandings and, 23; policy
recommendations and, 211–216;
poverty undermining, 190; problems
with teaching of, 206–11; as public
policy, 28–32, 210–211, 212; rationale
for, 15; recommended components of,
214–215; romantic love and, 23, 25–28,
39; structural factors and, 75–76;
universal relationship laws and,
37–38, 40–41. *See also* marriage
education programs; Thriving
Families
reliance (as attachment dynamic), 36
religion, 17, 43, 44, 82
resource-pooling, 89, 142
responsibility, 5, 40, 49, 55, 57, 58, 62,
69, 193, 209; parental, 108–112, 114,
131, 134, 145, 207
responsible fatherhood, 136, 137, 138–147,
163–165, 210
résumé workshops, 209
role models, 123, 154–155; fathers as, 157,
160, 164–165; for marriage, 66, 67,
68, 111
role-playing exercises, 22
romantic love, 25–50; beliefs about, 30,
31; as commitment, 106, 107, 128, 132;
competence and, 3; conflicted feelings
about, 29; conscious cognitive
processes and, 35; co-parenting and,
131–132; economic advantage and,
53–54, 56, 206; economic
disadvantage and, 4, 24, 54, 216;
individual choices and, 3, 66;
intentionality and, 65, 78; "logic" of,
36; marriage and, 25–26, 28–34, 47,
48–49, 50, 203; poverty undercutting,
132–135, 192, 193; pragmatic skills vs.,
32; public policy and, 28–34, 39;
rational choices and, 16, 60–61;
rationalization of, 31, 33–50; real vs.
infatuation, 38; relationship skills

and, 23, 25–28, 39; strengthening of,
110; therapeutic models of, 207. *See
also* skilled love
Roy, Kevin, 146–147

sadness, 46, 47
safe-zone rule, 36
same-sex marriage, 108
same-sex parents, 11, 12, 159–160, 166
savings plan, 71, 175–176, 177–178
Sawhill, Isabel, 12, 61, 79
Scafidi, Benjamin, 211
scarcity, 173, 175
segregation, 75
selection effect, 11, 117, 139–140, 203
self-awareness, 77, 207
self-change skill, 27
self-control, 47, 58, 76–77
self-esteem, 161–162
self-regulation, 57
sex: as attachment dynamic, 36; fidelity
and, 67; good decisions about, 45–46,
60–61; intentionality and, 65;
moral judgments and, 43, 58, 206;
promiscuity and, 57. *See also*
infidelity; premarital sex
sexual abstinence, 42, 46, 206
sexual attraction, 41
Shafir, Eldar, 173
Sherman, Jennifer, 55
Sigle-Rushton, Wendy, 12
single mothers, 57–58, 121; African
Americans as, 6, 58, 93; assessment
of marriage promotion programs and,
15; economic disadvantage and, 72,
88; marriage apprehensions and, 12,
94; racialized images of, 58; social
stigma of, 86, 87; valuation of
children by, 114; welfare assistance
and, 5, 6, 15, 58, 212
skilled communication. *See*
communication skills
skilled love, 23, 26–28, 34–50, 53, 89,
128, 174, 216; benefits of, 50, 64–65,
66; commitment and, 106, 107, 128;

competence of, 42–46; components of, 36, 39, 48, 49, 77; as economic investment, 64–65, 76, 103, 128–129; emotional control and, 46–48; inequalities and, 77–80; joint religious practice and, 44; logic of, 36–41; modern marriage dilemma and, 48–50; purpose of, 31–32; rational choices and, 60–61, 64; teaching of, 43, 59; upward mobility and, 53, 59, 77–79

skills-based approach, 213

skills training, 213. *See also* relationship skills programs

"smart" brain, meaning of, 63–64

S.M.A.R.T. goals, 4

Smart Steps for Stepfamilies (curriculum), 17, 70, 213

Smock, Pamela, 92

social class. *See* class; socioeconomic status

social inequality. *See* inequality

social institutions, 28, 78

social norms, 30, 31, 82, 86–87, 166; changes in, 205. *See also* gender norms

social safety net. *See* welfare system

social science studies, 26, 32–33, 49–50; simplistic interpretation of, 109; welfare policy and, 206

social stability, 41, 48; changed basis of, 29; government normative model of, 16

socioeconomic good, 125

socioeconomic opportunity, 12, 62–65, 77, 94, 107, 216

socioeconomic status, 4, 9, 10, 11–12, 95; discretionary spending and, 56; economic self-sufficiency and, 68–77; education and, 56, 57, 59, 60, 62, 77, 91; family stability and, 56; father's involvement and, 144; marriage gap and, 8–10, 56–57, 64, 86, 104, 204, 210–211; neoliberal ideology and, 57; relationship skills programs and, 14; relationship stability and, 93;

romantic decisions and, 216. *See also* class; inequality; middle-class marriage culture; upward mobility

Sparks, Anne, 15

speaker-listener technique, 35, 39

specialization thesis, 141

spiritual intimacy, 43–44

Stacey, Judith, 50

Stanley, Scott, 60–62, 63, 76

stepfamilies, 12, 83, 145, 213; healthy marriage program for, 17, 70

street-level bureaucracy theory, 109–111

stress: economic problems and, 54, 171–172, 173, 193–194, 200; of marriage program participants, 2, 193; reduction techniques, 47, 48, 65, 67, 133–135; relationship skills and, 208; romantic relationships and, 56

structural inequalities, 74–75, 93, 206–208

substance abuse. *See* alcohol; drugs

success sequence, 59–64, 79, 89–95, 102, 139–140, 142

Supporting Father Involvement (program), 213

Supporting Healthy Marriage (program): cost per-couple for, 210; evaluation of, 14, 174

Swidler, Ann, 30–31

TANF. *See* Temporary Assistance for Needy Families

tape exercise, 41–42, 45

taxes, 75, 211, 212

"Teach-Out-of-the-Box" (curricula), 18

teenage pregnancy, 65, 162

Temporary Assistance for Needy Families, 5–6, 182; cash assistance, 209, 210, 211, 212; goals for, 5–6; relationship education programs and, 15, 20, 61–62, 182

Ten Great Dates (curriculum), 17, 43–44, 70

Third Option (curriculum), 17, 36–37; leader's manual, 47

Thomas, Adam, 12

Thriving Families (program), 1, 19–24, 106–135, 146, 159–160, 169, 192–199; attendance incentives, 20, 21, 181–85, 192–193, 210; attendance requirements, 1–2, 20; central concern of, 110; committed co-parenting emphasis of, 23–24, 115–116, 125; communication skills and, 100, 170–171, 182–183, 185–196; curriculum design of, 21–22, 23, 124, 149; curriculum requirements of, 116, 119; description of, 20–22; effectiveness of, 2, 13–14, 174, 189–190; ethnographic in-depth study of, 10, 19–22, 109–110; evaluation of, 174–175; family yarn web exercise and, 125–132, 134–135; fatherhood and, 136–139, 142–143, 147–168; financial strategies and, 175–176; first-time parenthood stresses and, 186–187, 192–193; focus groups, 19; goal in studying, 109–110; goal-setting lesson of, 4–5; goals of, 1–2, 108, 109; goals vs. realities and, 110; government funding of, 7, 19, 107–108, 116, 210; group discussions and, 199; instruction focus and style, 21–22, 197–198; instructor training, 121–22, 123, 194–195; interviews with graduates of, 22; marital masculinity promotion and, 24, 157–68; marriageability redefinition, 147–168; marriage promotion strategy of, 108–113, 123–135; men's involvement and, 149; messages of, 15, 108–112; money management lessons and, 175–176, 179; most valuable message of, 175; as nonjudgmental forum, 192–199; participant assessment of, 182–200, 213–214; participant qualifications for, 182; participants' sharing of problems and, 192–194, 200–213; policy goal of, 23; policy implementation and, 109–135; positive effects of, 174–175, 193–195; poverty issues and, 171–201; pro-marriage moral beliefs and, 109; purpose and benefits of, 120–121; referrals to, 20, 96, 98, 120, 185, 198–199; relationship emphasis of, 128, 206, 207, 216; responsible fatherhood promotion and, 138–147; street-level analysis of, 109–135; true/false quiz and, 116–117, 119

time-outs, 35, 39

Townsend, Nicholas, 142

trust, 2, 9, 36, 67, 77, 94, 160; communication techniques and, 27, 28

two-parent married household: benefits to children of, 26, 134–135; government encouragement of, 6, 16, 50, 138, 139; social class and, 57–58. See also co-parenting

unemployment, 5, 56, 73, 75, 83, 86–87, 93, 104, 107, 133, 144, 165

universal laws of relationship, 37–38, 40–41

unmarried mothers. See single mothers

unmarried pregnancy, 20, 21, 60, 86, 96–97, 99, 103, 211; moral judgment and, 58; prevention program, 6; teenage, 65, 162

upward mobility, 114, 166, 175, 204; co-parenting and, 128–129, 134; keys to, 79; marriage and, 79, 81–82, 92, 110, 113, 146; teaching of, 3, 15, 23, 51–80

van Acker, Elizabeth, 31–32

Van Epp, John, 36, 37, 38, 40, 47; How to Avoid Falling in Love with a Jerk, 36, 47; Relationship Attachment Model (RAM), 36, 37, 40–41

violence: avoidance of, 206; relational, 47, 54, 55, 56, 75

vocational training, 209

wages, 9, 76, 92, 93, 104, 139, 144; discrimination and, 89; gender norms and, 90; low, 5, 12, 13, 165, 212;

"marriage premium" and, 139–140, 147; women's, 89–90. *See also* income

Wait Training: It's All About M.E. (Marriage Education) (curriculum), 41–42, 45, 46, 47, 65, 67–68

Watkins-Hayes, Celeste, 110

Weber, Max, 33–34

weddings, expense of, 84, 91, 92–93, 98, 101, 102, 119

Weiner-Davis, Michelle, 45

welfare reform (1990s), 211–212; assessment of goals achieved by, 13–16; cash assistance program and, 5–6; content/effects of, 5, 7, 79, 139–140, 167; employment and, 122, 138–139, 209, 212; individual responsibility emphasis of, 5, 193; marriage education and, 4–15, 209, 211; political themes of, 5, 58; responsible fatherhood and, 136, 137, 138–147, 163–165, 210; work and marriage promotion and, 7, 122. *See also* Healthy Marriage Initiative; Personal Responsibility and Work Opportunity Reconciliation Act; Temporary Assistance for Needy Families

welfare policy, 5, 6–7, 15, 57, 75, 79–80, 83, 110, 121, 215–216; asset-building initiatives and, 68–69; culture of poverty thesis and, 58; gender norms and, 145; missing male breadwinner and, 6, 145; single mothers and, 5, 6, 15, 58, 212; social science studies and, 206; stereotypical images and, 58; traditional approaches of, 6

welfare-to-work programs. *See* welfare reform

"What a Baby Wants" (exercise), 65

WIC (Women, Infants, and Children) nutrition program, 20, 98, 120, 185

Wilson, James Q., 57–58

Within My Reach (curriculum), 59–64, 65–66, 77

women: college degrees of, 88, 89, 90; earning gains by, 89–90; employment of, 89, 156–157, 212; financial instability of, 55, 62; gendered expectations of, 86, 140, 153–154; income potential for, 89–90; low-income men and, 92; marital age of, 88; marriage positive effects on, 211; marriage rate of, 88, 90; men's trust in, 160, 161; welfare stereotypes of, 58, 121. *See also* mothers

Women, Infants, and Children (WIC) nutrition program. *See* WIC

work. *See* employment

work ethic, 57, 64, 81

working mothers, 90, 212

workplace. *See* employment